Murat Gül is an architectural and urban historian, and is currently Associate Professor of Architecture at TOBB University of Economics and Technology in Ankara, Turkey. He has taught at Mimar Sinan Fine Arts University in Istanbul, Turkey, the University of Sydney, Australia, and the International University of Sarajevo, Bosnia-Herzegovina. He has extensive experience in the fields of urban planning and heritage conservation and has worked for various government agencies in Australia.

'A fascinating and highly readable account of the physical development of the city.'—*Jon Lang, Professor Emeritus of Architecture, University of New South Wales*

'Addresses an important and significant gap in the literature of the urban history of Istanbul; it is greatly needed, and fills the void in a scholarly and highly readable manner.'—*Trevor Howells, Director of Heritage Conservation Program, University of Sydney*

'A very important contribution to understanding Istanbul's architectural and planning history.'—*John Dee, Senior Lecturer in Architecture Program, International University of Sarajevo*

The Emergence of Modern Istanbul

Transformation and Modernisation of a City

Murat Gül

Revised paperback edition published in 2012 by I.B.Tauris & Co Ltd
6 Salem Road, London W2 4BU
175 Fifth Avenue, New York NY 10010
www.ibtauris.com

Distributed in the United States and Canada
Exclusively by Palgrave Macmillan
175 Fifth Avenue, New York NY 10010

Copyright © 2012, 2009 Murat Gül
First published in hardback in 2009 by Tauris Academic Studies, an imprint of
I.B.Tauris & Co Ltd

The right of Murat Gül to be identified as the author of this work has been asserted by the author in accordance with the Copyright, Designs and Patent Act 1988.

All rights reserved. Except for brief quotations in a review, this book, or any part thereof, may not be reproduced, stored in or introduced into a retrieval system, or transmitted, in any form or by any means, electronic, mechanical, photocopying, recording, or otherwise, without the prior written permission of the publisher.

ISBN: 978 1 78076 374 3

A full CIP record for this book is available from the British Library
A full CIP record for this book is available from the Library of Congress

Library of Congress catalog card: available

Printed and bound by CPI Group (UK) Ltd, Croydon, CR0 4YY
From camera-ready copy edited and supplied by the author

Cover images:
Front: Galata Bridge, Prints & Photographs Division, Library of Congress, LC-DIG-ppmsc-06061
Back: Galata Bridge, Yapı Kredi History Archives, Selahattin Giz Collection

To Ömer

CONTENTS

Preface	ix
Key to pronunciation of Turkish characters	xi
Introduction	1
1. The Demise of Classical Istanbul	7
2. Istanbul Between the Crimean War and the First World War	40
3. The Neglected City 1923–1933	72
4. Reshaping Istanbul under Kemalist Principles 1933–1950	92
5. Istanbul under Democrat Party Administration 1950–1955	127
6. Istanbul in Menderes' Hands 1956–1960	140
Conclusion	172
Notes	180
Figure Sources	217
Bibliography	220
Index	230

PREFACE

This book is the end product of extensive research into the planning history of Istanbul. Since growing up there in the 1970s, I witnessed how dramatically the city's social and physical morphology changed over four decades. However, as an architectural student living in Istanbul my interest in this subject first emerged during my undergraduate and postgraduate years at Mimar Sinan University. All the academic and professional activities I participated in and my private discussions with a variety of scholars during those years drew me back to the planning history of Istanbul. Specifically, I wanted to better understand the development of the city in the early Republican and Democrat Party periods. It was this deep interest that encouraged me to undertake my doctoral thesis on the planning history of Istanbul and this book is primarily produced from that research.

Throughout the preparation of the book many individuals, institutions and organisations have offered a wide range of support, assistance and encouragement for which I am grateful and happy to acknowledge. My deepest gratitude goes to Dr John Dee, my friend and colleague in Sydney, for providing guidance, making critical and valuable suggestions, reviewing my draft chapters but, above all, for encouraging me when I needed it most. I am also indebted to Trevor Howells for all his support and for reading the manuscripts and making valuable suggestions. To Professor İlgi Aşkun and her colleagues at the Restoration Department of Mimar Sinan Fine Arts University I owe a debt of gratitude for their kind help in providing access to the archival material held there. I would specifically like to thank Dr Mevlude Kaptı for her invaluable assistance with my research. I would like to thank other individuals from many different places for their generous support and assistance, including Professor Ataman Demir, Professor Angus Martin, Dr Aras Neftçi, Dr Bedriye Poyraz, Dr Derin Öncel, Nurhan Ercan and Megan Haig. I would also like to thank the Librarian and staff of the former Denis Winston Architecture Library at the University of Sydney for their friendly support and patience in attending to my endless interlibrary loan requests. I would also like to thank Jenna Steventon and Nadine El-Hadi at I.B.Tauris for their generous assistance throughout the preparation of this book. My very special thanks go to Lianne Hall, my copy-editor, who did a great job turning my manuscripts into a book.

To my family I should like to express my boundless appreciation for their unstinting support, assistance and encouragement throughout my education and in the process of this book. With delight I thank my sisters, Sevil Gül and Ebru Ünlühan, for their support in finding and sending invaluable books, articles and other source material. I profoundly appreciate my Mother and Father's support and their everlasting understanding since my undergraduate years. It is with deep gratitude that this book is dedicated to our son, Ömer, who grew up with this project during the first nine years of his life, for his forbearance for all the time I spent on this project that otherwise should have been his. And finally, I wish to thank my wife, Figen Gül, the one person who, from the beginning, supported me without reservation.

Murat Gül

Key to Pronunciation of Turkish Characters

The Turkish alphabet is composed of 29 letters. It is phonetic and hence every letter represents a certain sound without diphthongs. There are eight vowels and 21 consonants. Letters **Q, W, X** are not included in the alphabet but appear in foreign names. There are six more letters, namely: **Ç, Ğ, Ş, Ö, Ü, I**. The other letters are the same in both the Turkish and English alphabets, but they are pronounced differently. The sounds of Turkish characters that are not included in English are as follows:

    ç — *c* as in church
    ğ — soft *g* lengthens the preceding vowel
    ı — *i* as in insect or *u* as in radium
    ö — *u* as in urge
    ş — *ch* as in Chicago
    ü — *u* as in fruit or nude

Figure 1 Map of Constantinople published by the Society for the Diffusion of

eful Knowledge, Great Britain, and engraved by B. R. Davies, September 1840

INTRODUCTION

Today it can be clearly articulated that Turkey is still waiting for a statesman who is as enthusiastic and determined as Menderes regarding urban planning and redevelopment. There are many people who still remember Menderes eating his sandwich while he was giving orders to the officers of the municipality, who had not yet shaved in the very early morning, and his automobile following well behind him... In our opinion, Menderes is the only prime minister who went into the street and left his signature on the city and in the soil in his struggle for urban redevelopment.
Şevket Süreyya Aydemir[1]

Mid-nineteenth-century Istanbul was chaotic, overcrowded, poorly sewered, badly administered, prone to catastrophic fires and plagued with ineffective transportation systems. A century later the city was a metropolis with large avenues, postwar modernist architecture and city blocks which had swept away much of its traditional nineteenth-century street pattern and altered its urban form. In telling the story of such a dramatic transformation, this book investigates the social and political events experienced in Turkey that shaped the city's planning during the late Ottoman, early Republican and postwar Democrat Party periods. And it traces the impact of these changing policies in the very fabric of the city—in its streets, landscapes and buildings.

For Turkey, modernisation began in the early eighteenth-century Ottoman period and continued into the nineteenth century when it reached a high point. The establishment of the Turkish Republic in 1923, however, saw Turkey increasingly turn to the West to seek ideas about how to mould and direct the development of its modern culture. Under the 27-year, single-party rule and the principles advanced by Mustafa Kemal Atatürk, founder of modern Turkey, sweeping changes and reforms were made to Turkey's social, political and economic structures to align it more closely with Western civilisation and its ideas, practices and social mores. The political motto of the era was '*Muasır medeniyetler seviyesine ulaşmak*' ('To achieve the level of contemporary civilisations').

It was not until after the Second World War that Turkey saw its political system shift towards a Western democratic model of government. At a significant turning point in its history, the country tried to align itself with the Western block economically, militarily and politically. With a new political slogan, '*Memleketin imarı*' ('Development of the country'), and backed by foreign economic aid, Turkey's new Democrat Party administration took the opportunity in the 1950s to initiate significant infrastructure development, including the phenomenal mechanisation of agriculture.

Of all the areas of reform, it was in the transformation of cities that the desire to adopt Western ideas was most strongly expressed. Istanbul was the principal arena where this desire was realised, and where it can be most vividly understood. Its status, firstly as the capital of the Ottoman Empire and then as the strategic economic centre of Turkey, made Istanbul a theatrical stage where the different regimes displayed their political, ideological and social policies in the context of the built environment.

The long path to Istanbul's modernisation began in the nineteenth century when young Ottoman bureaucrats tried unsuccessfully to usher in several planning reforms at a time when the Empire was heading towards collapse. During this time major planning proposals were prepared for the city, mostly by foreign experts. With the exception of some local street regularisations, the majority of these plans remained on paper due to the severe economic conditions that prevailed.

Istanbul was neglected in the early years of the new Turkish Republic when Ankara was selected as the new capital of modern Turkey. Later, the Republican administration softened its stance against Istanbul and attempted to secularise and modernise the city in accordance with its new political agenda. This task was given to the French urban designer Henri Prost, whose considerable experience in the modernisation of Muslim cities under the French mandate of North Africa was highly valued by the Republican regime. Again, financial difficulties before and during the Second World War prevented Istanbul's transformation into a modern secular city, with the majority of Prost's proposals remaining on the drafting board.

The aftermath of the Second World War saw Istanbul enter a new era as prime minister Adnan Menderes' Democrat government launched a large-scale redesign of the city's urban form with the aim of putting an end to the 'long-standing negligence' of previous administrations. The mechanisation of agriculture in the 1950s brought massive and largely uncontrolled migration from the countryside to the cities, especially Istanbul. Immigration, coupled with Istanbul's acute housing shortage, led to the emergence of slums on the city's fringes. The increasing population, together with an improving economy, brought a rapid increase in the number of motor vehicles on Istanbul's streets, which put further pressure on the city's existing infrastructure.

These conditions set the stage for Menderes and his Democrat Party to modernise Istanbul in the late 1950s. In many ways, Menderes' redevelopment programme mirrored that of Baron Haussmann's spectacular transformation of Paris a century before. Istanbul saw thousands of buildings demolished, gigantic boulevards carved out within its historical core and the outward expansion of its urban area.

Despite its historic significance, Istanbul's massive urban transformation has remained somewhat immune from scholarly interest. Today, except for a few unpublished research dissertations, the literature fails to go beyond descriptive book chapters, journal articles and conference papers.[2] Moreover, the literature on Istanbul during the early Republican and Democrat Party periods is marginal at best, with the city's transformation being examined only through the narrow lens of physical change. Indeed, the oral histories that have been transmitted from older to younger generations, often ornamented by apocryphal tales, are the only other significant source providing critiques of Istanbul's urban redevelopment.

These same accounts are known to accommodate stereotypical images, prejudices and beliefs about Menderes based for the most part on his idiosyncratic behaviour and personality traits. While many existing historical accounts of the urban transformation of the 1950s provide fragmentary descriptions of physical change in the urban fabric, the reasons for Istanbul's redevelopment as seen from the perspective of underlying historical, cultural and political changes in the late-Ottoman and early Republican periods have been largely ignored.

The volatile political environment during the Democrat government years has also played a large part in the interpretations made by modern scholars about the urban redevelopment programme. The Turkish intelligentsia, who passionately adhere to Kemalist principles, describe the period of the Democrat Party administration as the 'dark age' of modern Turkish political history. They portray an idyllic picture of the 1930s and 1940s, which correspondingly debases Menderes and his administration as a corrupting influence on Atatürk's reforms. The Democrat Party's inclination towards a liberal economic model, its closer ties with the United States and its relaxation of strict control over religion are all regarded as practices that emasculated Atatürk's ideals of a modern, secular and independent Turkish state.

Hence these highly emotive and negative views of the Democrat government have strongly influenced the historical assessment of Menderes' urban redevelopment programme. Today he is labelled as the *bête noire* politician solely responsible for the destruction of much of the city's historical urban character. He is seen as personally staging the urban redevelopment works as a political showcase to camouflage his government's deficiencies in economic management. And he is branded the political representative of the *taşralı* (provincial) classes, the provincial politician who was not fully capable of understanding the city's problems, who did not listen to professional expertise and who executed all works without appropriately prepared plans.[3]

Historical Approach

The structure of this book follows the historical method of periodisation, or dividing the past into separate segments identified by recognisable symbols, landmarks and turning points. While it is recognised that periodisation is the subject of much debate among historians, for the purpose of this book it provides a clear structure for the reader to follow the influences and arguments along a logical path.[4]

The book follows the traditional periodisation of Turkish history employed by many social and political historians. Three main periods have been selected which represent important epochs of Turkish modernisation and, more specifically, the modernisation of Istanbul's urban morphology. These are: the late-Ottoman period, which consists of the eighteenth and, particularly, the nineteenth centuries; the early Republican period between 1923 and 1950; and, finally, the Democrat Party period of the 1950s.

These principal periods are further subdivided into smaller parts to reflect a more meaningful segregation. The late-Ottoman period, for example, is divided into three parts. The first covers the period between the early eighteenth and the early nineteenth centuries when cracks in classical Ottoman Istanbul first became visible. The second slice of the late-Ottoman period covers the beginning of Mahmud II's reign in 1808 to the Crimean War from 1853 to 1856. And finally, the last phase spans the era between the Crimean War and the collapse of the Ottoman Empire after the First World War. The early Republican period is divided between the decade after the establishment of the Republic in 1923, when the government channelled all its efforts into creating its new capital in Ankara, and the Prostian period up to 1950. The Democrat Party period can also be divided between the early

1950s when the government employed Turkish experts to revise Prost's plans and the last four years of the Menderes government between 1956 and 1960.

Based primarily on sources unearthed in Turkish archives, detailed reading of the existing literature and interviews with some of the key characters and witnesses of the Democrat Party era, this book aims to tell the story of how Istanbul was shaped and transformed. It also brings a critical perspective towards gaining a fuller understanding of the history of Turkish modernisation. The historical method employed in this book differs from mainstream urban history written primarily by architectural historians who focus on the physical manifestation of cities. Being trained as an architect in the city of Istanbul, one of the author's principal interests is the physical shape of the city—in the words of famous urban historian John Summerson, the 'bricks, mortars and steel'.[5] The aim of this book, however, is not limited to showing the physical change in the urban fabric, but to show how the 'roads, squares and parks' constructed in the different historical periods were themselves part of a complex interplay of the social and political conditions lying behind this remarkable transformation.

And, finally, some notes are necessary to explain the use of bibliographical material and translations from Turkish and contemporary spelling usage. As this book primarily targets the English-speaking reader, it has been referenced, wherever possible, with sources written in the English language, both by Turkish and non-Turkish authors. This approach will enable readers to acquire more in-depth information about the social and political history of Turkey. Many Turkish sources have been translated into English to allow the reader to form his or her own picture of the context. Turkish names follow the traditional spelling of words in the modern Turkish alphabet. Pre-1926 dates have also been converted from the Islamic Calendar to the Gregorian Calendar.

This book is structured as follows. Chapter One covers the first two periods of the late-Ottoman era between the early eighteenth and mid-nineteenth centuries. It provides a brief summary of the urban characteristics of classical Ottoman Istanbul, the early signals of its modernisation and the major attempts to redevelop the city in the first half of the nineteenth century. Chapter Two then explores the urban redevelopment of Istanbul between the Crimean War and the First World War. It looks at the establishment of municipal administration, the piecemeal urban regularisation works and some major, yet mostly unrealised, infrastructure initiatives. Chapter Three presents a brief survey of the political and social developments and their impact on Istanbul during the early years of the modern Turkish Republic. It specifically appraises how the peasantist movement of the 1930s and

1940s influenced Turkey's urban redevelopment polices. Chapter Four is dedicated to the Prost period. It analyses the images and ideas portrayed in his planning proposals and discusses his role in the broader context of the Kemalist modernisation project. The piecemeal implementation of Prost's plan during the troubled years of the Second World War is also presented in this chapter. Chapter Five begins with a historical account of related social, political and economic developments after the 1950 election and provides a detailed account of the Democrat Party's planning initiatives in the first half of the 1950s. And, finally, Chapter Six provides a meticulous survey of Menderes' redevelopment programme between 1956 and 1960. It undertakes an extensive investigation of the specific works from different historical perspectives to reinterpret the Menderes period and allow it to be seen in a more balanced historical perspective in terms of the modernisation of Istanbul.

1

THE DEMISE OF CLASSICAL ISTANBUL

Once or twice we rambled a good deal farther into the city than the square of the Seraskier Pasha; and on another occasion we rode from Pera across the Valley of the Sweet Waters, and along nearly the whole length of the landward walls of the city from the Golden Horn to the Propontis, and entering by the Selyvria gate, we took a devious course through the submural quarters to the heart of the old city, and then, by zig-zags, to the Serraglio, the acute angle of that triangle and end of Constantinople… Take away the mosques and the minarets, which show out always so beautifully, and sometimes so grandly, and you see hardly anything but mean wooden houses, nearly everywhere going to ruin, and threatening to fall upon your head.

Charles MacFarlane, 1850[1]

Two significant peace treaties signed in the late seventeenth and early eighteenth centuries marked the beginning of a long decline in the fortunes of the Ottoman Empire. The Treaty of Carlowitz in 1699 followed a series of defeats by the Holy League of Austria, Poland, Venice and Russia that started in Vienna in 1683. The Ottoman Empire, for the first time in its history, signed a peace treaty as a defeated power in a war and was forced to surrender long-held territories. The decline in military superiority over the West became even more apparent with the Treaty of Passarowitz, signed in 1718 after the Venetian–Turkish (1714–16) and Austro–Turkish (1716–18) wars, which resulted in further concessions of territory in Eastern Europe.

The impact of these humiliating defeats by the West triggered a long and harrowing debate in the Ottoman administration. Out of this debate emerged a radical change in the Ottoman perception of the West, which forced a new kind of relationship with Europe. Ensuing reforms first concentrated on implementing immediate change by adopting modern scientific knowledge in military organisation to stem the continuing loss of territories. However, it was soon realised that more fundamental reforms were required to open the Ottomans to Western ideas. The corollary was the emergence of a long process towards the modernisation of Turkey in a world which had become increasingly dominated by the European powers.

In the nineteenth century the Ottoman Empire initiated a long and painful series of reforms. The aim was to create a new modern army and to establish a more effective socio-economic structure to support the military reorganisation. The Ottoman reformers, particularly the young bureaucrats, aimed to transform the old Empire into an efficient and coherent social, political, cultural and economic system in line with the general modernisation processes evident throughout Europe. These changes dramatically influenced all aspects of Ottoman life. Most significantly, they had direct and indirect impacts on Istanbul's urban morphology, and brought to an end the period described as 'classical Ottoman Istanbul' which dated from the conquest of the city by Mehmed II in 1453.

Ottoman Istanbul had four traditional administrative districts: Dersaadet (Istanbul Proper),[2] Galata, Eyüp and Üsküdar, the latter three being referred to as the *Bilâd-ı Selâse* (the Three Towns). Dersaadet was the old triangular-shaped city surrounded by the Theodosian Walls to the west, the Bosphorus to the east, the Sea of Marmara to the south and the Golden Horn to the north. Galata, located across the Golden Horn, was home to Genoese merchants who had resided there since the Byzantine period. The district on the hill above Galata was named 'Pera' by Europeans, a Greek word meaning 'across the Golden Horn', and 'Beyoğlu' by the Turks meaning 'son of the Bey'. Pera gradually became the centre for Westerners who lived in the Ottoman capital and housed the European envoys and diplomatic missions. Eyüp, located outside the city walls towards the northern end of the Golden Horn, was named after Eyyüb el-Ensari, a companion of the Prophet who is believed to have died there during the siege of the city in 672. A mosque and tomb built in this district by Mehmed II the Conqueror became an important ceremonial centre where Ottoman sultans were girded and sworn. Üsküdar lay across the Bosphorus on the Asian shore, facing Dersaadet and Galata. It was captured by the Turks almost a century before the conquest of Constantinople, and had gradually expanded from the fifteenth to the nineteenth centuries. There were also a number of small villages spread along the shores of the Bosphorus and the Golden Horn.

Istanbul under Ottoman rule had a diverse population. Above all, it was demographically shaped by the inclusive policies of the Ottomans. Istanbul's population after the Turkish conquest was only around 50,000, but it increased sharply immediately after the conquest due to the Mehmed II's primary goal to return his new imperial capital to its glorious past. The Greeks who had left the city before and after the conquest were recalled by an imperial proclamation of *aman* (mercy) and provided with various incentives such as free housing and temporary exemption from taxation. Other methods employed to repopulate the city included *sürgün*, the forced relocation of households to Istanbul from every corner of the Empire, which proved very effective. Imperial decrees were issued for the relocation of Muslim and non-Muslim populations to Istanbul. Immigration from all over the world was also encouraged.[3] Particular emphasis was placed on the craftsmen and merchants who would regenerate the socio-economic life of Istanbul.

The Greeks formed the largest non-Muslim community in Istanbul. They were led by their own patriarch, with the consent of the Sultan. After the Turkish conquest, the patriarch was formally appointed under an imperial decree issued in 1454. The Greek community played a significant role in maritime trade and controlled a large share of the city's food supply. With the establishment of their patriarchate, a new Greek aristocracy emerged that increased its influence in the Ottoman court by supplying personal physicians and commercial agents to the sultans. Members of the Greek aristocracy also occupied the position of chief interpreter of the *Divan*, the Privy Council of the Empire.[4]

Jews formed the second largest non-Muslim population of Istanbul. Although their presence in the city went back to the Byzantine period, the number of Jewish inhabitants of the Ottoman capital had increased dramatically from the late-fifteenth century when many Jews, seeking refuge from Christian oppression, came to Ottoman soil from Spain, Portugal and other parts of Europe. By the mid-sixteenth century there were about 15,000 Jews living in the city, with 40 synagogues and schools serving their community. The Ottoman Jews played a significant role in banking with leading Jewish families, who had controlled large sums of money and trade in Europe prior to migrating to Istanbul, introducing modern banking and monetary reforms to the Ottoman Empire.[5]

There was also a sizable Armenian population in fifteenth-century Ottoman Istanbul. They were led by their own patriarch, a system established by the Ottoman administration in 1461. In the following centuries their number increased significantly, and the Armenians became the second largest non-Muslim group in Istanbul after the Greeks. The Armenian community, like other non-Muslim communities in Istanbul, played a significant role in the city's economic life. In the seventeenth century they began to control the silk trade between the Ottoman Empire and Italy, and from the early nineteenth century they worked mainly in banking and also administered the Imperial Mint.

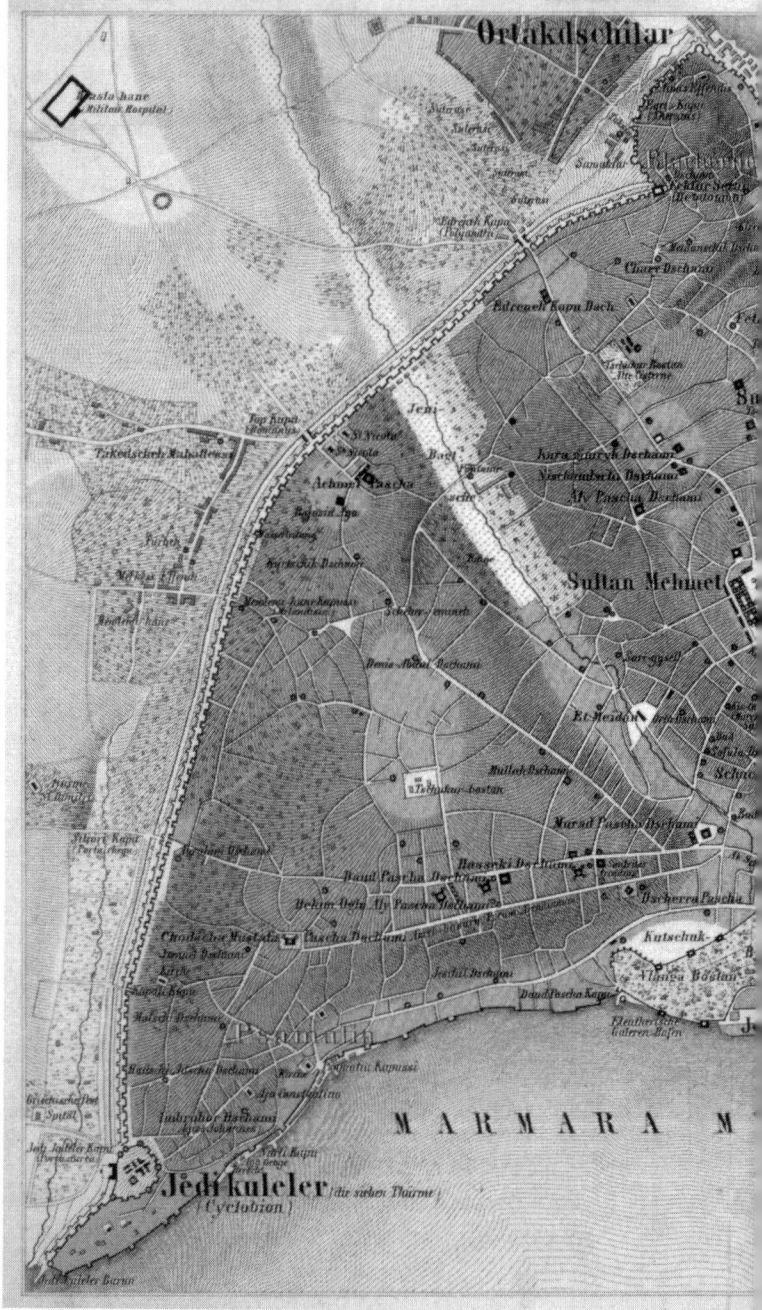

Figure 2 Istanbul Peninsula and Beyoğlu drawn by L. Kraatz, Berlin c.1840

The Greeks, Jews and Armenians, known as the 'People of the Book', were given the status of separate *millet*s (communities) and enjoyed autonomy in their internal affairs under the leadership of their respective patriarchs and rabbinate. Traditionally, the different religious and ethnic groups resided in separate quarters of Ottoman Istanbul. The Greeks were mainly located in Fener, Samatya and Cibali; the Armenians in Kumkapı, Yenikapı and Samatya; and the Jews in Balat and Hasköy. A significant Frankish population also resided in Galata, together with Greeks, Jews, Armenians and some Muslims who lived in the lower sections of the region along the Bosphorus and Golden Horn.

The Turks and other Turkish-speaking Muslims formed the majority of the city's population. From the very beginning of the Ottoman administration, one of its most significant policies was the creation and retention of Istanbul's Islamic character. Various measures were taken to ensure that the Turks always formed the majority population of the city, including strict regulations and restrictions on the construction of buildings for non-Muslim inhabitants. While the minority groups used their own languages, the most commonly used and official language of Istanbul was Turkish. A vivid illustration of this policy was the occasional use of the name 'İslambol' (where Islam abounds) in the official records during the reign of Mehmed II.[6] On 30 May 1453, the day after the fall of the city, Hagia Sophia, the church constructed by Emperor Justinian in 537, was converted into the Great Mosque of Istanbul. In 1459 all Ottoman dignitaries were asked to select an area anywhere within the city, which would then be named after them, to build a mosque, a bath and a marketplace.[7] The Sultan himself selected a site for his new palace at the easternmost end of the Istanbul Peninsula.[8] He also chose a topographically significant location in the centre of the city, previously occupied by the Church of the Holy Apostles, for his new grand mosque. Completed in 1471, the Fatih Mosque together with its surrounding buildings formed Istanbul's first large *külliye* (building complex consisting of a mosque surrounded by a group of public buildings such as hospitals, schools, baths, libraries or hospices). The Fatih complex, with its eight *medrese*s (Islamic colleges) and dormitory buildings, was not only a major place of worship but also a significant centre of learning where medicine, law and Islamic sciences were taught.

In the following centuries all Ottoman sultans, their family members and high-ranking officials adorned every part of the city with a large number of mosques and complexes. Istanbul witnessed immense construction activity during the reign of the two Turkish rulers following Mehmed II:

Bayezid II (1481–1512) and Selim I (1512–20). However, it was the reign of Süleyman I (1520–66), known in the West as Süleyman the Magnificent, that completed the transformation of the old Byzantine capital into a complete Turkish Islamic city. The most significant masterpieces of classical Ottoman architecture were created under the patronage of the great sixteenth-century architect, Sinan. His works, in particular the Süleymaniye Complex constructed for Süleyman the Magnificent, form a fundamental element of the celebrated image of Istanbul. The construction of such religious and public buildings continued until the very end of the Ottoman Empire, although the number of new mosques and their dimensions decreased after the eighteenth century. It is these buildings that give Istanbul the distinctive shape for which it is known today.

Figure 3 Süleymaniye Mosque from the Golden Horn

Another significant characteristic of classical Ottoman Istanbul was its marketplace. Similar to other traditional Middle Eastern cities, Ottoman Istanbul was shaped around the idea of a well-established class of merchants and craftsmen under the control and governance of a ruling military class.[9] A *bedesten* (central marketplace) surrounded by various *han*s (lodges for accommodation and storage) for merchants who engaged in inter-regional trade was the principal element of this model. Unlike the residential pattern, which was based on the idea of separating those of different religious and ethnic origin, the marketplace was occupied by Muslim and non-Muslim tradesmen and merchants working side-by-side without any discrimination by the regulatory authorities.

The *bedesten* of Istanbul was constructed immediately after the Turkish conquest in a former Byzantine commercial district between the former Forum Constantini and the Forum Tauri. With its 15 domes and fortress-like structure, it surpassed previous examples of traditional Ottoman *bedesten* architecture found in the former Ottoman capitals of Bursa and Edirne. The *bedesten* was gradually extended over the next two centuries and became an immense marketplace (*Kapalı Çarşı*) containing thousands of shops, with covered streets and 32 gates leading to the city in every direction.[10] Many *han*s were also constructed in the area between the marketplace and the shores of the Golden Horn. Another significant type of commercial building in Ottoman Istanbul was the *kapan*, where commodities imported to Istanbul were inspected, weighed and taxed by the authorities. They were generally established alongside the port area, and the most significant were: *un kapanı* (for flour), *bal kapanı* (for honey), *yemiş kapanı* (for fruit) and *yağ kapanı* (for oil). The traditional commercial district also included customs houses: one named *gümrük kapanı* in Eminönü for goods imported by the sea and one named *kara gümrüğü* in Edirnekapı on the Theodosian Walls for goods imported overland.

The urban pattern of the city included narrow twisting streets, many of them with cul-de-sacs. There was no planning involved in the street pattern as many of the residential neighbourhoods had come into existence haphazardly around mosques or other buildings of worship in the non-Muslim districts. Even the fires, which in most cases resulted in the loss of entire neighbourhoods, did not alter the crooked and twisted street network as reconstruction of burnt areas always followed pre-existing alignments. The main thoroughfare of the city was Divanyolu, through which had passed caravans, armies and imperial parades. This major road followed the route of the old Byzantine *mese*, and lay on the east–west axis between Hagia Sophia and Çemberlitaş (Forum Constantini), extending to Beyazıt (Forum Tauri) and terminating at the Theodosian Walls in Edirnekapı.[11]

Istanbul's population continued to grow and reached an estimated 300,000 in the sixteenth century.[12] This represented a six-fold increase in a period of 150 years making Istanbul, according to some sources, the world's most populated urban centre. It brought with it severe difficulties such as inadequate food and water supply and lack of security. The city's problems deepened in the late-sixteenth century when immigration from Anatolia further increased as a result of serious social unrest caused by the *Celâli İsyanları*, revolts organised by brigands who were mostly dissident military leaders. The rapid population increase continued in the eighteenth century forcing the Ottoman administration to implement serious measures including the refusal of entry to new immigrants to Istanbul and the forced return of unmarried men to their towns and villages.[13]

Figure 4 Yeni Mosque and Eminönü, late-nineteenth century

Figure 5 An aerial view of the western part of Istanbul Peninsula: Fatih Mosque, Valens Aqueducts and the residential urban pattern of the city, late-nineteenth century

Figure 6 An aerial view of the eastern part of Istanbul Peninsula: Topkapı Palace, Hagia Sophia and part of the Nuruosmaniye Mosque (right) surrounded by the dense urban pattern, late-nineteenth century

The overall administration and security of the city was the responsibility of the *kadı*, the juridical authority under the *Şer-i* (religious law). The *kadı*, in addition to his duty to implement the law, was also responsible for financial, administrative and civic matters. Larger cities often needed several positions. In Istanbul each of the four administrative districts—Dersaadet and the other three districts forming the *Bilâd-ı Selâse*—was governed by a *kadı*. The *kadı* of Dersaadet, also known as *İstanbul Efendisi* (Master of Istanbul), was first in the hierarchy with a direct link to the *Sadrazam* (Grand Vizier).[14]

Dersaadet was subdivided into 13 principal quarters called *nahiye*, emulating the administrative structure established by Emperor Constantine in the fourth century.[15] The establishment of the 13 quarters was based on the order of Mehmed II to his high-ranking military and bureaucratic officials to construct mosques and other civic buildings to encourage the repopulation and prosperity of the city. Each *nahiye* was further subdivided into small neighbourhoods called *mahalle*. Settled around a mosque or a church or synagogue in non-Muslim quarters, the *mahalle* was an entity that represented the common identity of its inhabitants. Every *nahiye* had its own *naib*, the official delegate of the *kadı* in his district, and *imam*, the religious leader of the mosque who was the administrative head of the *mahalle*.[16] In non-Muslim neighbourhoods this task was performed by a priest or rabbi who represented their community in dealing with the state authorities. Beyond its primary function of providing a collective cultural and religious solidarity for its inhabitants, the *mahalle* was also a self-contained administrative unit for performing civic duties. The inhabitants of the *mahalle*, for example, had joint responsibility for their neighbourhood in the maintenance of order, street-cleaning, tax collection and other general obligations to the state. The residents guaranteed each other to ensure the security of their neighbourhood. In this capacity they had to employ street-cleaners and watchman and, in certain neighbourhoods, some of the young men were required to serve as firefighters.[17]

The *kadı* performed his tasks with the help of assistants from the *ulema* (scholars of religious sciences) and the military. For example, the *muhtesip*, a member of the *ulema*, was responsible for the control of commercial activities in the markets. Other military assistants were the *subaşı* (police superintendent), *çöplük subaşısı* (superintendent of garbage collection in the cities) and *Acemi Oğlanlar* (Janissary Corps responsible for monitoring city cleaning). The *Hassa Mimarlar Ocağı* (Corps of Royal Architects) and *Hassa Mimarbaşılığı* (Office of the Royal Architect) were in charge of building activities in the city. All those posts, however, did not establish an effective municipal organisation and, in the absence of such authority and without adequate planning controls, the city grew spontaneously around large public works such as the sultanic mosques and other major public buildings.

At the beginning of the eighteenth century Istanbul saw the first cracks appear in its traditional urban and architectural form. The crushing defeats by Western armies were followed by a relatively peaceful political atmosphere which allowed the Ottomans to carry out some modest changes to the life of the ruling elite. The reign of Ahmed III (1703–30) and his last grand vizier, Nevşehirli Damat İbrahim Paşa, for example, represented one of the most luminous periods in the court life of the Ottoman Empire. Owing its popular name to the extreme tulip-mania of the time, the *Lâle Devri* (Tulip Era) of 1718–30 sowed the embryonic seeds of the secularism that was to enter Ottoman life through increased contact with the West.[18] Significant indicators of change were the exchange of ambassadors, the extensive non-religious or non-official construction activity, the introduction of foreign concepts of architecture, literature, fashion, entertainment and new modes of art. All these changes were partly based on non-Ottoman and, to a certain extent, non-Islamic sources of inspiration that were mostly Persian and French in origin. Hence Ottoman society, or at least the ruling family and high-ranking officials of the court, experienced a way of life that had never existed before.

The Tulip Era saw the Ottoman ruling class extend its daily practices beyond the walls of Topkapı Palace, with the Sultan vacationing in newly constructed imperial residences outside the boundaries of the city in Kağıthane, Üsküdar, Beşiktaş and other palaces along the shores of the Bosphorus. Visits to these residences were often accompanied by extravagant parties such as *lâle çırağanı* (tulip garden illuminations), where candles were placed under tulips and tortoises were to be seen meandering over beds of tulips bearing night-lights on their shells. The festive season continued throughout the year, and not even winter could interrupt the entertainment as *helva sohbetleri* (halva soirées) brought poets, dancers and singers to perform in the imperial palaces.[19]

The effect of the new social practices and entertainments of the ruling elite flowed through the Ottoman capital with the general population of the city being able to observe, for the first time, the life of the ruling class and, to a limited extent, participate in this new mode of life. In addition to the special religious days and occasions, such as the end of Ramadan or the commemoration of the birth of the Prophet, secular events such as royal births, weddings, military victories and betrothals began to be celebrated, with entertainments and carnivals occurring in several major quarters of the city. Illumination of the great mosques, especially during Ramadan, was encouraged by several imperial decrees and, in addition to religious occasions, they began to be illuminated for secular celebrations. A further initiative was the use of the newly created parks and meadows for public events and entertainments such as the great picnics, sightseeing, music and sporting displays, including wrestling and archery.[20]

While the Tulip Era is characterised by this extravagant joy, it is also known for various intellectual initiatives by the high-ranking officials. New libraries opened, including one at the imperial palace of Topkapı by Ahmed III. Grand Vizier İbrahim Paşa established a society to translate masterpieces of Arabic and Persian literature and forbad the export of rare manuscripts. But even more importantly, the Tulip Era saw the introduction of the first Ottoman printing press in 1729 by İbrahim Müteferrika, a Hungarian-born Ottoman who professed to Islam, and Said Efendi, the son of the first Turkish ambassador to France. Although the Christian and Jewish minorities of the Empire had established their own presses long before, printing in Turkish was not permitted because of strong opposition from the calligraphers who were responsible for making copies of the Koran and other religious books. However, Said Efendi and Müteferrika secured permission from the Sultan to print non-religious books under the liberal atmosphere of the era.[21] The establishment of the Turkish press was the first example of a technology transfer from the West in the cultural arena.[22]

The more relaxed attitude to social life and the diplomatic contact with the West during the Tulip Era brought with it extensive construction activity, particularly along the shores of the Golden Horn and the Bosphorus, which pushed the city limits outside the established boundary defined by the Istanbul Peninsula, Galata and Üsküdar. The Ottoman Sultan, grand vizier and many other high-ranking elites constructed hundreds of timber mansions, marine villas, summer palaces and gardens in Kağıthane, Üsküdar, Beşiktaş and along the shores of the Bosphorus. The *Sa'dabad* in Kağıthane, at the upper end of the Golden Horn, was the most significant complex constructed in this period. It was completed in two months in the early 1720s and included imperial residences, approximately 170 timber dwellings and numerous gardens, fountains and canals. The palaces and residences constructed during this period presented a hybrid identity. As noted by various European travellers, as well as Marquis de Bonnac, the French ambassador in Istanbul at the time, the concept may have been borrowed from drawings of French palaces and gardens brought back by Yirmisekiz Çelebi Mehmed Efendi, the first Ottoman exploratory ambassador to Europe, who was sent to France in 1720–21. In particular, the kilometre-long canal in *Sa'dabad* owed its design to

Fontainebleau. The architectural inspiration for the buildings, however, was Eastern and the names given to the places were all poetic Persian words such as *sa'dabad* (abode of happiness) and *hürremabad* (abode of joy).[23]

Notwithstanding these cultural and intellectual developments, the economic and political structures of the Ottoman Empire were unstable. The defeat by the Austrians in 1683 and the Russian campaigns of 1678–81 brought structural changes to the Ottoman military system and a significant increase in the number of paid soldiers.[24] In order to pay the army, gold and silverware were melted down to increase the supply of currency and the *akçe* (silver coin), the major currency used in Anatolia and the Balkans during the Ottoman Empire, was decreased in weight in 1685.[25] These financial and political problems worsened in the first quarter of the eighteenth century when the wars against Persia in 1723 added new tax burdens and brought about a spectacular increase in the existing levies. A significant decrease in crop production in Anatolia also created unprecedented immigration flows from rural areas to urban Istanbul. This intense immigration would not only place increased pressure on Istanbul's social fabric, but would also lead to a significant decline in the Empire's agricultural production and revenue.[26]

In 1721 Ahmed III attempted to reduce the pressures of population by issuing an order to the governors of Anatolia and Rumelia to forbid immigration to Istanbul. This order and further decrees failed to stop the influx of people to the Empire's capital until, finally, in November 1724 the Sultan ordered the Janissaries to control the gates of the city and to turn back the immigrants.[27] Despite these drastic measures, Istanbul's population continued to grow leading to an explosive political climate. Excessively high population densities within the city walls eventually resulted in crowds of jobless protesters and anarchy. High prices and taxes and lack of food caused deep resentment among Istanbul's population. In addition, unbridled expenditure by the court on entertainment and construction, together with corruption in moral values and the bad news from the wars against the Persians on the eastern front, all led to increased public dissatisfaction and much unease in conservative political circles. Arson became one of the most devastating and effective ways for the poor and jobless to express their resentment and anger towards the extravagant life of the Ottoman court.[28] As a consequence, a large number of fires, many of them started by arsonists, occurred in Istanbul, especially after 1724.[29]

The volatile conditions of the Ottoman Empire brought an abrupt end to the Tulip Era and culminated in a violent riot led by Patrona Halil, a former marine of Albanian origin in the Imperial Navy, in late September

1730. Within two days of the riots Ahmed III was deposed and his grand vizier, Damat İbrahim Paşa, was executed. Although Mahmud I, the new sultan, eventually took back control of the city and executed the leaders of the insurgency in late November of the same year, the riots left Istanbul extensively fire-damaged, with the timber houses and mansions along the Golden Horn and the Bosphorus completely destroyed.[30]

Anarchy and riots, however, did not put a stop to the reforms. After a short period of interruption the printers started to operate, ambassadors were sent to Europe and European military staff were employed to introduce Western-style military techniques and education.[31] The increasing contact with the West was echoed in the architectural vocabulary of Istanbul. During the mid-eighteenth century the city witnessed the adoption of baroque and rococo styles in both architecture and decoration. Many buildings were decorated with shell-like curves or S and C-shaped figures. Corinthian and composite column heads were used instead of the traditional decorative shapes of Ottoman architecture. The very early examples of baroque and rococo motifs found in Ottoman architecture, such as fountains and *sebils*, go back to the 1740s.[32]

The most significant demonstration of the change in architectural styles, however, can be found in the construction of the Nuruosmaniye Mosque in Istanbul in 1755.[33] With its unprecedented, and never repeated, horseshoe-shaped courtyard, the Nuruosmaniye Mosque was the first Ottoman mosque to adopt the major characteristics of the French baroque style, such as scrolls, shells, cable, heavily formed cornices, concave and convex facades, round arches and fluted capitals.

The changes to the Ottoman social structure were further accelerated under the reign of Selim III (1789–1807) who broadened communication channels to the West. Selim III's reforms were a decisive change from the classical approaches of earlier Ottoman rulers who saw the restoration of the traditional order and the institutions of the past as the best recipe to solve the problems of the Empire. In fact, he was the first Ottoman sultan who, in Stanford Shaw's words, genuinely tried to pierce the 'iron curtain' between the Ottomans and the West, and he was partially successful.[34]

The humiliating defeat of the Ottomans by the Russians and the harsh outcome of the peace treaty of Küçük Kaynarca, signed in 1774 after the Ottoman–Russian war, demonstrated the deficiency of the classical Ottoman military apparatus. Once again, Selim III launched a new reform programme, named the *Nizam-ı Cedid* (New Order), with the aims of strengthening state authority to solve both external and internal problems and establishing a new army to compete with European military supremacy.[35]

Figure 7 Nuruosmaniye Mosque and the aerial view of the *Kapalı Çarşı* (the Grand Bazaar), late-nineteenth century

The new sultan appointed European advisers to the newly opened Western-style military schools, posted staff to Europe and established permanent embassies in several major European capital cities, including Paris, London and Vienna.[36] Paris, especially, became an educative destination for young Ottoman bureaucrats, similar to Rome for English gentlemen on the Grand Tour. These initiatives resulted in a revamped Ottoman bureaucracy, familiar with Western-style urban ways of life and its built environment and possessing a fervent desire to transform Istanbul into a modern capital like its European counterparts. These same initiatives also led to an understanding of planning principles in relation to managing the urban environment and culminated in the implementation of building regulations and other institutional reforms in the first half of the nineteenth century.

The city's increasing population, together with the strengthened relationships with Western institutions, led the Ottomans of the late-eighteenth century to look at urban problems from a very different perspective. A significant indication of this new perception can be found in Tatarcık Abdullah Efendi's memorandum to the Ottoman court in 1792. This memorandum to Selim III is the first known proposal for modernising the urban structure of Istanbul. As a member of the *ulema* and a member of Selim III's advisory council, Abdullah Efendi recommended ways to improve the quality of the urban environment in the Ottoman capital. Apart from other areas of concern such as the military, legislation, economics and navigation, the fourth clause of his memorandum was titled *Siyaset-i Belediyye* (Politics of Municipal Affairs) and described the essential works required to improve the quality of urban life and to ameliorate the problems of municipal management in the Ottoman capital. According to Abdullah Efendi, nations who established 'sovereignty and states' should pass from a 'nomadic' to a 'sedentary' system and should act in accordance with 'sedentary rules' to solve the problems of such civilisations. For example, the need to collect garbage in Istanbul directly corresponded with the city's population increases, and had to be carried out in accordance with hygienic rules. Significantly, Abdullah Efendi recommended the opening of large streets in the areas destroyed by the great fires, establishing clean and hygienic urban spaces and converting residential buildings from timber to masonry construction.[37] These recommendations were formulated as early as 1796 in the *Ebniye Nizamı* (Building Regulation), the first statutory planning instrument in the history of Ottoman Istanbul.

Istanbul during the Reign of Mahmud II

The reforms introduced by Selim III at the end of the eighteenth century ended violently with an uprising in May 1807 by the Janissary Corps against his newly established army, the *Nizam-ı Cedid*. The rebellious Janissaries, backed by the *ulema*, installed Selim III's cousin, Mustafa IV, on the throne on 29 May 1807. Mustafa's reign, however, proved to be short-lived. He was toppled by a counter uprising organised by the remnants of the *Nizam-ı Cedid* under the command of Bayrakdar Mustafa Paşa, a provincial notable of Rusçuk in the Balkans. This resulted in Selim III's other cousin, Mahmud II, claiming the throne on 28 July 1808.

Mahmud II was a strong supporter of the *Nizam-ı Cedid* and continued the process of reform. For him, the rebellious Janissaries posed a major problem. The Janissary Corps initially emerged as an elite guard responsible for the protection of the sultan, and since the sixteenth century had assumed a highly influential, almost pivotal, role in the Ottoman army by dramatically increasing their numbers and power. Settled in their barracks within the city, they performed important civic duties such as firefighting and the maintenance of law and order and, most importantly, the regulation of economic life. As artisans and tradesmen during peacetime, the Janissaries were a very significant and distinctive element in the development of Istanbul's urban morphology. Over time their growing lack of discipline formed a state within a state, giving rise to numerous revolts and rebellions that resulted in the overthrow, and even murder, of sultans, not unlike the Praetorian Guard of Imperial Rome.

Backed by low-ranking *ulema,* the Janissaries vigorously opposed any attempt at reform as a threat to their power and privilege. Despite their critical position as internal political players, the Janissary troops could no longer claim a distinguished record in defending the Ottoman Empire against enemies. Their humiliating defeat during the Greek campaigns in the mid-1820s provided a strategic opportunity for the new sultan to destroy their power base. Unlike his cousin Selim III, Mahmud II was now able to secure the support of the religious establishment and city population who had suffered from the Janissaries terror. The Janissary Corps was eventually crushed in a bloody massacre on 15–17 June 1826, which was reinforced by subsequent operations over the following months.

The abolition of the Janissary Corps, labelled *Vak'a-i Hayriye* (The Auspicious Event), brought substantial changes to the administrative structure of the Empire. Three independent administrative branches were created: *kalemiyye* (civil bureaucracy); *ilmiyye* (religious-judicial hierarchy); and *seyfiyye* (the military). The new army, named *Muallem Asakir-i Mansure-i Muhammediye* (Trained Victorious Troops of Muhammed), was placed under the control of the *serasker* (commander-in-chief). The *ulema* also lost their privileged status as their religious endowments, or *evkaf,* were taken away and placed under the government control of the *şeyhülislam,* the head of the *ilmiyye*. The grand vizier, the absolute deputy of the Sultan, was lowered in rank having equal status with the *serasker* and the *şeyhülislam,* and given the title of 'prime minister' with responsibility for the civil bureaucracy. The grand vizier's former deputies were made ministers for Internal and External Affairs and Finance. Finally, these reforms were formalised by the establishment of consultative councils, the most important being the *Meclis-i Vâlâ-i Ahkâm-i Adliyye* (Supreme Council of Judicial Ordinance).[38]

These changes had significant impacts on the urban management of Istanbul. The abolition of the Janissary Corps saw the *kadı* lose his administrative power in the city as he became responsible only for juridical duties.[39] Soon after, the *İhtisab Nazırlığı* (Ministry of Taxation and Urban Affairs) was established and given responsibility for the collection of taxes, security and the coordination and implementation of public works. The post of *muhtar* (headman), responsible for the administration of the *mahalle,* was introduced into the urban government. Non-Muslim quarters were also to be administered by a *kocabaşı,* an equivalent of the *muhtar,* and both the *muhtar* and *kocabaşı* and the religious leaders of the *mahalle* were authorised to issue official paperwork and ensure the security and order of their quarters.[40] The reforms were followed by the replacement of *Hassa Mimarlar Ocağı* by *Ebniye-i Hassa Müdürlüğü* (Directorate of Royal Buildings) in 1831. The *Şehreminliği* (Office for Construction Activities for Royal Buildings) was also amalgamated with the *Ebniye-i Hassa Müdürlüğü* and attached to the *Nafia Nezareti* (Ministry of Public Works).

Another important political event which was to impact deeply on Istanbul's urban morphology occurred in August 1838. Despite all the attempts of reform during Mahmud II's reign, the Ottoman Empire could not overcome its inherent military and economic weakness. For many young Ottoman reformers integration with industrialised Europe and world markets was the only way to save the Empire from collapse. This precarious situation, amplified by the increasing military threat from Mehmed Ali Paşa, the rebellious Ottoman Governor of Egypt, forced the Ottomans to seek British support in the mid-1830s. This resulted in the signing of a commercial treaty in 1838 known as the Anglo–Ottoman Commercial Treaty. Subsequently, similar treaties were made with other major European states which lowered the custom tariffs in favour of European merchants permitting them to make direct contact with local producers without the involvement of government officials. Although the increase in foreign trade benefited middle class merchants, the result was catastrophic for local craftsmen and farmers who were unable to compete with the influx of cheap industrial products with minimal tariffs.

As a result, all Ottoman ports and particularly Istanbul attracted a large number of merchants, bankers and businessmen from Europe and the former Eastern European provinces of the Empire. This highlighted the ineffectiveness of Istanbul's existing urban infrastructure. Increasing international trade required an efficient transport system, effective port facilities, reliable postal services and communications, and appropriate new commercial accommodation. New public buildings such as hotels and entertainment venues and, more importantly, an effective urban infrastructure were also needed to satisfy the city's new residents. Consequently, the economic centre of the city shifted from the traditional marketplace and *han*s to European-style commercial and bank buildings constructed in Galata on the northern shore of the Golden Horn. Galata and Pera, especially from the 1840s, began to appear as the European face of Istanbul. With its Western-style shops full of imported European goods, places of entertainment and schools, Galata consolidated its European distinctiveness in the Ottoman capital. The multi-ethnic population drawn from many nationalities mixed with young Ottoman bureaucrats who were embracing a Western lifestyle.

The political reforms of the first part of the nineteenth century gathered pace in 1839 with the declaration of an imperial edict commonly known as the *Tanzimat Fermanı*. The edict was prepared by a group of Ottoman bureaucrats led by the Minister for Foreign Affairs, Mustafa Reşid Paşa, and was announced on 3 November 1839. Also known as the *Gülhane Hatt-ı Şerifi* (The Noble Edict of the Rose Garden), the edict guaranteed the subjects of the Empire their life, honour, property and equality before the law regardless of ethnic or religious origin. This edict was, in fact, the official announcement of proposed changes to the Ottoman administrative, social and cultural structure, which had their origin in the early years of the eighteenth century. The *Tanzimat* reforms (1839–76) included: abolition of the patrimonial taxation system; creation of a monetised system to levy taxes; secularisation and formalisation of education and justice; differentiation of the administrative structure along functional lines; introduction of a new provincial administration; creation of a new elite bureaucratic system; and, finally, the establishment of an Ottoman parliament and constitution.[41]

During the *Tanzimat* era the Sultan's power shifted into the hands of bureaucrats who had close European contacts and saw the establishment of Western institutions as the only way to rescue the declining empire.[42] Many of the young Ottoman bureaucrats who had been stationed in major European capitals wanted to emulate in Istanbul the type of urban life they had enjoyed abroad. Mustafa Reşid Paşa's political correspondence with the Sublime Porte, the ministerial office of the grand vizier and other ministers, whilst working as diplomat in London advocated that architecture and urban planning based on rational geometrical rules could be used to regularise the labyrinthine street pattern of Istanbul. He also argued for the adoption of European building technology, especially the replacement of timber with masonry for residential construction in order to reduce the risk of fire. To help further these aims Turkish students were to be sent to Europe to study architecture and building technology. Interestingly, Mustafa Reşid, a passionate believer in the political advantages of the Anglo–Ottoman alliance, favoured the English residential pattern of detached houses on individual lots over the French style of multi-storeyed apartment blocks because he believed the former was much more appropriate to the Islamic way of life.[43]

Reorganisation of the Urban Pattern: the 1839 Development Policy

Like most old European cities, Istanbul entered the nineteenth century troubled by a range of major social problems, including dramatic population growth, insufficient land for new urban settlements to house immigrants, and increasing outbreaks of major fires that resulted in the loss of thousands of buildings annually.[44] From the mid-1830s the city's inadequate infrastructure and cumbersome commercial practices in a time of expanding international trade represented the most immediate problems for the Ottoman administration. And, most importantly, despite the changes to the administrative structure, Istanbul still lacked an adequate municipal organisation to deal with these problems.

The condition of the existing building stock was another significant problem confronting the urban administration. The houses of Istanbul were made of timber, using a construction tradition that originated in the Byzantine period. Since the beginning of the eighteenth century the number of fires and their intensity had increased at an alarming rate.[45] These fire outbreaks were exacerbated by the increasing population and the narrow, crooked street network with innumerable cul-de-sacs built over with crowded timber dwellings. The development of new residential areas outside the traditional city quarters was subject to the Sultan's approval. This was not usually granted to new immigrants so new arrivals were largely accommodated in existing neighbourhoods within the old city, resulting in rapidly increasing densities and deterioration of the spatial qualities of settlements. The city in general developed a chaotic character.

Ottoman administrators also confronted difficulties caused by the lack of reliable infrastructure in their capital. Istanbul did not have an effective transport network as movement within the city's narrow and labyrinthine street pattern was simply based on pedestrian circulation with commercial goods being carried by *hamal*s (porters). In 1844 there were about 8,500 registered *hamal*s responsible for the carriage of commercial goods.[46] Not even the principal streets had pavements or sewerage. Postal services, traditionally provided by the military, proved inadequate to service the growing commercial enterprises of the city, and port facilities required major upgrading in order to handle rapidly increasing freight and passenger traffic. In a similar way, the traditional business district located within the *bedesten* and around the many *han*s was unable to provide the new types of commercial accommodation required for banks, offices, warehouses and hotels as international trade expanded and intensified.

A significant milestone in solving the problems of the existing urban pattern came in 1839 with the first known attempt to apply Western urban planning concepts to Istanbul.[47] This occurred just a few months prior to the announcement of the *Tanzimat Fermanı*. A document found in the Ottoman

State Secretariat's archive gives a meticulous description of a development policy and related physical planning controls for the Empire's capital. The policy seems to represent the suggestions made by Abdullah Efendi in 1792. This policy, however, provides both principles and detailed planning controls for the city in a way that had never been applied before. By comparison, the earlier building orders, regulations and codes did not go beyond basic controls and general precautions against the danger of fire. The 1839 policy was quite different from the Ottoman urban planning concepts that preceded it and, despite the fact that no other part of the development concept has yet been found, it clearly indicates planning policy directions and specific design features for the built environment. A brief summary of an English translation follows:

> All buildings to be constructed in the future shall not be built of timber and will no longer be constructed without plans. Muslims and non-Muslims who want to construct a masonry house shall be provided with sites which are regularised according to geometrical rules and have large streets. Such sites may be enlarged by construction works in the future. If other such *mahalle*s are to be created, standardised sites will be produced by the works of persons who have expertise in engineering. No one is permitted to build timber houses amongst the masonry ones. However, poor people may be permitted to construct timber houses on outer suburban sites. After preparation of a detailed map of Istanbul, the following streets shall be constructed 20 *zira'* [15 metres] in width: a road starting from the *Bab-ı Hümayun* and crossing Divanyolu to Beyazıt and Aksaray and then to Silivrikapı and to Mevlevihanekapısı; a road from Beyazıt to Edirnekapı; and roads from Çarşamba Pazarı to Eğrikapı, from Kadırga Port to Yedikule and from Bahçekapı to Eyüp. Both sides of these roads will be planted with trees and provided with pedestrian footpaths of four *zira'* [three metres] width. In order to allow the passing of carriages, 12 *zira'* [nine metres] width shall be provided. The rest of the streets are to be 12 and 15 *zira'* or at least 10 *zira'* [7.5 metres] in width. No cul-de-sacs are permitted. The coastal lines between Yalıköşkü in Sarayburnu and Unkapanı and between Tophane and *Cisr-i Cedid* [bridge over the Golden Horn] are to be provided with masonry wharves. The roads shall be planted with trees and provided with pedestrian footpaths which are to be 4 *arşın* [three metres] in width. In appropriate locations the masonry wharves shall be provided with *meydan*s [squares]. *Meydan*s are also to be created within the proximity of mosques and other large buildings. The [financial]

loss of private *evkaf* [endowments] due to the expropriation of land for street widening will be compensated for by the *Evkaf Nezareti* [Ministry of Endowments]. Individuals who lose their homes are also to be provided with rental assistance. The new masonry houses shall not be more than three storeys and 20 *zira'* [15 metres] in height, and no cantilevered balcony is permitted. Mosques and cemeteries are to be excluded from expropriation. However, fountains and similar structures can be relocated to appropriate places. In principle, houses shall be masonry; however, someone who cannot afford to build a masonry house can construct a timber house. Nevertheless, a masonry wall must be constructed between these timber houses and the walls must exceed the uppermost level of the roof. All these works are to be carried out in accordance with prepared plans, and the Director of *Ebniye-i Hassa* shall be responsible for the application of this regulation of development.[48]

The document on which the above translation is based was found in the Ottoman archives and published in 1922 by Osman Nuri [Ergin].[49] It clearly shows that the Ottoman administration had already begun to see the planning and development of their capital's built environment through very different eyes.

Today this document is described as a 'redevelopment plan' or a 'master plan' in several literary sources. However, careful examination reveals that its contents are not sufficient to determine whether it was a redevelopment plan, as understood in modern terms, or rather a general conceptual guide providing overarching planning principles for the future development of the city. As no primary evidence has been found, the determination of this matter is open to question. It is not known if it was illustrated with plans or architectural drawings. However, the document was detailed and prescriptive and, at the same time, proposed a regulatory policy to reposition the structural components of the urban form to achieve a better built environment for Istanbul. For these reasons it is probably more appropriate to call this document a development policy.

The 1839 development policy for Istanbul promulgated a proper street network consisting of wide roads with pedestrian pathways, proper wharves and large open spaces. Rather than opening new routes, the proposed arteries mainly followed existing roads that connected the major commercial and administrative districts to the gates of the Theodosian Walls. The old Byzantine *mese*, the Divanyolu, was envisaged as one of the main arteries in the proposed network and would connect *Bab-ı Hümayun* (the main gate of the Topkapı Palace) to Beyazıt Square and Aksaray to Silivrikapı and Mevlevihanekapısı (gates on the Theodosian Walls). Another proposed artery followed a route towards the north, connecting Beyazıt Square to Fatih and then travelled to Edirnekapı and Eğrikapı. In addition, two main littoral roads were proposed. The first one was to start from the Port of Kadırga and follow the Marmara shores before terminating at the southern end of the Theodosian Walls. The second proposed coastal artery would follow the southern shores of the Golden Horn, connecting Eminönü to Eyüp. The width of these roads was to be approximately 16.5 metres. Along the verges of the roads there was provision for three-metre-wide pedestrian paths lined with trees, plus a nine-metre-wide easement for carriages. Other roads, depending on their importance, were to be approximately 7.5, 9 or 11.25 metres in width. Several stone wharves were also to be provided alongside the shores of the Bosphorus (between Tophane and the Bridge) and the Golden Horn (between Yalıköşkü and Unkapanı).

Building heights were restricted to three storeys or 16.5 metres. Property resumption was another new practice designed to enable the widening of streets and to provide sufficient space for a regular street network. Expropriation provisions would also allow for reclamation of land and wharf buildings on the waterfronts, although mosques and cemeteries were exempted from the resumption. Fountains and other public structures that did not conform to the provisions of the policy were to be relocated to more appropriate places. The 1839 policy also provided for several public open spaces to be created around the great mosques. Most importantly, maps and plans of the city were required before these works could be carried out. This was the first time in Istanbul's known Islamic past that such cartographic documents, as understood today, were required for the purpose of the development of the city.

The authorship of the 1839 development policy is a controversial issue. Several scholars have identified Helmuth von Moltke as the author of this development policy. A Prussian military advisor to the Ottoman Empire, Moltke is sometimes represented as an engineer and the author of a 'grand scheme'.[50] As a serving military officer in the Prussian army, he arrived in Istanbul in 1835 to participate in the modernisation of the Ottoman army.

Moltke worked primarily as a military adviser and resided in Istanbul until 1839.[51] His skill as a topographic cartographer was recognised by Mahmud II who asked him to prepare surveys of the Dardanelles and both shores of the Bosphorus, including Istanbul.[52] Moltke's survey was completed in February 1837, winning him a medal of recognition, İftihar Nişanı, from Mahmud

II.[53] It is noteworthy that Moltke's surveys of Istanbul and the Bosphorus were not only applauded by the Ottomans, but also highly praised by the Prussian government as they provided valuable military information, such as the position of fortresses on the Bosphorus and the number of cannon in each bastion.[54] Moltke's map was first published in Berlin in 1842 and then reprinted in 1853.[55]

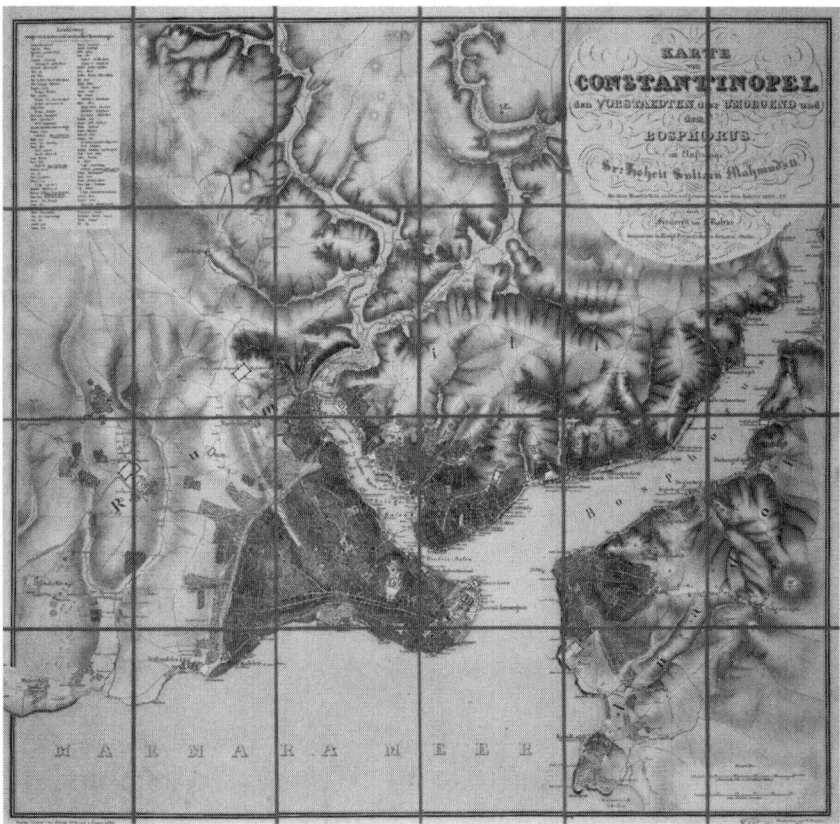

Figure 8 Moltke's Map of Istanbul, printed by Verlag von Simon Schropp and Company, 1842

In a letter of 22 February 1837 Moltke writes: 'I have completed the survey of Constantinople; certainly in no other capital could I have worked in such a way without disturbance, like here on the roads. Harita means a map to the Turks'.[56] In this letter Moltke used the German word *aufnahme* to describe his map. The basic meaning of this word is a 'survey' or 'map'. However, *aufnahme* was interpreted as 'plan' when Moltke's letters were published in Turkish, and the above mentioned statement was translated as, '*İstanbul'un planını bitirdim*' ('I have completed the plan of Istanbul').[57] The word 'plan' in the Turkish translation of Moltke's letter is interpreted as the '*İmar Planı*' (redevelopment or master plan) and hence the above statement concerning the completion of the map has been construed by many contemporary architectural and urban historians as conclusive evidence of his authorship of the separate and different urban development policy of 1839.

Further reading of Moltke's other letters from Istanbul, which are not translated into Turkish, provides an opportunity to interpret his statement more correctly.[58] One of these letters published in volume four provides an important clue to understanding what Moltke actually meant when he wrote, 'I have completed the survey of Constantinople'. In this letter of 6 February 1837 Moltke wrote:

> I have been settled here in Pera for a fortnight, because the Sultan has ordered me to make a plan of Constantinople ... I only need another week to finish my map ... The map I have made of this neighbourhood has already cost me 100 thaler, but in the future it will be one of the 'most pleasurable' results of my residence in Turkey. It includes, at present, the whole of the Bosphorus from the entrance to the Black Sea for five miles down towards the Sea of Marmara and inland for between one to one and a half miles on both sides. It includes: Büyükdere where the ambassadors live; Tarabya where Medea culled her magic herbs; the Cyaneæ which was circumnavigated by the Argonauts; Hisar which was fortified by the Turkish Sultans; Constantinople with its walls built by the Greek Emperors; the Seraglio which occupies the site of ancient Byzantium; Pera and Galata which were founded by the Genoese; Kadıköy, the ancient Chalcedon; the Plain of Davud Paşa where the Janissaries met and where they were given the Sancak-ı Şerif or the standard of the Prophet as they were setting forth to conquer Christendom; the aqueducts of Valens and of Süleyman; the last spurs of the Balkans; and the first mountains of Bithynia ...[59]

In addition, Moltke mentions his survey of Istanbul in several other letters. In one letter dated 27 September 1836 he writes, 'At this moment I am very busy with some work which at the same time gives me much pleasure: a survey of the lands on both sides of the Bosphorus'.[60] And in another letter written to his mother, dated 17 March 1837, Moltke comments, 'I think, as I mentioned in my last letter, I have finally finished the survey completely'.[61] Similarly, in his autobiography Moltke writes:

> In those times promotion in the General Staff was not as quick as it is now. For seven years I was a Captain of the second class. Four years

of that period, from 1836 to 1839, I spent in Turkey. My letters on "Turkish Affairs, &c." have been published, as well as my survey of the Dardanelles and of Constantinople and the Bosphorus.[62]

An analysis of this primary source material casts doubt on the association of Moltke with the 1839 development policy. There is no evidence that he drafted it. A careful reading of Moltke's letters clearly indicates that the statement in his letter dated 22 February 1837 simply describes his survey of Istanbul. In none of the letters is there any reference to involvement with a development plan or policy. Moreover, his letters show that he uses 'plan' and 'map' interchangeably when describing his survey of Istanbul. Moreover, apart from the publication of a Turkish version of Moltke's map by the Military School of the Ottoman Empire in 1849, there is no evidence to show that Moltke's work was used by the Ottoman administration in urban planning and development. And there is no evidence that the 1839 policy was implemented by the Ottoman administration, although it may have influenced thinking about planning generally.

On 30 June 1839 Mahmud II died and his son, Abdülmecid, acceded to the throne. Shortly after, in November 1839, the imperial decree of *Tanzimat* was issued. Istanbul's first grid street pattern was laid out in 1856, seventeen years after the introduction of the 1839 development policy. The first street widenings in Istanbul began in 1866.[63]

Despite the doubtful authorship of the 1839 development policy, it can still be considered as the first major attempt to reorganise the city according to Western planning principles. The provision of pedestrian paths, public spaces and regular streets were all innovations which had not formed part of Istanbul's Islamic past. It is clear that during the second half of the nineteenth century changes in Ottoman thinking about development planning were related to the provisions of the 1839 policy, even if they were not specifically prescribed by them. Indeed, the major planning principles for the modernisation of Istanbul in the twentieth century, particularly the regularising of streets and establishment of an effective road network, are all consistent with the 1839 development policy. Another important aspect of this plan is its recommendation for regularising spaces around the great mosques and large public buildings to liberate them from the 'ugly' clutter of squatters. This was a common feature of future plans for the city in both Ottoman and subsequent Republican periods.

The first serious planning control instrument for Istanbul came nine years after the 1839 development policy. Although the Ottomans had issued various building codes since the late-eighteenth century, the 1848 *Ebniye Nizamnamesi*

(Building Regulation) was the first meticulous document prepared to regulate building activities in the city. In 1849 it was revised slightly and reissued with a total of 33 clauses, of which the majority referred to the most urgent problem of the city: the threat of fire. According to the 1849 regulation, the newly opened streets could not be narrower than 6, 10 or 12 *arşın* (4.5, 7.5 or 9 metres) and cul-de-sacs were to be eliminated. Masonry was preferred to timber in all new construction and building heights, except for public buildings, were restricted to 14 *arşın* (10.5 metres) for timber buildings and 20 *arşın* (15 metres) for masonry buildings. No new permits would be issued for buildings around squares and mosque courtyards. However, what makes this building regulation more interesting is that the concepts of 'public interest' and 'land resumption' for public interest were firmly incorporated into planning jargon for the first time in Ottoman history.

The 1849 building regulation was followed by a raft of statutory planning control instruments issued over the forthcoming decades. The 1863 *Turuk ve Ebniye Nizamnamesi* (Road and Building Regulation) determined the minimum acceptable road widths and the 1863 *Rıhtımlar Nizamnamesi* (Quays Regulation) envisaged the reorganisation of the quayside to accommodate changing commercial and transport activities. Finally, in 1882 the *Ebniye Kanunu* (Building Act) was passed.

Changed Urban Morphology

Beyond the changes experienced in urban planning legislation, Istanbul also saw various cultural, social and technological initiatives. The first was the establishment of an Ottoman newspaper, *Takvim-i Vakayi* (Calendar of Events), launched in 1831 as an official gazette and published in both Turkish and French.[64] Despite the very low literacy rate, coffee-houses provided an opportunity for the ordinary people to have access to newspapers and so familiarise themselves with general politics. Censuses were undertaken in 1828 and 1831 which counted the Empire's male population to be about 3.5 million.[65] Education was another social issue to which Mahmud II paid great attention, and a medical school for the military was established at Galatasaray in 1827 with the curriculum taught in French. The School of Military Music was founded in 1831 by Giuseppe Donizetti, brother of the famous Italian composer Domenico Gaetano Maria Donizetti. Giuseppe Donizetti had arrived in Istanbul in 1828 and had composed the first Ottoman military march, *Mahmudiye,* which became the first Ottoman national anthem.[66] These initiatives were followed by the opening of a military academy in the Maçka district of the city in 1834. Perhaps one of the most significant developments in the cultural area was the opening of the *Tercüme Odası* (Translation Office) in 1833. This office went beyond its bureaucratic role of servicing the increasing diplomatic and commercial contact with European countries and functioned as a school to familiarise young Ottoman bureaucrats with Western civilisation.[67]

Reforms in the army and educational sector significantly impacted on the urban expansion of the imperial capital. Almost all new military barracks and schools constructed from the late-eighteenth century were outside the city walls, particularly in the Beyoğlu district. The construction of these buildings intensified the increasing importance of the Beyoğlu region. This trend was further accelerated from 1830 onwards by the relocation of the Ottoman sultans from Topkapı Palace to Western-style palaces along the shores of the Bosphorus. The Ottoman sultans had constructed imperial residences and marine villas along the shores of the Bosphorus since the sixteenth century, and spent time there during summers. However, from the *Tanzimat* period the palaces on the Bosphorus were preferred as permanent residences for the ruling family. In the large part, this was the result of the psychological harm suffered in childhood by Mahmud II who had witnessed the revolts of the Janissaries and the murder of Selim III within the walls of the Topkapı Palace. Mahmud II spent more and more time in imperial residences outside Topkapı Palace and eventually ordered the construction of the old Çırağan Palace in 1834. Designed by Abdülhalim Bey, the Director of *Ebniye-i Hassa*, Çırağan Palace was completed in 1839, shortly after the death of Mahmud II. The new palaces and mansions were significantly different from the former palace in terms of their architectural styles. Although it had housed the Ottoman sultans during the Empire's golden ages, the Topkapı Palace was a very modest imperial residence formed by pavilions and small buildings. In contrast, the new imperial palaces of the *Tanzimat* period with their sumptuous exteriors and interiors represented the latest European architectural fashion. This dramatic change in architectural expression was an inevitable result of a process of reform in political and cultural areas which reflected European values.

The striking change in architectural taste was not limited to the imperial palaces and residences. Military and government buildings, as well as private residences, designed by European or Christian Ottoman architects who began to monopolise the architectural profession, reflected the changing status of the newly emerging bourgeoisie. The military and government buildings with their imposing presence and immense size began to dominate the city's silhouette and formed a distinct topography which had been formerly the preserve of the monumental sultanic mosques constructed from the mid-fifteenth century. One significant example was *Darülfünun*, the university building constructed next to Hagia Sophia. Designed by the

Swiss architect Gaspare Trajano Fossati who was the designer of many other Istanbul buildings and restorer of Hagia Sophia, *Darülfünun* was a three-storey, neo-Renaissance building that had a great visual impact on Istanbul's urban character.

Among the many military buildings constructed in this period, the Selimiye Barracks in Üsküdar was the most significant. This building was first constructed in timber under the reign of Selim III, and later destroyed by fire during the Janissary uprising of the early nineteenth century. It was reconstructed in masonry in 1829 for Mahmud II's new army. Built in a quadrangular form with gigantic dimensions (268 metres by 200 metres), Selimiye Barracks became a landmark building on the Asian side of Istanbul.[68]

While the old walled city of Istanbul witnessed the sporadic construction of a number of new buildings, the most radical transformation of the city's urban morphology occurred across the Golden Horn. After the great fire of 1831 the northern section of Galata underwent a complete transformation, with the construction of new embassies, commercial buildings, hotels and entertainment venues. New Western-style shops, cafés and patisseries appeared along the Grande Rue de Pera, and in 1831 a theatre opened in this district. It was here that Donizetti, who was then given the title of Paşa, scheduled an annual Italian opera programme.[69] As a vivid indication of the transformation of this area, between 1838 and 1847 land values in Pera increased by about 75 per cent, whereas rents in the traditional Grand Bazaar fell by about 90 per cent. Only 222 of a total of 1,159 merchants and bankers registered in *Indicateur Constantinopolitan* were located within the traditional walled city of Istanbul.[70]

Again, in this period various industrial sites were introduced into Istanbul. New gunpowder factories operated from the late-1790s outside the city walls in the west at Yeşilköy and Bakırköy. A new paper mill was established in 1804 at Beykoz, a small village on the upper Asian side of the Bosphorus, and a spinning mill opened in Eyüp in 1827. In 1839 a steam-powered mill of thirty horsepower was established by a Belgian speculator, M. L. Moine.[71] A glass factory, *Billur Fabrika-i Hümâyunu*, was opened in Beykoz in 1846, and this small plant was improved in 1866 and 1899 to become a full-scale industrial unit for the production of glass and porcelain. During this period Yedikule-Zeytinburnu became an important industrial centre with new factories for the manufacture of muskets, leather, copper, wool and steel. However, the most significant industrial plant to open was the state-of-the-art *Feshane* in Eyüp. Established for the production of *fez*, a new type of headgear adopted by Mahmud II for his new army, *Feshane* first started to operate in 1835 with hand-powered machinery in Küçükayasofya within the walled city.

Figure 9 Topkapı Palace, c.1890s

Figure 10 Fossati's *Darülfünun* building, 1852

It was later relocated to Eyüp in 1839 because of increasing demand for the *fez*, and then modernised and re-equipped with steam-powered machinery in 1846. With further improvements, the production capacity of *Feshane* reached 70,000 metres of fabric per year in 1855. Following its destruction by a fire in 1866, *Feshane* was reconstructed with annual production capacity reaching more than 500,000 metres in the 1890s.

As well as *Feshane*, other textile factories were opened in İzmit in 1842 and Hereke in 1845, both of which were small towns on the eastern shores of the Sea of Marmara outside Istanbul. The industrial sites that were opened in and around Istanbul prompted an English traveller to comment that the region could soon become a 'Turkish Manchester, Leeds or Birmingham'.[72] However, the technical and scientific environments were far from that required to establish a sustainable industry similar to the industrial cities of England and other European countries.

The industrialisation of the Golden Horn—which still causes major environmental problems for the city—dates from this period. New factories were established along its shores to produce cloth and other goods for the new army and military establishments. Although the shores had been occupied since the fifteenth century by depots, shipyards and an arsenal, it was the establishment of *Feshane* which launched the era of industrialisation of the Golden Horn in the modern sense. The opening of *Feshane* was followed in the late-nineteenth century by the establishment of new industrial sites along the shores of the Golden Horn, including factories, powerhouses, dockyards and abattoirs.

The most important change in Istanbul during the first half of the nineteenth century was the construction of two bridges across the Golden Horn linking the walled city of Istanbul to Galata. The first bridge was constructed between Azapkapı and Unkapanı in 1836 during the reign of Mahmud II. Moltke described in his letters the opening of this bridge as the 'newest development in Istanbul'. According to him, the bridge was constructed over a 'forest of timber piles' driven into the seabed and was 23 metres wide and 582 metres long.[73] Charles White, an English traveller, portrayed this bridge as a floating structure and gives the construction date as 1838. White suggested the plan of the bridge was conceived by a local Greek mast-maker named Georgi, who worked in the shipyards where the construction was carried out. White provided a detailed description of the bridge, including a schematic section, and stated that the southern central span was constructed as a swing bridge to allow the passage of large vessels.[74]

The second bridge was constructed in 1846 near the mouth of the Golden Horn between Karaköy and Eminönü. In a similar way to the first bridge, it was formed by floating pontoons moored firmly into the seabed. The construction of these two bridges over the Golden Horn was revolutionary. They not only provided rapid transportation between two significant parts of the city, but they were also vivid signs of the more determined works undertaken by the subsequent Ottoman administrations in the second half of the century to modernise the city. Similarly, the early planning control documents prepared in the 1830s and 1840s inspired the Ottoman bureaucrats to take more courageous steps to regulate and control the city's expansion in the following decades.

2

ISTANBUL BETWEEN THE CRIMEAN WAR AND THE FIRST WORLD WAR

As I followed the hammal, who was proceeding towards the lodging reserved for me, I entered a labyrinth of streets and narrow lanes, tortuous, ignoble, horribly paved, full of holes and pitfalls, encumbered with leprous dogs and asses carrying beams or rubbish. The dazzling mirage presented by Constantinople at a distance was rapidly vanishing, Paradise was turning into a slough, poetry into prose; and I asked myself, with a feeling of melancholy, how these ugly hovels could possibly assume at a distance such a seductive aspect, such a tender and vaporous colour.

Théophile Gautier, 1852[1]

The mid-1850s marked the opening of a new era in the history of the Ottoman Empire, with the increasing influence of Europe and an array of modernising endeavours. Significant change occurred on political, social and cultural fronts and, within a short space of time, this had a deep impact on Istanbul's urban morphology. While overall city planning was never achieved, parts of Istanbul saw piecemeal urban renewal projects implemented by both local and foreign experts. Regulations and codes which were drafted in the first half of the nineteenth century were further developed and began to be applied in parts of Istanbul. The administration of the city, including civil services, was assigned to European-style municipalities though the desired outcome was not always achieved. At the same time, the city would see some remarkable infrastructure projects, although not all proposals would be implemented.

The Crimean War of 1853–56 put Britain and France in alliance with the Ottoman Empire against Russia. After the war the Ottoman Empire joined the 'Concert of Europe', the system established at the Congress of Vienna in 1814–15 by Great Britain, Prussia, Austria and Russia to maintain the balance of power in Europe. The weak financial and military structure of the

Ottoman Empire, however, did not make it an equal member of the alliance and it provided further opportunities for the European powers to influence internal Ottoman politics.[2] The Ottoman demand for the abrogation of capitulations, commercial privileges given to European states since the mid-sixteenth century, was not accepted as the Ottoman legal system, according to the European states, 'was too alien for Europeans to live under'.[3] All these political circumstances forced the Ottomans to intensify their modernisation attempts. The reforms instituted by the 1839 imperial edict were underpinned by the declaration of another decree, *Hatt-ı Hümayun*, on 18 February 1856. This edict, which was dictated by Britain and France in pledging their support during the Crimean War, confirmed the reforms of 1839 and promised equality of legal rights to all subjects of the Empire, regardless of ethnicity or religion.

The immediate impact of the Crimean War on Istanbul was direct contact between the city's inhabitants and British and French troops. Since the beginning of the *Tanzimat* era, contact between Ottomans and Europeans had gradually increased, but it was limited to high-ranking bureaucrats and officials only. After their arrival in 1854, the European troops were barracked in various parts of the city, before being sent to Sebastopol and other fronts to fight against the Russian army. The military hospitals for French and British soldiers in Fatih and Üsküdar further exposed Istanbul's inhabitants to European culture.

A significant economic impact of the European–Ottoman alliance flowed from substantially increased Ottoman trade with Europe, beginning with the Anglo–Ottoman Commercial Treaty of 1838. One notable indicator of this activity was a dramatic increase in naval traffic, which forced the Ottoman authorities to introduce new regulatory measures on maritime passage through the Bosphorus and Golden Horn.[4] During the Crimean War Istanbul, for the first time in its history, was connected to the European telegraph network with a line constructed between the capital and Edirne. Steam ferries began service to the Asian side of the city and the shores of the Bosphorus, allowing easy access for the city's well-to-do population. More importantly, this period saw the ruling family abandon the old Topkapı Palace and move permanently to the new European-style palace built in Dolmabahçe in 1856.

The Crimean War also impacted on Istanbul's socio-cultural geography by intensifying the separation between the old walled city of Istanbul and the Galata–Pera region. The contrast between the two centres became visibly more explicit, leading Steven Rosenthal to describe Pera as a 'boom town'.[5] The wartime shortages, together with the weakness of the Ottoman economy, helped the merchants and bankers of Galata to increase their economic and political power. According to the 1882 census records, approximately 220,000 people, a quarter of the whole urban population, lived in Galata making it the second most populous district of Istanbul after Fatih. The population of Galata was also heterogonous, as almost half of its inhabitants were foreign subjects, Europeans and non-Muslim Ottoman citizens. They enjoyed the privileges they had gained under the infamous capitulations, as well as immunity from Ottoman law as they were under the protection of their respective embassies. Such privileges often extended to the local Greeks, Armenians and Jews who had commercial connections with European embassies. These conditions gave an unprecedented opportunity for the non-Muslim stratum of Ottoman society to increase their power, both economically and politically. The merchants and bankers, who had already begun to benefit from increased trade with Europe since the 1838 Commercial Treaty, were now hired by the Ottoman government to arrange loans from Europe.[6]

The wealth acquired by these merchants and bankers was invested in premises along the Grande Rue de Pera, bringing a distinctly European flavour to this part of Istanbul. The newly opened shops in this street, with their displays of imported European goods, not only attracted the European and Levantine inhabitants of the city but also Muslim bureaucrats and high-ranking officials. Moreover, Pera became the hub of Western-style entertainments, a new phenomenon introduced during this period. Attractions included European-style hotels, restaurants, cafés, an Italian circus, a French theatre and an opera house.[7]

Despite these developments, the urban quality of the city, even in its most Europeanised districts, was far from satisfactory. The narrow streets of Pera, for example, like most of the city, were poorly maintained and lacking in appropriate infrastructure. In addition to such physical shortcomings, there were growing social problems. Increased trade and wartime black markets had attracted to the city a large influx of shady fortune seekers and criminals. The lack of a modern and effective municipal administrative system became more apparent, prompting the British and French military to take matters into their own hands. They provided their own police and fire brigades, as well as health services to combat cholera, plague and other diseases.[8] The demands of Europeans for a better built environment induced the new Ottoman bureaucrats to force their government to reassess fundamentally the issue of the urban administration of Istanbul.[9]

Figure 11 A view of the Dolmabahçe Palace, c.1890s

Municipal Reform

In 1855 these political and social conditions prompted the establishment of the *Şehremaneti* (Municipality) in the form of the French *préfecture de la ville*, a significant milestone in the urban administration of Istanbul. The organisation of the *Şehremaneti* established the office of a *Şehremini* (Mayor) appointed by the Sultan, with two deputies and a city council consisting of 12 representatives, in addition to the *Şehremini* and his deputies, drawn from various strata of the population and its trade and commercial guilds. The *Şehremaneti* was to be given responsibility for the regulation and collection of taxes, construction and repair of roads, cleaning and general improvement of the city. The works assigned to the *Şehremaneti* were to be supervised by the *Meclis-i Vâlâ-i Ahkâm-i Adliyye* (Supreme Council of Judicial Ordinance) established by Mahmud II immediately after the abolition of the Janissaries.[10]

Despite the new administrative structure, these changes produced no practical outcomes since the new municipality could only execute functions previously carried out by the *kadı*, such as the control of market prices and the administration of guilds. The lack of technical expertise and experience, coupled with financial shortages, did not allow the undertaking of the urgent and necessary works assigned to the *Şehremaneti,* and eventually led to a chaotic situation. The power and responsibility of the *Şehremaneti* was very limited as all decisions required final approval in the *Meclis-i Vâlâ*. Furthermore, having no source of income to pay the salaries of municipal staff, the municipality had to rely on the central government for funding. Within a matter of months this led to the removal of Salih Paşa, the first mayor, and the appointment of deputies and the establishment of the city council was deferred.[11]

This first, unsuccessful attempt to create a Western-style municipal system led to the creation of an advisory council called *İntizam-ı Şehir Komisyonu* (Commission of the Order of the City) in 1856. This was an initiative of Emin Muhlis Efendi, who as a young diplomat worked at the Ottoman Embassy in Vienna and later became an official translator for the Ottoman government and a chief officer at the Ministry of Foreign Affairs.[12] The major aim was to utilise the knowledge and experience of Ottomans and established European residents of the city who had observed municipal administrations in Europe.[13] The commission, in a similar way to the *Şehremaneti*, aimed to establish municipal regulations in order to improve public infrastructure, hygiene in market places, street cleaning and illumination, and regularisation of the street pattern.[14]

The head of the *İntizam-ı Şehir Komisyonu* was Hacı Hüssam Efendi, who was also the *Şehremini*. Members of the commission, however, included non-Muslim Ottoman subjects who had good command of a European language and Europeans who had settled in the city and accumulated wealth during the Crimean War. Commission members included: Antoine Alleon, a member of a very rich French family which had fled to and settled in Istanbul after the French Revolution; Avram Camondo, a Jewish banker and real estate speculator under Austrian protection; Ohannes Miğerdiç, an Armenian banker; David Revelaki, an Ottoman Greek merchant under British protection; Ferhad Paşa, an Austrian military advisor; Franko Efendi, a member of the government's Translation Office; Mehmed Salih Efendi, the chief physician to Sultan Abdülmecid; Refik Mustafa; and Yusuf Efendi.[15]

As an advisory body, the *İntizam-ı Şehir Komisyonu* achieved little to improve the urban infrastructure of the city. Among the few works it carried out were the regulation of garbage collection and the selling of goods on streets, the trial laying of European-style road pavements and the installation of gas lighting along parts of the Grande Rue de Pera. French engineers were hired to supervise the pavement works, with stones and labour supplied by the Imperial Arsenal. The gas was supplied by a plant at Feriköy that was originally set up to service the Dolmabahçe Palace. By 1857 the commission had become greatly frustrated, having achieved very little in practical terms. It therefore made various recommendations in the form of a memorandum, almost an ultimatum, to the Ministry of Commerce on issues such as street construction and illumination, sewerage, garbage collection, financial support for the municipal programme and an effective administrative structure.[16]

The proposals of the *İntizam-ı Şehir Komisyonu* were accepted by the government and Istanbul was subsequently divided into 14 municipal districts in 1858.[17] As noted by Rosenthal, the commission's proposal was made to the Ottoman government at the most opportune time as the Ottoman Empire, being a new member of the Concert of Europe, wished to demonstrate its ability to implement European models of administration, including municipal affairs.[18] Financial difficulties and lack of expertise, however, meant it was impossible to begin the intended works across the city. As an exemplar, a municipal administration was established only in the Sixth District, comprising Galata, Pera, Taksim, Pangaltı, Kurtuluş, Kasımpaşa and Tophane. Since it was in this district that European settlers, bankers and merchants were located, as well as European embassies, it was possible to collect taxes and other charges to fund the required works.[19] The privileged status of the Sixth District was highlighted by its direct link to the *Sadrazam*, whereas the other 13 districts were under the supervision of the *Şehremaneti*.

The Municipality of the Sixth District, chaired by a *müdür* (director), was comprised of a *meclis* (municipal council) of seven members appointed by the government. The members of the council were required to be property owners within the municipal borders of the district and to have resided in the city for more than ten years. These were Antoine Alleon and Avram Camondo, who were also amongst the members of the previous *İntizam-ı Şehir Komisyonu*, Septime Franchini, an Italian, and Charles Hanson, a member of the British merchant community of Istanbul. Kâmil Bey, the chief of protocol in the Ministry of Foreign Affairs, was the first director of the Sixth District. During his service in the Foreign Office, Kâmil Bey had visited many European cities and headed the commission that organised the Ottoman pavilion at the Universal Exhibition in Paris in 1856. This experience, as well as his previous administrative positions, was recognised by the award of the French *Légion d'honneur*, and positioned Kâmil Bey as the ideal person for the task. The other members of the council included two local Greeks, an Ottoman Armenian, two Muslims and Theodore Naum, an Ottoman citizen under French protection who had established the first opera of Istanbul in the mid-1840s. Four foreign advisors were also to be selected by the government to assist in civic services.[20]

The responsibilities of the new municipality were very broad, including all civil services such as road construction, water supply, sewerage, street cleaning and the regulation of markets.²¹ Legislative power given to the Sixth District was also unprecedented. The district was allowed to draft its own budget, to appoint staff, to collect property tax and even to enter into contracts to obtain loans to carry out its works. With its extensive powers the Sixth District, until the loss of its privileged status in 1868 with the introduction of a new municipal model for the whole city, undertook some noteworthy works such as street widening, improvement of roads, street lighting, garbage collection and the installation of water and sewerage systems.

The Sixth District had a technical bureau consisting of a cadastral chief and two officers, an engineer and an architect to administer and service approximately 12,000 buildings within the new municipality.²² For tax collection purposes, a detailed cadastral map of the area at 1:2,000 scale, the first of its kind in Istanbul, was prepared between 1858 and 1860 by G. Coficci, under the directions of the chief engineer, G. d'Ostaya.²³ Work then began on various street levelling works and enlargements. At the northern end of the Galata Bridge demolitions were carried out in Karaköy, the busiest section of Galata, to permit the construction of a new commercial office building for the municipality, financed by local bankers. In another important project, Karaköy was linked to the western end of the Grande Rue de Pera by the construction of a new street. Although many of them could not be fully implemented, new regulations were issued to administer civil services such as street cleaning, provision of street lighting, sewerage and gas, inspection of businesses and shopkeepers, and supervision of services.²⁴

Despite its achievements, the municipality encountered severe difficulties, both financially and administratively. Tax revenue was far below what was necessary to maintain a viable financial base. In part, this was caused by the refusal of the European and non-Muslim inhabitants of the district, who were under the protection of European embassies, to pay taxes. These financial difficulties, coupled with poor management and corruption, led the Ottoman government to intervene in 1862 and appoint Server Efendi, the former chief secretary of the Ministry of Foreign Affairs, as the new director of the district in 1863. While the majority of the municipal council was still formed by non-Muslims and foreigners, four Muslim Turks were appointed to the council by the government which now more strictly controlled and supervised the works of the Sixth District. Server Efendi's appointment also brought the government's full support to the municipality, enabling it to increase its range of municipal services. A municipal doctor, for example, was appointed to provide clinical services to the poor, as well as a free immunisation programme for the children of the area. Regular municipal duties such as garbage collection and street cleaning were also resumed.²⁵

The most significant of the Sixth District's work, however, began in November 1864 with the demolition of the ancient Genoese ramparts under the supervision of the municipal advisor, Marie de Launay.[26] Like the demolition of Vienna's city walls in 1857, the aim was to link the old inner city to the new and growing outer sections of the region.[27] Other major works executed by the Sixth District were the opening of a new tree-lined road between Taksim and Pangaltı, the relocation of cemeteries in Taksim to Şişli and the establishment of a *Beaux-Arts* style park in their place, and the planning of a new public park in Tepebaşı.[28] In the early 1870s construction began on a new 'Municipal Palace' in Şişhane as a new administration office for the Sixth District—the last major work of the Sixth District before it lost its privileged status.[29]

Regardless of these works, Pera still remained far from a modern urban centre in European terms. Despite all efforts made by the Sixth District, most of the streets still lacked basic infrastructure. By 1875, seventeen years after the establishment of the Municipality of the Sixth District, the Grande Rue de Pera, according to a British correspondent, was not more than a lane and the streets which branched from it 'would be dignified if the name of "lane" were applied to them'. Most of the streets were paved with 'huge, uneven, sharp-pointed stones' suggesting that they were laid down during the Middle Ages. There were 'no drains, or gutters' and the mud that covered the streets was 'deep, black and slippery'.[30]

The Great Fire of Pera in 1870 created an opportunity to change the filthy appearance of the area. The fire, which started on the night of 5 June, resulted in the loss of more than 3,500 buildings with almost the entire Grande Rue de Pera burnt down, as well as 63 streets and 103 residential quarters. On 19 September the government announced a redevelopment plan that required the redesign of all burnt areas. The new plan envisaged a regularised street pattern with large streets up to 20 metres wide. A 30-metre-wide grand boulevard between Taksim and Tepebaşı, parallel to the Grande Rue de Pera, was also proposed. The new plan, however, attracted severe criticism from the residents and property owners whose interests would be adversely affected by the implementation of new streets. After long debates the government withdrew the plan and announced that the reconstruction of the burnt areas was to proceed according to the existing plan.[31] Perhaps the most practical outcome that the government achieved following the Pera fire was the establishment of a modern firefighting department by two experts brought from Hungary for this purpose.[32]

Figure 12 The Sixth District's Municipal Palace, c.1890s

Although the municipal scheme was not ideal, the achievements made in Galata prompted the Ottoman government to extend the scheme in 1864 to other parts of the city in Tarabya on the upper European shore of the Bosphorus and the Princes Islands in the Sea of Marmara. Both areas, like Galata, were predominantly inhabited by non-Muslim residents of Istanbul, foreigners and the well-to-do stratum of Turkish society.[33] Finally, in 1868 the government decided to broaden the experimental municipal administration to the entire city. In a similar way to the first municipal model of 1856, Istanbul was divided into 14 municipal districts. The Sixth District lost its privileged status to a great extent and was linked to the office of the *Şehremaneti*. Each district was to have a municipal council of eight to twelve members and a mayor elected by the members of the council. A general municipal council of 56 members would also be established for the *Şehremaneti* comprising representatives from each of the districts' municipal councils. Server Efendi, who had made noteworthy contributions in the Sixth District, was appointed as the new *Şehremini*. Despite the government's enthusiasm and optimism, the bitter economic and physical conditions did not help it to implement the new municipal scheme successfully. Firstly, the municipality could not collect the intended property tax it needed to achieve its goals. Except for Galata, no other parts of Istanbul had the cadastral maps that would enable an accurate estimation of tax income to be made. Moreover, the sporadic fires had resulted in a bulk loss of houses and other buildings which made tax collection even more difficult. Viable financial support from the government, which was struggling with the dire financial crisis, was also out of the question. Under these harsh conditions some of the 14 municipal councils could not be established and the general municipal council never met. In the end the new municipal model did not bring about any practical results outside the Sixth District.[34]

Street Regularisations in Istanbul

While the government failed to extend the municipal works outside Galata, the Istanbul Peninsula saw its first street regularisations in the mid-1850s. Luigi Storari, an Italian engineer who had previously prepared a cadastral plan of İzmir between 1854 and 1856, was engaged to prepare new street maps of previously burnt-out areas. He worked in Istanbul from 1856 to 1863 and carried out various street regularisation projects in parts of the city.[35] In 1862 Antoine Figuière, a French entrepreneur, was hired by the Ministry of Public Works to carry out construction of European-style pavements in some major streets of Istanbul. The thoroughfares Figuière paved included Bahçekapısı Street between the Babıâli and Yeni Mosque in Eminönü, some streets in Tophane and a street between Üsküdar and Büyük Çamlıca on the Asian side of the city.[36] However, the Istanbul Peninsula had to wait until May 1866 with the establishment of the *Islahat-ı Turuk Komisyonu* (Commission of Road Upgrading) before a coordinated approach to street regularisation projects was undertaken.

This initiative came after a devastating fire—a problem that had plagued the city throughout its entire history. The fire started in a local café in Hocapaşa district at 11 o'clock on the night of 5 September 1865, and with the aid of a north-easterly breeze spread throughout the city in a short space of time.[37] The fire caused great destruction. It consumed almost one-third of the Istanbul Peninsula, from the Golden Horn to the shores of the Sea of Marmara, destroying all buildings, including government offices and mosques. The conflagration became known in Ottoman history as *Harik-i Kebir*, the Great Fire. This catastrophic inferno, as observed by Ergin, provided an opportunity for the Ottoman administration to introduce a new regularised urban pattern and to construct large streets in the burnt-out areas.[38] The 1849 building regulation and, in particular, the experience gained in Galata prompted the Ottoman administration to set up a more effective administrative mechanism to deal with problems concerning the narrow, labyrinthine street patterns and fire-prone timber buildings.

The nine members of the *Islahat-ı Turuk Komisyonu*, unlike those of the Sixth District Municipality, were all Muslim. The existing street patterns of Istanbul were harshly described in the commission's reports as 'narrow crooked holes which do not allow the passage of humans, let alone carriages, and are not worth calling streets'.[39] The commission first mapped the burnt areas and then prepared a master plan which envisaged the opening of new roads between 4.5 and 16.75 metres wide according to their importance and function. No timber buildings were permitted and 20 per cent of all land parcels, except those for mosques and other religious buildings, were required to be excised for future road reservations. Financial incentives, such as waiving the levies on building materials and construction and providing cheap materials and transportation, were also included in the plan.[40]

The commission constructed many new streets, both within the burnt-out areas and in other parts of the city, until its closure in 1869. Newly opened-up streets were paved in stone by a local tradesman named Ali Ağa and provided with drainage and sewerage. The major thoroughfares opened in this period were Aziziye Street (the present Ankara Street) which linked Babıâli to Sirkeci Quay, Beyazıt–Aksaray Street (the present Ordu Street), Mercan and Fincancılar streets. The environs of Hagia Sophia and the Beyazıt Mosque were also tidied up and transformed into public squares.[41] Of the other street projects carried out by the *Islahat-ı Turuk Komisyonu*, the most significant was the enlargement of Divanyolu to a width of 25 *zira'* (16.75 metres). This street had formed the backbone of the city since the Byzantine period (the old *mese*) but had been gradually narrowed by uncontrolled building construction that had reduced its width to less than three metres at various locations.[42] With the reconstruction of Divanyolu, for the first time in its history, Istanbul's historic street pattern was significantly modified according to modernisation principles. This brought about the demolition of shops in the vicinity of Constantine's Column in order to achieve a straight alignment. Additionally, parts of the *medrese* of the Atik Ali Paşa complex and the Elçi Han were demolished and the dome of the *hamam* of Çemberlitaş cut away.

The modernisation of the historic precinct caused a reactionary response in some parts of the community. The demolition of historic buildings and graveyards, for example, attracted severe criticism, especially within conservative circles. In this respect, it is of interest to note the colourful exchange between Fuad Paşa, a leading bureaucrat of the *Tanzimat*, and an elderly city dweller during the relocation of the graveyards of Köprülü Mehmed Paşa and his family for the enlargement of Divanyolu. 'Paşa, you have been ordering the destruction of these mosques and tombs but the people will shit on your grave,' said the elderly man. The Paşa answered, 'It will not be a problem, old fellow. If they really defecate on my grave, their children will definitely sweep it away into the sea'. In another conversation Fuad Paşa repaid a compliment made by the *Şehremini*, Hüseyin Bey, with the following words: 'We have made these roads with the stones thrown at us'.[43]

Figure 13 Newly enlarged Divanyolu, Constantine's Column and the sliced dome of the *hamam* of Çemberlitaş, c.1890s

In the early 1870s a major event occurred with the visit of the important historical figure of Georges-Eugéne Haussmann, who created modern Paris in the mid-nineteenth century. The initial contact with Haussmann was made during Sultan Abdülaziz's visit to the 1867 Universal Exhibition in Paris at the invitation of Napoleon III. Abdülaziz was the first Ottoman sultan to venture into Western Europe for other than military reasons. His visit allowed him to inspect at first-hand the French capital, which since 1853 had been transformed by extensive public works under the prefecture of Haussmann. Following the expiration of his contract in Paris, Haussmann arrived in Istanbul in February 1873 on the invitation of İsmail Paşa, the Viceroy of Egypt, who had also visited the 1867 exhibition and had carried out noteworthy modernisation works in Cairo.

During his visit to Istanbul Haussmann was accompanied by a Monsieur Caméré, a road and bridge engineer, and a Monsieur Duparchy, a building contractor.[44] Whilst there he also visited the gardens in Tarabya which were designed by his ex-gardener, Monsieur Barillet-Deschamps, who had worked in Istanbul between 1869 and 1871. At this time Haussmann had several meetings with the Grand Vizier and the Sultan.[45] After spending a couple of months in Istanbul, Haussmann returned to Paris in June of the same year.[46] Today little evidence remains concerning Haussmann's contribution to the urban renewal of Istanbul during this visit. According to Fâzıl Halil Edhem Bey, director of the Imperial Museum, Haussmann worked on the preparation of maps after the fires that took place in the Aksaray region. Again, architect Mazhar Bey claimed that Haussmann worked on the opening of a new boulevard around Hagia Sophia, but this project, requiring five million liras, was not approved by the Sultan.[47] Despite this slender evidence of Haussmann's contribution to Istanbul's urban planning, it is now known that he saw the dire financial conditions of the Ottoman Empire as a promising business opportunity. Haussmann offered to establish a subsidiary of his finance company, *Crédit Mobilier*, in Istanbul through which he would organise loans for military and other purposes. His local contact in Istanbul was the famous land speculator, Avram Camondo, who played a significant role in the municipal organisations of Galata. After the Ottoman government defaulted on its loan repayments to *Crédit Mobilier*, Haussmann proposed a model for collecting taxes which was accepted by the Ottoman administration eight years later.[48]

While the street regularisation projects were carried out in a piecemeal fashion, additional planning legislation was introduced in the second half of the nineteenth century. These legislative reforms included the 1859

Sokaklara Dair Nizamname (Regulation on Streets), the 1863 *Turuk ve Ebniye Nizamnamesi* (Road and Building Code), the 1863 *Rıhtımlar Nizamnamesi* (Code for Wharves), the 1875 *İstanbul ve Bilâd-ı Selâsede Yapılacak Ebniyenin Suver-i İnşasiyyesine Dair Nizamname* (Regulation on Construction Methods in Istanbul) and the 1882 *Ebniye Kanunu* (Building Act).[49]

Improved Transport

An important initiative to follow the Crimean War was the improvement of the city's public transportation. Chief amongst these improvements was the renovation of bridges over the Golden Horn in 1853 to provide a more convenient connection between the two shores. The first bridge constructed between Unkapanı and Azapkapı was replaced with an iron bridge in 1872. Regular steam ferry services between the European and Asian shores of the Bosphorus had been started in 1850 by two foreign investors. A year later the *Şirket-i Hayriye*, a maritime transport company owned by members of the ruling family, high-ranking bureaucrats and Galata bankers, was established to provide regular ferry services.[50] In 1869 Istanbul welcomed a new mode of public transport with the establishment of the *Dersaadet Tramvay Şirketi* (Istanbul Tram Company), which operated a horse-drawn tram service in the Istanbul Peninsula and Pera. The first line was opened between Beşiktaş and Tophane with horses brought from Hungary and Austria. This was followed in 1871 by the opening of new tram routes in the Istanbul Peninsula between Azapkapı and Aksaray, Aksaray and Yedikule, and Aksaray and Topkapı.[51]

By far the most ambitious public transport project was the opening in 1875 of an underground railway tunnel between Karaköy and Galata, designed by the French engineer Eugène Henri Gavand in 1869. In 1872 the Metropolitan Railway of Constantinople from Galata to Pera secured a 45-year concession from the government to operate a rail link between the two busiest financial districts of the city, which were occupied by Levantine and European inhabitants.[52] The railway tunnel, which was the second of its kind in the world, consisted of a 554-metre funicular system operated by steam engines with stations at each end.[53] This short line remained the only underground railway in Istanbul until a new line opened between Aksaray and Topkapı in 1989.

This period also brought with it the first international railway line connecting Istanbul to Europe. The contract for this ambitious project was granted in 1869 to the *Société des Chemin de Fer Orientaux*, a company established by Baron Maurice de Hirsch, a Belgian-based banker, and financed with Austrian, British, French and Belgian capital. Istanbul was connected first to Edirne by a 355-kilometre line in 1871. In 1873 a 91-kilometre line was constructed between Haydarpaşa and İzmit on the Asian side of the city. The Istanbul–Edirne line was further extended to Dedeağaç (Alexandropolis) in 1872 and Sofia in 1874. Leaving Istanbul, the European railway followed the shore of the Sea of Marmara where it pierced the southern city walls at various points. Because the terminal was located at Sirkeci, the commercial hub of the walled city to the west of Seraglio Point (Sarayburnu), the railway was forced to pass through the lower reaches of the gardens of the Topkapı Palace. This controversial decision was made after Sultan Abdülaziz's famous statement, 'The railway must come to Istanbul, even if it has to pass through my own back'.

Although the major reason for the construction of the railway lines was to link Istanbul to Anatolia and Europe to facilitate increasing international trade and commercial activity, the railways on each of the European and Asian shores soon began to run suburban train services linking the outer sections of the city to the historic centre. The steam ferry services and the newly opened suburban train services pushed Istanbul's urban growth on an east-west axis around the shores of the Sea of Marmara and on a north-south axis along the Bosphorus.

Istanbul during the Hamidian Years

The infrastructure works of the 1850s and 1870s were carried out to modernise Istanbul at a time when the Empire was surviving on borrowed European money. The loan capital was spent on endless wars, the construction of a modern navy and financing modern educational institutes and Western-style palaces. This excessive level of spending brought the Ottoman Empire to financial ruin and bankruptcy in 1876. The ensuing bitter economic conditions led to a bureaucratic coup that ended with the removal of Sultan Abdülaziz from the throne on 30 May 1876. He was found dead in the Çırağan Palace shortly after. The short-lived rule of Murad V, who suffered from serious psychiatric problems, was followed by the stable 33-year reign of Abdülhamid II from 1 September 1876.

Sultan Abdülhamid came to the throne after promising to establish a constitutional monarchy. This was a reflection of the reaction to the extreme Westernisation of the state apparatus and bureaucratic oligarchy, which first crystallised in the political movement known as *Genç Osmanlılar* (Young Ottomans, also known in the West as *Jeunes-Turcs*). The reforms of *Tanzimat* were not based on popular demands, but were the initiatives of an elite who saw the introduction of Western institutions and practices as the only way to save the Empire from collapse. The reforms, however, held little appeal to the wider Muslim stratum of Ottoman society since they only helped non-Muslims to increase their wealth and power within the current political system. The reforms, moreover, failed to establish a sustainable modern economy and only intensified Ottoman dependence on the Great Powers, forcing the Empire into a subordinate and increasingly indebted role in the international financial system.

Criticising this growing dependence, the Young Ottomans—who had grown up under the *Tanzimat* regime and were influenced by the European ideals of liberalism and nationalism—advocated a political ideology called *Osmanlılık* (Ottomanism). They believed that liberalism and nationalism could be merged with Islamic culture to help create an Ottoman national identity. All Ottomans, regardless of their religious and ethnic differences, would be unified under the political ideology of Ottomanism, which required loyalty to the new concepts of *vatan* (fatherland), *hürriyet* (freedom) and *millet* (nation) and not necessarily to the absolute power of the ruling sultan. The Young Ottomans, despite the lack of a common and clearly defined ideological standpoint in the group, demanded the establishment of a constitutional monarchy in the mid-1860s and early 1870s.[54]

Abdülhamid II kept his promise and the first Ottoman constitution was drafted in December 1876 and the Ottoman Parliament met in March 1877 after a two-tiered election process. This first constitutional experiment, however, was short-lived. The 1877–78 Ottoman–Russian War led Abdülhamid to suspend the parliament and assume absolute rule of the Empire. This was a decisive end to the *Tanzimat* era's bureaucratic hegemony, whereby the power of the sultan had largely been usurped by senior bureaucrats who had assumed Western values and management practices.

Financial and economic conditions worsened with the Russian declaration of war on the Ottoman Empire in 1877. The Russian armies reached the outskirts of Istanbul a year later, and the invasion of the city was averted only by the intercession of the European powers. The Ottomans, however, lost control of Bosnia-Herzegovina and Bulgaria in Eastern Europe and Kars and Batum in the east. As compensation for their help with the war against Russia, the Ottomans ceded Cyprus to Britain. This dramatic territorial loss resulted in a flood of refugees into the Empire, numbering in the hundreds of thousands, from former Ottoman provinces. In the three years to 1885 Istanbul's population increased from 382,376 to 873,575.[55]

Reforms in technological areas, however, continued and even accelerated under Abdülhamid's reign. During the Hamidian years the Ottoman Empire undertook significant infrastructure projects in agriculture, railways and mining, all of which further contributed to Ottoman integration into world markets. The telegraph network was extended and Istanbul was now connected to every corner of the Empire by newly constructed telegraph lines. The existing rail network also saw a significant increase with new lines opened in Anatolia, Syria and the Arabic Peninsula. In 1892 Istanbul was first connected to Ankara and then in 1894 to Konya. In 1903 a German company proposed the famous Baghdad Railway project to extend the Anatolian railways to Baghdad and Basra.[56] Education was one of the other significant achievements experienced during the Hamidian years. In the 1880s many primary and secondary schools were opened and modern imperial colleges established to supply much-needed public servants to the bureaucracy and educated administrative staff and medical doctors to the army.[57]

Another significant characteristic of the Hamidian years was the rise of political Islam. During his 33-year reign Abdülhamid used Islam as a political tool in his struggle, not only against his opponents who demanded constitutionalism and liberalism, but also against Western imperialism. He presented himself as the 'Protector of the Islamic World' in the hope that this new title would give him more leverage in dealing with the European powers. His international policy resulted in a close relationship between the Ottoman Empire and Germany, the new rising imperial power in Europe following the country's unification in 1871. German Kaiser Wilhelm II, the leader of the only European power without Muslim colonies, visited Istanbul and other parts of the Ottoman Empire in 1898.[58] His visit to the city was commemorated by a public fountain, *Alman Çeşmesi* (the German Fountain), which was built in Germany and transported to Istanbul where it was assembled in Sultanahmet Square.

The rise of Ottomanism and political Islam was reflected in the fabric of the city of Istanbul from the late 1870s. This inspired a new movement that advocated a revivalist architectural style drawn from classical forms of the Ottoman and Islamic traditions. The initial signals of this movement appeared early in 1873, with the codification of Ottoman architecture in the famous text called *Usul-i Mimari-yi Osmani* (Principles of Ottoman Architecture). Written by İbrahim Edhem Paşa, Minister of Public Works, this was the first book about Ottoman architecture and was prepared for the 1873 Universal Exposition in Vienna. Its aim was to represent the 'universalistic aspirations' of Ottoman architecture to the Western world.[59] Although the Young Ottomans were soon crushed by Abdülhamid's autocratic rule, the influence of their ideas in the 1870s led to embryonic examples of Islamic Revivalist architecture in the following decade. Whilst there is no conclusive evidence that this architectural language was supported by Abdülhamid's regime, it was either intentionally or coincidentally represented in large-scale Ottoman public buildings in the late-nineteenth century.

Interestingly, Islamic Revivalist architecture was practised by European architects who taught at the *Sanayi-i Nefise Mektebi Âlisi* (School of Fine Arts) established in 1883 on the model of the French *École des Beaux-Arts* and the *Hendese-i Mülkiye Mektebi* (School of Civil Engineering) founded in 1884. Both were initiatives of Abdülhamid's educational reform. However, the architects' knowledge of Islamic architecture was only sufficient to allow them to decorate Western-style buildings superficially with Islamic decorative motives. One of the most significant examples of this revivalist architecture was the Sirkeci Train Terminus, which was constructed at the tip of the Istanbul Peninsula in 1890. Designed by the German architect August Jasmund, who was sent to the Ottoman Empire by the German government and taught at the School of Civil Engineering, the Sirkeci Train Terminus represented the principles of *Beaux-Arts* composition, such as symmetry, spatial hierarchy and eclecticism, overlaid with decorative elements borrowed from North African Islamic architecture. Another noteworthy example of the style, based on classical Ottoman forms, was the Office of Public Debt Building designed in 1897 by French architect Alexandre Vallaury, who conducted the architectural education at the School of Fine Arts.[60] However, Vallaury's most spectacular building was the *Mekteb-i Şahane-i Tıbbiye* (Imperial School of Medicine) completed in 1903 between Üsküdar and Kadıköy on the Asian side of the Bosphorus. He worked on this building with Italian architect Raimondo D'Aronco who practiced in Istanbul for sixteen years.

One of the noteworthy events that occurred in the Hamidian period was the introduction of a new municipal model for Istanbul. In 1877 two municipal acts were proposed in the Ottoman Parliament: *Dersaadet Belediye Kanunu* (Istanbul Municipal Act) and *Vilayet Belediye Kanunu* (Cities Municipal Act). Separate municipal legislation for Istanbul, despite the severe criticisms of the members of parliament from other parts of the Empire, simply formalised Istanbul's pre-existing privileged status in the new legal system. Emulating the municipal model of Paris, the 1877 *Dersaadet Belediye Kanunu* divided Istanbul into 20 municipal districts.[61] The new legislation abrogated the few remaining concessions of the Sixth District. Despite the optimistic approach, the implementation of the new municipal model was difficult. The government had previously tried, but failed, to implement a 14-region municipal model in 1868. Increasing the number of the districts obviously made it more complicated for the government which was already struggling with major financial problems. Also the 1877–78 Ottoman–Russian War did not even allow the Ottoman administration to attempt this new scheme. The government eventually divided Istanbul into 10 municipal districts in 1878 and appointed directors in each district. This model, although it did not bring about any practical outcomes for most of the city, remained until 1908.[62]

Unrealised Proposals

While Istanbul was witnessing the experimental stages of revivalist architecture, another significant impact of the economic and political crises of the 1870s on the city was the injection of international finance into major projects. The monetary crisis was solved by the establishment of the *Duyun-u Umumiye* (Office of Public Debts) in 1881, a model suggested by Haussmann eight years earlier. The office was authorised to collect taxes to secure debts directly on the behalf of European creditors, thus providing wider assurances to foreign investors and merchants. With the establishment of the Office of Public Debts, the Ottoman Empire's integration into the world economy was further accelerated, bringing with it some major project initiatives by Western entrepreneurs in Istanbul and many other parts of the Empire.

A remarkable proposal of the time was to connect Asia to Europe by construction of a bridge over the Bosphorus. This exciting idea generated various bridge designs from leading international engineers, though none of them were to be realised. While preliminary discussions had started in the late 1870s, a viable bridge proposal was first prepared by Captain James Buchanan Eads, an American engineer who specialised in the construction of bridges and pontoons. Eads was assisted by A. O. Lambert, a civil engineer specialising in the construction of railways and bridges in Europe and America. Eads and Lambert's proposal called for an iron bridge carrying a railway connection between Rumelihisarı on the European shore and Anadoluhisarı on the Asian shore of the Bosphorus. The planned bridge would be 1,828 metres long, 30.5 metres wide and have fifteen spans. According to the design, the Bosphorus Bridge would have a 228-metre-wide span in the centre, then the longest span yet constructed in the world. The wide span was to be carried by two 15-metre-wide central masonry piers built of granite from nearby quarries. There would also be two spans of 152 metres adjoining the central span. The cost of the project was an estimated $US25 million and the designers envisaged a six-year construction period. The proposed bridge was considered an extension of the intra-city transportation between the European and Asian sectors of the city which had been provided by steamships since the early 1850s. The construction of the bridge would make the Asian side of the city easily accessible, which in turn would open up new residential areas for the city's wealthier citizens who had their businesses in Pera and Galata. The revenue generated from the sale of new building allotments was intended to finance the bridge.⁶³

The Eads and Lambert proposal was followed by another bridge project put forward by a French syndicate in 1890. Again, the proposal intended to connect Rumelihisarı to Kandilli, but with only a single span over 800 metres long and 70 metres high.⁶⁴ A decade later a more ambitious project was announced by an international consortium called the *Compagnie Internationale du Chemin de Fer de Bosphore* and submitted to Sultan Abdülhamid II on 19 November 1900. The aim of this project was to connect the Asian and European railways by means of two bridges over the Bosphorus. The first bridge was to be constructed between Seraglio Point (Sarayburnu) and Üsküdar and the second from Rumelihisarı to Kandilli.⁶⁵ The bridges were to be connected by a circumferential rail route around Istanbul. The project bore the signature of Ferdinand Joseph Arnodin, a French engineer who was the principal inventor of the 'transporter bridge'.⁶⁶

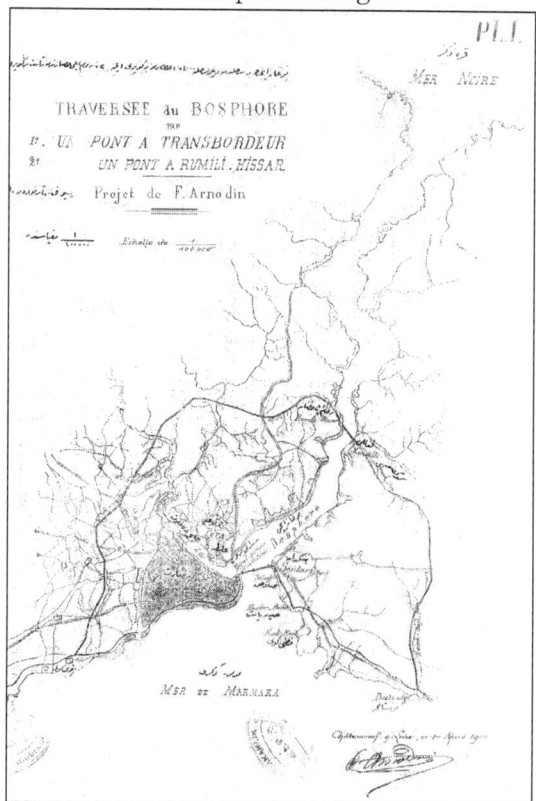

Figure 14 Arnodin's rail-ring proposal associated with two bridges over the Bosphorus

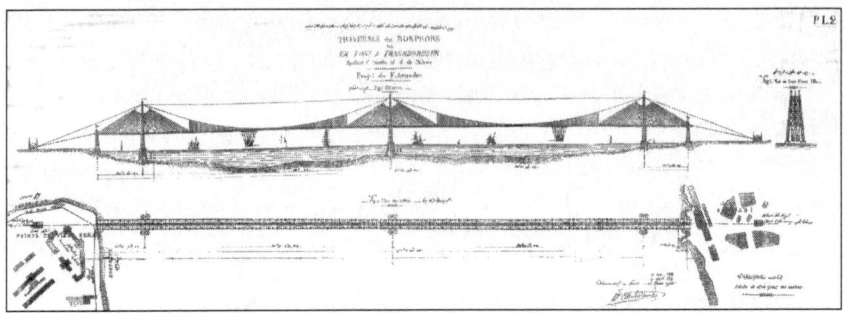

Figure 15 Arnodin's proposed transporter bridge between Sarayburnu and Üsküdar

Arnodin's intended bridge between Sarayburnu and Üsküdar was an impressive engineering proposal. Based on his earlier works constructed in Bizerte (1898) and Rouen (1899) in France, it was a suspended cable steel structure comprising three main pylons. As a transporter bridge it was designed to carry goods and people from one shore of the Bosphorus to the other and, contrary to some contemporary interpretations, a rail connection over the bridge would not have been possible as its structure was not designed for this purpose and could not carry the required load.[67] On the other hand, the second bridge, Hamidiye Bridge, being a suspension bridge with at least five massive masonry pylons was designed to carry a railway, as well as vehicular and pedestrian traffic.

The Hamidiye Bridge, with its highly ornamental design, differs sharply from the lighter and unadorned transporter bridge. It was ornamented with bold eclectic Islamic architectural elements, such as domes and minarets, to create a series of small mosques above the piers. While no evidence has been found, the extraordinarily whimsical and overtly architectural character of the bridge suggests the involvement of an architect, perhaps Jasmund who designed the Sirkeci Train Terminus in a related style.[68]

Arnodin's project is today interpreted as a major urban design scheme, with comparisons to Otto Wagner's proposal for Vienna and Arturo Soria Mata's for Madrid.[69] This assumption, however, seems improbable and requires closer scrutiny. All available evidence indicates that the project was specifically prepared as part of the famous Baghdad Railway project. A German book by Siegmund Schneider published in the spring of 1900, at almost the same time as Arnodin's proposal, throws light on the purpose of the latter's project and calls into question descriptions of it as a major urban design scheme.[70] Schneider provided a detailed description of the Hamideye Bridge and published an artistic drawing of it (the same drawing that was attached to Arnodin's rail-ring project). Schneider saw the Hamidiye Bridge as a vital part of the Baghdad Railway project and promoted it as one of the most triumphal examples of German technology.[71] According to Schneider, Victor Sasemann, a German engineer, dedicated his life to this project and conducted a geological survey of the Bosphorus 20 years before Arnodin's project.[72]

The connection linking the rail bridge over the Bosphorus to the Baghdad Railway project is also mentioned in official documents from the Ottoman archives. A document translated by the Translation Office of the Ministry of Foreign Affairs, at the time when Arnodin's drawings were submitted to the Sultan, states that the idea of constructing a bridge over the Bosphorus was a vital part of the Baghdad Railway project. It suggests, in part, that:

> The idea of construction of a bridge over the Bosphorus was first considered before the Ottoman–Russian war (1877–78). This idea has now been re-emphasised together with the forthcoming Anatolia–Baghdad Railway project that was franchised to the Germans. The Bosphorus Railways Company aims to connect the routes of the South, South-West and the Central European Railways to the Baghdad Railway by a great bridge passing the Bosphorus at its narrowest points: Rumelihisarı and Kandilli. The military bridge over which Darius passed with 800,000 Persians and which was constructed by Mondrokles, the Corinthian architect, in 500 BC was also erected at this point of the Bosphorus…[73]

These sources make it clear that there was a strong intention to connect the Baghdad Railway to the European rail network. What is worth noting here is that the descriptions of the bridge and its purpose in Schneider's book are almost identical to those contained in the archival document from the Ministry of Foreign Affairs. In both sources it is clearly articulated that Rumelihisarı and Kandilli were preferred because of their geographical position as the two closest points between the Asian and European shores of the Bosphorus, rather than because they were part of a major urban regional development scheme. And it is reasonable to assume that crediting a French structural engineer, who may never have visited Istanbul, as being the author of a large urban regional development project requiring detailed knowledge of the city and experience in urban planning is unrealistic and highly unlikely.[74] The most likely explanation is that the sponsors of the Baghdad Railway project commissioned Arnodin to prepare a preliminary scheme in accordance with German geopolitics in the Middle East.[75]

None of these bridge projects were built, remaining only on paper as concepts which reflected the intense foreign interest in major projects in Istanbul in the late-nineteenth century. As the Ottoman Empire became increasingly integrated into European economic markets, such projects were seen to be good investments by international financial entrepreneurs. However, Istanbul would have to wait another 73 years before a bridge over the Bosphorus connected Asia to Europe.

Figure 16 An illustration showing the Hamidiye Bridge, c. 1900

Beside the various unrealised bridge proposals, another noteworthy proposal of the Hamidian period was the reorganisation of the Ottoman capital in accordance with European urban planning principles. At the beginning of the twentieth century Istanbul's problems relating to population pressure, inadequate transportation, lack of sanitary facilities and poor development standards featured prominently in the observations and writings of European travellers. These critiques were echoed in the Palace and Salih Münir Paşa, the Ottoman ambassador in Paris, was given the task of finding a European expert to redevelop the Ottoman capital.[76] In 1901 the ambassador approached Joseph Antoine Bouvard and offered him a commission to prepare a master plan for Istanbul. At this time Bouvard held various prestigious positions, such as inspector-general of the Architecture Department in the City of Paris and chief of the Architecture Department for the 1900 Universal Exposition in Paris. Significantly, for the first time, a European architect was invited to prepare a holistic redevelopment plan for Istanbul.

Bouvard, however, neither visited the city nor produced a master plan. Instead, he simply prepared a series of imaginative design concepts based on photographs of the city. His concepts included several artistic impressions of important quarters such as the Hippodrome, Beyazıt Square, Yeni Mosque Square and Galata Bridge.[77] In reality, Bouvard's perspectives were nothing more than imprecise images inspired by scenes from European cities and applied to several central locations in Istanbul.[78] In Bouvard's proposal each square selected was considered independently, with no means of connection to the surrounding city. The existing street pattern and, most importantly, the highly dominant topography of the city were completely ignored in his designs. Apart from saving some monumental buildings, such as mosques and prominent government buildings, Bouvard's sketches required the demolition of the existing urban form and its replacement by large, open, rectangular piazzas ornamented with European-style buildings, parks and wide roads. Overall, his design can be seen as a series of independent islands surrounded by the existing architectural character of the city.

Despite the unrealistic nature of his designs, Bouvard's perspectives influenced the Ottoman administration so deeply that an imperial order to implement his project was issued.[79] However, the financial conditions in which the Ottoman Empire found itself did not allow for the construction of such a costly project. Like other major projects prepared for Istanbul in the nineteenth century, Bouvard's imaginative proposals never left the page.

Young Turks and Istanbul

Abdülhamid made many efforts to modernise the Empire, yet his extreme fear of, and paranoia about, conspiracies led him to impose a harshly autocratic regime. The whole of Istanbul became a virtual open-air prison with spies on every corner reporting perceived, imagined or manufactured political conspiracies back to the palace at Yıldız. The Sultan's fear of a coup against him impacted all parts of the state apparatus. The navy, for example, was not allowed to leave its docks in the Golden Horn and the army had to conduct its military training without bullets.[80] Curiously, his extreme paranoia led him to prohibit the introduction of electric trams, telephones and electrical appliances because he feared that such technological tools could be used against him. Even electric lamps imported from the United States were impounded at customs. It took long and protracted negotiations by their Western importers, who had the Sultan's personal trust, before an imperial order was secured to allow their entry into the city.[81]

Opposition to the Sultan's absolutism began to crystallise in the 1880s when a group of military cadets, with the support of students and young bureaucrats, demanded the end of autocratic rule and the resumption of the Ottoman Parliament. The group—who like their predecessors of the 1860s and 1870s named themselves the Young Turks—formed a political organisation called *İttihat ve Terakki Cemiyeti* (Committee of Union and Progress or CUP). In 1908 they were able to force Abdülhamid to resurrect the parliament which had been disbanded for 30 years. They eventually brought about the overthrow of Abdülhamid in the following year, but hopes for a democratic constitutional system had to be set aside as the Ottoman Empire witnessed more turbulent political times. Numerous plots, conspiracies and oppressive rule occurred under the CUP until the Ottoman defeat in 1918 at the end of the First World War.

The Ottoman Empire lost its last remaining territories in Europe after the Balkan Wars of 1912 and 1913. This brought another significant wave of immigrants flooding into Istanbul, and the population rose to about 1.6 million. Despite the political setbacks, Istanbul saw some remarkable achievements in urban affairs during the first quarter of the twentieth century. According to Bernard Lewis, the 'Young Turks may have failed to give Turkey constitutional government. They did, however, give Istanbul drains'.[82]

In fact, the achievements of the CUP administration of this period were considerably greater than the mere laying out of drains. A new municipal model which divided the city into nine municipal districts was developed by the *Dersaadet Teşkilat-ı Belediyesi* (Istanbul Municipal Organisation) in 1912. In the same year a new municipal tax, *Rüsum-u Belediye*, was introduced as a source of revenue, as well as a new mode of financing civil works through the use of municipal loans. The first of these loans was based on a decision taken in the Municipal Council on 10 November 1909 and was approved by an imperial *irade* (order issued in the name of the Sultan) the following day. The loan of £1 million carried an interest rate of 5 per cent per annum for a period of 50 years and was floated on the London stock market. Loan bonds and coupons were exempt from any sort of taxes or stamp duties in the Ottoman Empire. While the obligations arising from the loan were the responsibility of the municipality, it was fully and unconditionally guaranteed by the Ottoman government. Tolls from the bridges across the Golden Horn and receipts from the petroleum depots in Paşabahçe, a small village located on the upper Asian bank of the Bosphorus, were given as security for the interest payments.[83]

The money obtained from municipal loans enabled the *Şehremaneti* to order the much-needed modern bridge between Karaköy and Eminönü. The old Galata Bridge had been replaced by a new pontoon bridge in 1875. Yet it was not sufficient to accommodate the increasing pedestrian and vehicular traffic across the Golden Horn. After various projects were prepared by European engineering companies, the new bridge was finally awarded to the German firm *Maschinenfabrik Augsburg-Nürnberg* in 1907, though construction was delayed until 1910 due to the political turbulence.[84] Completed in 1912 at a cost of 350,000 Turkish gold liras, the new bridge was an iron structure floating on pontoons 467 metres long and 25 metres wide.

Figure 17 Galata Bridge connecting Istanbul Peninsula to Galata, c.1870s

The CUP carried out other noteworthy improvements during this period. Priority was given to the introduction of technological devices banned by Abdülhamid. In 1909 a commission was established by the Ministry of Public Works to investigate opportunities to establish street lighting and a power supply for Istanbul.[85] A year later a Budapest-based firm was contracted to install a power station in Istanbul. The proposal included the installation of a total of 600 lamps along the major streets of the city.[86] The construction of the first power station in Silahtarağa was completed in 1914 and the same year electricity began to be supplied to various parts of Istanbul. In 1911 the *Société Anonyme Ottomane des Téléphones de Constantinople*, an international syndicate established by British, French and American firms, was given a concession to establish a long-delayed telephone service in the Ottoman capital.[87] According to the proposal, the Istanbul Peninsula, Galata, Üsküdar, the Bosphorus and the coastal settlements along the Sea of Marmara up to

Yeşilköy would be provided with 10,000 telephone lines at a total project cost of about £300,000.[88] By February 1914 a total of 12 telephone exchanges had been constructed at various locations in the city, including three major centres in Istanbul, Galata and Kadıköy. These centres were equipped with modern technical plants, and a total of 112 kilometres of telephone conduits was laid along the streets of Istanbul.[89] Electric-powered trams were first put into service in 1912 between Ortaköy and Karaköy. The network was extended in 1914 as the Silahtarağa power station began to supply power to the tram network.

One of the government's first initiatives in urban planning during this period was to renew the invitation to Bouvard to prepare a master plan for the city. In 1908 Bouvard had been working on a master plan for Buenos Aires. This time Bouvard, who had been offered 25,000 francs by the Ottoman government, travelled to Istanbul, but he later declined the job as there were no adequate maps to form the basis of the master plan. His refusal forced the Ottoman administration to engage foreign expertise to remedy this shortcoming.[90] A French surveying company was commissioned by Halil Edhem Bey, the *Şehremini* of Istanbul, to prepare a detailed set of maps of the city.[91] This task was completed in 1911 under the supervision of an engineer, a Monsieur Schreider. Between 1913 and 1914 a German firm, *Deutsches-Syndikat für Städtebauliche Arbeiten in der Türkei*, was given the task of completing the surveys of the city.[92] Upon the completion of these maps, known as the *Alman Mavileri* (German Blues), Istanbul for the first time in its history had sufficient and reliable cartographic material on which to build an urban planning system to guide its future development.

Istanbul also enjoyed a second phase of revivalist architectural style inspired by Ottoman forms during the early years of the twentieth century. Although various buildings were designed by European architects in Western styles in the early twentieth century—a notable example here is Otto Ritter and Helmuth Cuno's Bavarian-style railway terminus in Haydarpaşa in 1908—Istanbul encountered mature examples of the Ottoman Revivalist style in this period. In contrast to earlier examples designed by European architects with only a superfluous knowledge of Ottoman culture, the retrospective style of this time was created by Vedat and Kemalettin, two prominent Turkish architects who had developed their architectural vocabulary under the strong influence of the ideas of Ziya Gökalp, the founder of Turkish nationalism. Retrospectively named the *Birinci Milli Mimari* (First National Style Architecture) in Turkish architectural historiography, this revivalist style derived its artistic expressions from the classical period of Ottoman and Seljukid architecture and used elements such as wide-roof overhangs, tiled ornamentation and arches. Under the influence of Turkism, which became the official political ideology of the CUP era, especially after the Balkan Wars of 1912–13, Ottoman Revivalism became the national architectural style and enjoyed wide popularity and acceptance. Many public buildings such as post offices, ferry wharves, bank buildings and schools were built in this style in the early twentieth century.[93]

Figure 18 Galata Bridge from Eminönü, c.1890s

Auric's Redevelopment Scheme

André Auric, an engineer from the Municipality of Lyon, was another significant figure of this period.[94] In 1910 he was appointed head of the Infrastructure Department of the Municipality of Istanbul for a period of three years[95] and given the title 'Director of the Roads Service of the City of Istanbul'. His responsibilities were comprehensive, covering the organisation, surveillance and control of public works such as water, gas and trams as well as road planning, quays, sewers, bridges, water works, gas, electricity and communication systems.

Auric worked primarily on projects concerning the water supply to the city and wrote detailed reports about the design of water canals, reservoirs and distribution centres in both the European and Asian parts of the city.[96] Perhaps the most remarkable part of his work was the preparation of a development scheme for the entire city which was published in a technical journal in Istanbul in the early twentieth century.[97] The proposal was titled 'The Embellishment and Cleaning up of Istanbul'. The two main sections of the report were the construction of large boulevards and the establishment of main trunk sewers.

The large boulevards were designed to connect significant centres of the city. They were described by Auric as rectilinear, broader, sunnier and more airy streets. Borrowing the well-known proverb 'Where air and sunlight penetrate, the doctor does not go', he termed the boulevards the 'bronchial tubes of big cities' and the streets and lanes as 'bronchioles' of a vast system of aeration. The planting of trees along large boulevards was strongly emphasised in his report. Trees were seen as not only giving 'a more majestic appearance for cities' but in terms of their environmental benefits were known to absorb carbon. He argued that boulevards should have a minimum width of 32.5 metres and should be augmented by squares, parks and public gardens. Furthermore, Auric considered Istanbul's redundant military properties such as barracks, fortifications and earthworks as prime sites to be transformed into public gardens or promenades. The costs of creating squares and parks were not seen as sumptuary or luxury expenses, but as essential outlays for public health. They embodied the picturesque and architectural beauties and the historical and archaeological memories that every city possessed.

The Auric report recommended constructing the trunk sewers simultaneously with the boulevards to help coordinate the construction phases of the infrastructure works. He proposed two main sewer lines ending near Seraglio Point at the easternmost end of Istanbul Peninsula where the presence of a strong and permanent current would allow the discharge of waste waters without preliminary treatment. The first sewer was to run along the Golden Horn starting near Eyüp, and the second along the shores of the Sea of Marmara starting near Yedikule where the Theodosian Walls merge with the sea.

The road network was reminiscent of that proposed in the 1839 development policy. Aurics' two littoral boulevards terminated at Sarayburnu with two large squares in Eyüp and Yedikule. In addition, the plan proposed the creation of new vehicular arteries between Aksaray and the various gates on the Theodosian Walls at Silivrikapı, Mevlevihanekapısı, Topkapı and Edirnekapı.

Aksaray was an important crossroad in Auric's scheme where he proposed a large square with roads connecting it to the gates on the Theodosian Walls and to Beyazıt in the east. Finally, the two littoral boulevards he proposed along the Golden Horn and the Sea of Marmara were to be connected by a transversal boulevard from the new square at Aksaray to Unkapanı and Yenikapı.

In Pera, Auric proposed similar principles for the discharge of sewage and believed it would be necessary to go up as far as Ortaköy, where there was a permanent and sufficiently strong current, to discharge the waste waters into the Bosphorus. He beleived that Tophane would eventually be transformed and used for the enlargement of the commercial port. For this reason, it would be necessary to plan two boulevards on the hillside, one finishing at Galatasaray and the other at Taksim. He also proposed new roads starting from Kasımpaşa connecting the Golden Horn to Taksim, Feriköy and Tatavla (Kurtuluş) and a new road between Kabataş and Beşiktaş. And finally, his road scheme ended with the duplication of the Grande Rue de Pera between Taksim and Şişhane with two squares.

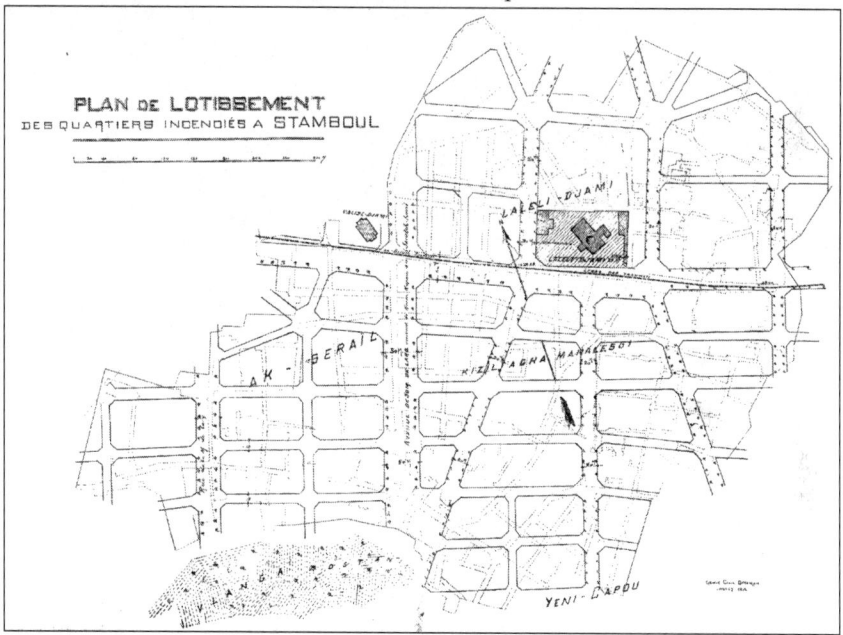

Figure 19 A plan published in *Génie Civil Ottoman* in 1912 showing the new roads proposed by Auric after the 1911 Aksaray fire, including the 50-metre-wide artery connecting Yenikapı to Aksaray

Although most of Auric's proposals never went beyond a set of general ideas, they were significant as a first attempt to plan Istanbul as a whole city and, even more importantly, to go beyond aesthetic concerns by including infrastructure projects. Auric's legacy in Istanbul could be said to be the replanning of Aksaray after a great fire that occurred on 23 July 1911. The 50–metre-wide boulevard between Yenikapı and Aksaray, which later became part of a major traffic route of modern Istanbul, together with the construction of other large axial roads and the large boulevard between

Aksaray and Beyazıt were the only works implemented in accordance with Auric's plan. This gave Istanbul, for the first time in its history, infrastructure services and aesthetic parks and gardens designed according to geometric rules and modern planning principles.[98]

Figure 20 Regularised street pattern proposed by Auric after the 1911 Aksaray fire shown on a map published by *Deutsches-Syndikat für Städtebauliche Arbeiten in der Türkei*

The Last Years of the Ottoman Empire

Perhaps the last influential figure to play a significant role in the modernisation of Ottoman Istanbul was Cemil Paşa, the ambitious mayor of Istanbul in 1912–14 and 1919–20. During his term of office Istanbul saw major civic works implemented, such as improvement in hygiene, regulation of commercial activities, improvement of streets, construction of parks, upgrading of fire services and many other works for improving the city's infrastructure. Cemil Paşa's position as personal doctor to the Sultan, the ruling family and other high-ranking officials gave him an unprecedented opportunity to secure approval for some of the works executed during his time in office. The creation of Gülhane Park, for example, designed within the gardens of the Topkapı Palace, was only possible because Cemil Paşa took advantage of his personal relationship with the Sultan to seek agreement.[99]

This range of civic works, however, was carried out in bitter and harsh political conditions. The Ottoman Empire had entered the First World War aligning itself with Germany, Austria and Hungary against the Triple Entente of Britain, France and Russia. The war interrupted many projects as the municipality was fully engaged in the war effort and all resources were needed for the army and hospitals. The First World War ended with the victory of the Entente on 11 November 1918. The Ottoman Empire signed the Treaty of Sèvres with the Allies on 10 August 1920, resulting in the occupation of its last remaining territories in Thrace and Anatolia by Britain, France, Greece and Italy. Istanbul had already been occupied by British troops on 13 November 1918, immediately after the signing of the Armistice of Mudros between the Ottoman Empire and the Allies on 30 October to mark the end of the war. On the same day the troops landed, the Allied navy sailed into the Bosphorus and faced their cannons towards Dolmabahçe Palace. Finally, on 8 February 1919, the French General Franchet d'Espèrey entered Istanbul, emulating Mehmed II the Conqueror in 1453 by riding a white horse through the streets of the city and giving a clear message that after four-and-a-half centuries Ottoman sovereignty of the imperial city was over.

3

THE NEGLECTED CITY
1923–1933

It was thus inevitable that Istanbul should seem to one who had known it in old days but a pale and unhappy shadow of itself. It was true that there were marked improvements in some ways—the mosques were 'swept and garnished', the streets were cleaner, the museum and its incomparable treasures were rightly cared for and the tourist could see and enjoy them as never before. But Constantinople, now officially Istanbul, was becoming more and more a city of memories, while a bleak village on a bare mountain plateau in the heart of Anatolia was being transformed into a town of immense public buildings and offices, with railways stretching out in every direction and with an administration where Government officials, instead of spending their afternoons over coffee and cigarettes, were worked every day from early morning until at night.

Sir George Clerk, 1938[1]

Political pandemonium in the five years following the First World War ended with a decisive victory by the national resistance movement which had pursued a successful campaign against military invasion and occupation by British, French, Italian and Greek forces. The struggle was led by Mustafa Kemal, a celebrated officer in the Ottoman army who first came to prominence in the Gallipoli campaign and later founded the modern Turkish Republic and adopted the surname Atatürk, 'Father of the Turks'. The Lausanne Treaty recognised Turkey's sovereignty on 24 July 1923, and the Grand National Assembly in Ankara proclaimed the new modern Republic of Turkey on 29 October of the same year. This new era marked the beginning of an intensive phase of Turkish modernisation and brought fundamental institutional change to the country's political social and economic structure.

While it is a truism that the modernisation process had its origins in the eighteenth and nineteenth centuries, the reform programme undertaken in the Republican period was radically different. It aimed to transform the traditional Ottoman (understood to mean Islamic) society along Westernised modern and secular lines. Secularism, or more correctly *'laiklik'* as it is referred to in Turkish, was the foundation stone of Turkish modernisation.[2] The major aim of these reforms was the removal or destruction of the political figures, symbols and institutions of the Ottoman Empire, and their replacement by a new secular order in which religion was strictly under state control. Above all, the reform programme had the wider purpose of creating a Turkish nation-state and Turkish identity from the ashes of the multi-ethnic and multi-religious Ottoman Empire.

Political reform had already begun prior to the proclamation of the Republic, with the abolition of the Ottoman Sultanate in 1922 followed by the exile of the last sultan, Mehmed VI (Vahdettin), who fled to Malta on a British warship. Thereafter, the rate of reform accelerated and targeted traditional institutions. The Caliphate was first demoted to a symbolic religious position, and subsequently abolished in 1924. Religious schools and courts were closed, and the juridical duties of the *mufti* (the official head of religion in the Ottoman Empire) were abolished. The Ministry of Religious Affairs and Pious Foundations was closed, and all members of the former Ottoman dynasty were forbidden residence in the new Turkish state. The restructuring was further reinforced by legislative reforms, which included the adoption in 1926 of the Swiss civil legal code, the Italian penal code and a new commercial code largely based on the German and Italian commercial codes.[3]

Despite the iconoclastic character of the regime, the Republican modernisers, like their Ottoman predecessors, opted for a top-down social transformation programme. This was led by Mustafa Kemal who had progressively consolidated his power as the leader of a single-party regime. The regime believed that the existing social order based on traditional Islamic institutions was the major reason for the backwardness of the country. The new elite demanded a radical ideological transformation, which could only be realised by cutting all ties with the past. In this respect, *'Muasır medeniyetler seviyesine ulaşmak'* ('Achieving the level of contemporary civilisations') became the major ideological target to motivate the Republican reforms. The reformers, again emulating their Ottoman predecessors, used recognisable symbols of Western civilisation such as dress, lifestyle, eating habits and the modern built environment as the principal tools to transform the country into a modern state.

Nothing shows the process of transformation better than the *Şapka Kanunu* (Hat Act), which was adopted on 25 November 1925. The *fez*, introduced as modern headwear a century earlier by Mahmud II, became a symbol of conservatism. The European-style hat was introduced personally by Mustafa Kemal in one of his public speeches in Kastamonu, a small Anatolian town, in August 1925. The legislation required all members of the Turkish National Assembly and public servants to wear Western-style hats in public spaces. In his celebrated 36-hour speech at the Congress of the Republican People's Party (RPP) in October 1927 Mustafa Kemal explained:

> Gentlemen, it was necessary to abolish the *fez*, which sat on the heads of our nation as an emblem of ignorance, negligence, fanaticism and hatred of progress and civilisation, to accept in its place the hat, the headgear used by the whole civilized world, and in this way to demonstrate that the Turkish nation, in its mentality as in other respects, in no way diverges from civilized social life.[4]

The meaning of 'other respects' refers to the inclusion of almost every dimension of Turkish culture in the transformation programme. The government closed the religious lodges, forbad the visiting of tombs and shrines and abolished the use of religious titles such as 'sheikh' and 'dervish'. In 1926 the Islamic lunar calendar was replaced by the Gregorian calendar, and in 1928 the Arabic script, deemed unsuitable for the Turkish language and the main reason for the low literacy rate of below 10 per cent, was replaced by the Latin alphabet.[5]

By the end of the 1920s the reform agenda had accelerated. The unexpected success of the *Serbest Cumhuriyet Fırkası* (Free Republican Party), an opposition party which was formed with the encouragement of Atatürk in August 1930, and a religious revolt which occurred in the small Aegean town of Menemen in December the same year forewarned the government that its public support was neither guaranteed nor unconditional.[6] Alarmed by these signals, the government took serious measures against a potential counter-revolution. Firstly, it forced the opposition party to disband in November. Then it took measures to consolidate its powerbase by codifying its political ideology. At the Third Congress of the ruling RPP in May 1931 the party defined its six basic principles: republicanism, statism, populism, revolutionism, nationalism and laicism. Together they came to be known as Kemalism, and were represented in the RPP's emblem as six arrows. The principles were eventually incorporated into the constitution in 1937.[7] All these measures merged to consolidate the single-party character of the regime and removed the last remaining separation between the party and the state. In the 1930s almost all public servants were members of the ruling RPP. The secretary-general of the party was the Minister for Internal Affairs and the provincial party chairmen were the governors of their respective cities.[8]

The next step for the Kemalists was to consolidate all social, cultural and intellectual organisations under strict government control. The brief democratic experience of the *Serbest Cumhuriyet Fırkası* vividly showed that the regime needed dedicated institutions to propagate its principles in the national psyche. In the name of the 'unification of forces' many cultural and intellectual organisations without strict government control were forced to join the official institutions. Amongst them, *Türk Ocakları* (Turkish Hearts), founded in 1912 to promote Turkish nationalism on the eve of the collapse of the Ottoman Empire, was the country's most important autonomous intellectual and political institution. Perceived by the regime as a potential political threat, Turkish Hearts was abolished in 1931 and replaced by *Halkevleri* (People's Houses) in 1932.[9] Initially, 14 houses were opened in various cities in Anatolia. Their number increased dramatically over time, and they were established in every corner of Turkey. Before their closure in 1950 there were 473 People's Houses and over 4,300 People's Rooms (a smaller version of the People's House that opened in small towns and villages). Between 1932 and 1935 seven houses were opened in various locations in Istanbul. This figure became 11 in 1940. Managed and financed by the ruling RPP, these houses served as adult education centres similar to those of the authoritarian regimes of Germany and Italy. Official ideology was propagated to the masses through lectures, concerts, art performances, theatre and sport. In many towns the People's House was located in buildings formerly occupied by Turkish Hearts. In others, new buildings were constructed in the most prominent locations of the city and town centre.[10] With their modern architectural features, the People's Houses aimed to compete with the dominant role of the mosque in the silhouette of Anatolian towns and cities.[11]

The reforms of the Kemalists, as many scholars have observed, reflected the extreme Jacobin revolutionary reforms of 1793–94 in which every visible trace of the *ancien régime* was forbidden, outlawed or removed. Amongst the innumerable measures were the following: the gazettal of an act in 1927 requiring the removal of all Ottoman coat-of-arms and insignia from official and public buildings;[12] the sale of Ottoman archival documents to Bulgaria as recycled paper;[13] the proposal of Sultan Ahmet Mosque as an art gallery for young artists of the Republic, mirroring the rededication of the Notre Dame de Paris to the Cult of Reason during the French Revolution; the conversion of Hagia Sophia into a museum; the renaming of streets that commemorated Ottoman sultans; the removal of classical Turkish music from primary and secondary school curricula; the closure of the Turkish section of the Istanbul

Conservatorium; and the temporary banning of Turkish music on radio in the 1930s.[14] Additionally, the metric system of measurement was introduced in 1931. The passing of the Surname Act in 1934 required all Turkish people to adopt the use of surnames. The government also banned the use of all courtesy titles such as '*bey*', '*paşa*' and '*efendi*', and declared Sunday the official holiday instead of the Muslim Friday.

The features of traditional Ottoman culture were also discredited in posters as symbols of backwardness, whereas the reforms of the Republic were celebrated as essential tools to 'Achieve the level of contemporary civilisations'. The strident nature of official propaganda can be seen in an excerpt from a book published by the Office of the General Directorate of Press extolling the virtues of the new regime:

> The republican, Kemalist Turkey is one of the new, vigorous countries that originated from the post-war times. Established on the part of the Ottoman territory inhabited by the denominating Turkish race, it certainly descends from the old empire, but on comparing the civilisation, the social and practical structure, or the economic system of the two states, one sees that this descent is of a purely historic nature. As for the social bodies or constitutive elements of the two states, one would look in vain for anything but contrasting relations.[15]

The introduction of women's rights was another important instrument of the Kemalist reforms. Atatürk explained this aspect of his reforms as, 'Republic means democracy, and recognition of women's rights is a dictate of democracy; hence women's rights will be recognized' and 'If knowledge and technology are necessary for our society, both our men and our women have to acquire them equally'.[16] The appearance of women in public, therefore, was one of the most effective symbolic expressions of Turkish modernism.[17] Images of women, often juxtaposed with images of modern buildings, were widely used in official propaganda. Women were pictured in front of Istanbul's major mosques and these images were often published in popular magazines of the early Republican period such as *Yedigün* and *Moda*.[18] In this atmosphere political equality for women was granted in the early 1930s and Islamic rules governing inheritance and other aspects of marriage were outlawed and reorganised according to the new civil code. These reforms abolished polygamy and banned religious marriage ceremonies. Women were also given the right to choose their spouses and to initiate divorce. The first Miss Turkey beauty contest was held in 1929, followed by the opening of public beaches to women in the early 1930s.

In line with the programme to create a 'new nation', Turkish history had to be rewritten. Much historical and linguistic research focused on the origins of the Turks and their language. Hence the *Türk Tarih Tezi* (Turkish Historical Thesis) and the *Güneş Dil Teorisi* (Sun Language Theory) represented the ultimate arguments of the Kemalist regime. The Turkish Historical Thesis was based on the idea that the 'Turks contributed to civilisation long before the existence of the Ottoman Empire'.[19] It argued that the Turks had developed a civilisation in their homeland in Central Asia, a place that had witnessed the birth of many other civilisations. A great drought had then forced the Turks to migrate to different parts of the world, including Europe, Africa and the Americas. Earlier inhabitants of Anatolia and Mesopotamia, the Hittites and the Sumerians, were therefore accepted as the ancestors of present-day Turks.

Similarly, the Sun Language Theory claimed that ancient Turkish was the origin of many, if not all, languages in the world. To establish the basis for these claims, the Turkish Historical Society and the Turkish Language Society were opened in 1931 and 1932 respectively, under the personal leadership of Mustafa Kemal. The Faculty of Linguistics, History and Geography at Ankara University was founded to theorise the Kemalist theses further and departments of Sumerology and Hittitology, Ancient Greek and Latin were established to support the assertion that many civilisations in Anatolia were founded by the Turks. School textbooks were written to include this new historical perspective which formed the basis of primary and secondary educational curricula. In parallel with these endeavours, the Turkish language was 'purified' by the removal of many Arabic and Persian words.

The Kemalist regime, in common with revolutionary regimes the world over, saw architecture and urban design as the most important visual indicators of cultural modernisation. Curiously, the Ottoman Revival style continued to be the preferred architectural expression throughout the 1920s. The new capital of Turkey, as well as many other Anatolian towns, was adorned with the finest Ottoman-style buildings during the early years of the Republic. The first and second National Assembly, the State Railways Headquarters, the Ministry of Foreign Affairs, the Ethnographic Museum and the Ankara Palace Hotel are all important examples. Celâl Esat Arseven, a professor of architectural history at the *Sanayi-i Nefise Mektebi,* explained this trend:

> Almost all architects walked this path which was forged by Mimar Vedat and Kemalettin [two leading architects of the Ottoman Revivalist style]. The government also supported this, and insistently requested

that schools, barracks, train stations and such kinds of buildings be built in the national style. Furthermore, an Act was passed to force even private owners to construct their buildings in this style.[20]

This paradoxical acceptance of Ottoman Revival as an official architectural style of the new regime was, in fact, a reflection of the duality in the political ideology of early twentieth-century Turkey.[21] In the early years of the new Republic political power was still shared by a modernist elite, who proposed a radical transformation programme, and by significant figures of the national movement, who advocated a smoother reform agenda that did not totally deny former Ottoman heritage. The acceptance of Ottoman forms in architecture was only possible in this political atmosphere.

The reign of Ottoman Revivalism, however, was short-lived and it was abandoned in the late 1920s in favour of European Modernism. The first significant crack in architectural revivalism appeared when Kemalettin Bey, a pioneer of the Ottoman Revival, died in 1927. The final demise of this architectural style came in 1931 when, as noted above, the new regime consolidated its power and eliminated its political opponents. From this time the Kemalist administration totally rejected the use of Ottoman forms in new buildings. This brought about changes to the facades of some Ottoman Revivalist buildings in Ankara.

Political rejection was also shared by young Turkish architects who began to see Ottoman Revival as anathema to their architectural expression. The cubic compositions of European Modernism, known in Turkey as *Yeni Mimari* (the New Architecture), were promoted as the most appropriate way to express the rationalist and secular ideals of Kemalism.[22] As can be seen in the writings of Behçet Sabri and Bedrettin Hamdi, two young architects of the era, the architecture of the Turkish revolution was completely different from that of Ottoman times. According to them, the Turkish revolution did not attempt to modernise the *fez* but had replaced it with the hat and, equally, did not try to revise the old Arabic script but had abandoned it for the Latin alphabet. Hence they advocated that modern Turkish architects reject the old stylistic forms and embark on a 'new and logical path' towards modernisation.[23] As a result of this decisive shift in favour of European Modernism, new government buildings and public centres such as cinemas, clubs, public domains, large boulevards, parks, picnic areas and promenades were designed in keeping with the reformist and secular character of the Republic. These cubic buildings became the platforms for the Kemalist regime to show the modern face of its political power.[24]

The radical transition to European Modernism was completed with the reconfiguration of architectural education in Turkey in the early 1930s. Giulio Mongeri, a leading figure of the Ottoman Revivalist style, resigned from his post at the *Sanayi-i Nefise Mektebi* in 1928. In the same year the name of the school was 'modernised' and changed to the *Güzel Sanatlar Akademisi* (Fine Arts Academy). This was followed by the resignation of Vedat Bey from his post in 1930. Responsibility for the sole architectural school of Turkey was then given to Swiss architect Ernst Egli. The classical Beaux-Arts model in the architectural curriculum was abandoned and the principles of European Modernism were incorporated into the Fine Arts Academy. A year later in 1931 *Mimar*, a new architectural journal, was published and in its pages many Turkish architects promoted the new architectural styles of Turkey. Like everything else that represented Ottoman culture, the title of the journal *Mimar* (a word of Arabic origin) was replaced in 1934 by *Arkitekt* (derived from the German spelling).[25]

Istanbul, however, was immune from this radical shift in Turkish architecture in favour of European Modernism. As the city had lost its privileged status and much of its population, almost no new large-scale public buildings were constructed in Istanbul until the 1940s. Amongst the few modern buildings constructed in this period were the Presidential Summer Mansion in Florya in 1935, the Karaköy Harbour Passenger Terminal in 1938 and the Kadıköy People's House building in 1939. The impact of the 'New Architecture', however, was mostly felt in the smaller scale private buildings, in particular the residential apartment blocks constructed in the Taksim and Gümüşsuyu districts. Perhaps the most noteworthy development in Istanbul's architecture was the emergence of the Art Deco style, especially in residential apartment blocks in the Taksim, Şişli, Gümüşsuyu and Cihangir districts of the city.

As the new Republic shifted abruptly towards European Modernist architecture, the traditional urban form of the cities became a target. Atatürk's reforms, as noted by Şerif Mardin, aimed to establish a 'new collective identity' where religion was no longer of any determining power, and were intended to liberate the individual from the 'idiocy of traditional, community-oriented life'.[26] The secularisation of daily social life and the independence of individuals could only be realised by breaking the traditional social relationships and destroying the power of the *imam* at the local level of the *mahalle*, the local neighbourhood unit.[27] The *mahalle* was the core of social life in traditional Ottoman culture. As well as serving administrative and civic purposes, the *mahalle* was an enclosed world where the average Ottoman citizen would undertake his primary education, obtain his professional or occupational skills, arrange his marriage, celebrate the birth of his children and receive a funeral ceremony on his death.[28] The most significant targets of the Republican reform agenda—equality between men and women and the participation of women in daily social life—were not possible in the *mahalle* which was under the strict control of the *imam* and governed by traditional cultural norms. Hence it was the moral control of the *mahalle* that the Republican reforms were intent on abolishing and replacing with a modern system, one that provided more independence for individuals.[29] In this political and ideological atmosphere new planning schemes to modernise the traditional urban pattern of Anatolian cities, as well as Istanbul, were put on the Republican reform agenda.

The 1920s and 1930s brought a raft of new legislation in urban planning. First was the *Ankara Şehremaneti Kanunu (*Ankara Municipal Act) of 16 February 1924. According to the Act, which mirrored the municipal model developed for Istanbul in the late-Ottoman period, the municipality was to be governed by the *Cemiyet-i Umumiye-i Belediye* (General Committee of the Municipality) comprising a mayor, who was brought from Istanbul, and 24 members appointed by the government. *Ankara'da İnşaası Mukarrer Yeni Mahalle İçin Muktazi Yerler ile Bataklık ve Merzagi Arazinin Şehremanetince İstimlâkine Dair Kanun* (The Act of Acquisition of Marsh Lands for the Establishment of New Development Areas by the Municipality of Ankara) was adopted on 24 March 1925 to create new development areas. This was followed by the foundation of the Ankara Directorate of Development on 28 May 1928.[30]

The National Assembly introduced the following legislation in the 1930s: *Belediyeler Kanunu* (Municipality Act) 1930; *Belediyeler Bankası Kuruluş Kanunu* (Foundation of Municipal Bank Act) 1931; *Belediyeler Yapı ve Yollar Kanunu* (Municipal Public Works Act) 1933; *Belediyeler İstimlak Kanunu* (Municipal Acquisition Act) 1934; and *Belediyeler İmar Heyeti Kuruluş Kanunu* (Foundation of Municipal Development Council Act) 1935. The Municipality Act ended the old *Şehremaneti* and required the establishment of new *belediye*s (municipalities) across the country. This new legislation necessitated the preparation of urban development plans for all cities and towns that had populations greater than 10,000. A five-year plan for municipal construction was introduced in 1934. Between 1930 and 1948 approximately 240 towns were mapped and 300 city plans were completed for towns and cities in Anatolia.[31] These schemes portrayed Ankara as the ideal city planning model with its secular, youthful and healthy image. It was this image which led Cemil Topuzlu, the former mayor of Istanbul to observe: 'In my opinion, in order to transform Istanbul into a contemporary city, there is no solution but total demolition, with the exception of Istanbul's monuments, and gradual reconstruction'.[32]

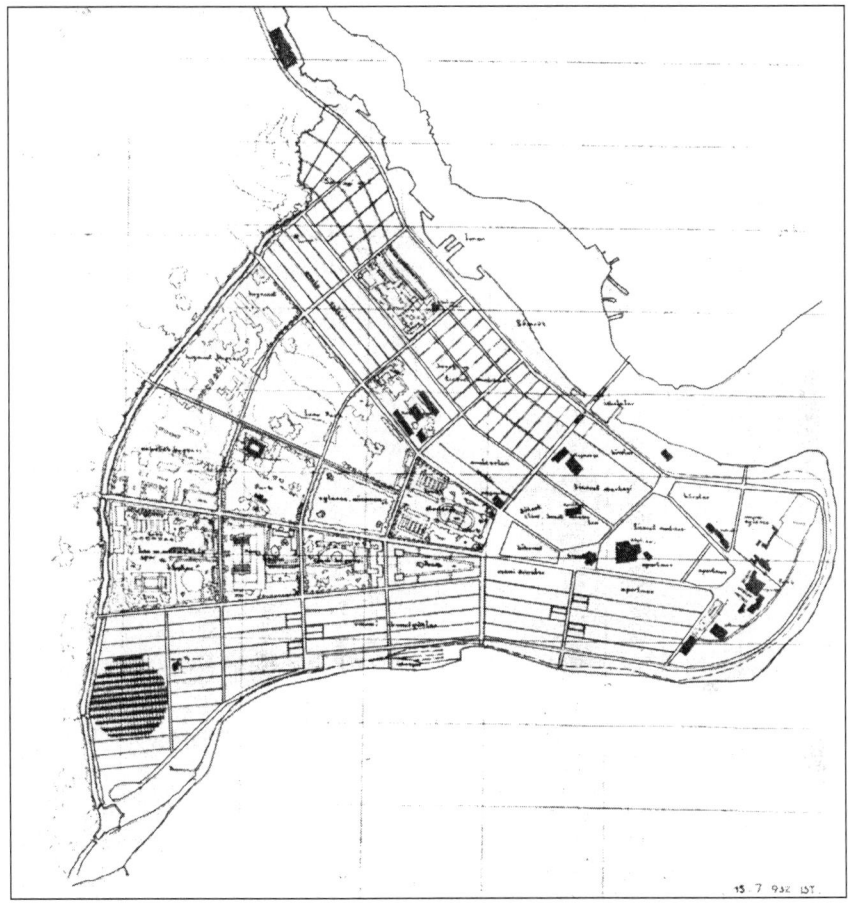

Figure 21 A redevelopment proposal reconfiguring Istanbul Peninsula on a grid pattern prepared by a group of final year architectural students in the Fine Arts Academy, 1931–32

Another significant aspect of the Republican government's urban policy was the retention of the existing social structure. Turkey in the 1930s was overwhelmingly an agrarian country, with more that 80 per cent of the population living in rural areas. In the absence of opportunities for industrial employment, immigration to the big cities would have created a chaotic situation and made the Kemalist objective of maintaining control almost impossible. As understood by the lessons of the short-lived democratic experience, even in the big cities where the literacy rate was relatively high the spirit of the Kemalist reform could have only limited success. The influence of the reforms in the vast majority of the 33,000 villages, many of which had very little communication with the cities and towns, was almost nonexistent. The policy, therefore, was to keep the peasants in their villages, discourage immigration, downplay the attractions of city life and educate the rural population about the virtues of Kemalist ideology. Hence for village children a distinct style of education was needed that emphasised practical knowledge rather than theoretically based learning. To achieve this goal, special educational organisations called *köy enstitüleri (*village institutes) were established in 1940, after a three-year trial period, to train village teachers.[33] As candidates from cities could have potential problems adjusting to village life, students for these institutes were selected from the peasantry and required to work for many years in their assigned villages. The importance of the village and its contribution to national development was often propounded in the official declarations and political propaganda of the Republican government. Mustafa Kemal's rhetoric during the national struggle was that 'the peasants are the real masters of the nation'. This became one of the most frequently used political slogans of the early Republican period. In this strong ideological climate the 'scientific planning of villages' became a distinct focus for Turkish architects of the 1930s, with the preparation of several 'model village' projects.[34]

This policy was not only a political choice but also an inevitable outcome of the influence of the peasantism of the mid-1930s. In fact, it was the intellectual articulation of this ideology that brought the village institutes to life. Peasantist ideology first appeared in the late-Ottoman period, and gained new momentum in the 1930s to become one of the most influential socio-political movements in Turkey.[35] This movement became mainstream, especially in the academic circles of Istanbul University, during the early 1930s. Turkish academics in the social sciences who had completed their education in Germany and France, such as Ömer Lütfi Barkan, Ziayeddin Fahri Fındıkoğlu and Ömer Celâl Sarc, together with German professors who had sought refuge in Turkey and now worked in Istanbul University, adopted a strong anti-urban position. They regarded the city as the source of all evil, with its degenerate class struggles, unemployment, economic depression and social unrest. These same academics also took a strong stand against political and economic liberalism and saw the peasantry as the real motive behind the Turkish revolution. Strongly influenced by the German *Sozialpolitic,* this movement advocated the creation of small-scale farmer homesteads (based on the model of *Erbhof* in National Socialist Germany) to prevent mass immigration from rural areas to big cities. According to Wilhelm Röpke, one of the German professors employed in Istanbul University, the ideal city should have a maximum of 30,000 inhabitants.[36] Even the most developed industrialised countries, according to Barkan, had learned their lessons from the result of the 1929 Great Depression and had taken all possible precautions to preserve village life against policies that attracted peasants to the cities.[37]

The anti-urban bias was not limited to some influential academics in the 1930s Turkish universities. The regime's ideologists at every level had also taken strong pro-peasant positions at various institutions. For example, the prominent peasantist ideologue of the early Republican period, Nusret Kemal Köymen, who was the editor of *Ülkü*, the semi-official propaganda journal of the Ankara People's House, portrayed the importance of the village and the creation of a classless society in his writings:

> Kemalism sees the village and the peasant as indispensable elements of society, while it considers cities as the centre of districts, and it prioritises the development of social order among its other ideals. By not allowing the abuse of villages and agriculture by cities and industry, by aiming to establish harmony and unity between agriculture and industry, by trying not to cause a conflict between the village and the city and agriculture and industry, Kemalism is a leading and, at the same time, sophisticated kind of regime which is progressing in the most positive way towards achieving a classless society.[38]

According to Köymen, the 'materialist viewpoint' which had begun to dominate the world since the nineteenth century was totally an urbanist idea and its aims were to terminate villages, heap people into big cities and organise them into a 'highly complex collaborative division of labour'. This division, Köymen suggested, would be so complicated that in a similar way to 'millions of cogwheels in a factory' an individual's place in society would have no specific character. Similarly, the entire administration and production mechanism would be managed by a complex bureaucratic and technocratic hierarchy, and individuals would obey the orders that were given to them like 'soldiers in a great army'. He then argued that the works would be so complicated and power would be held by so few people that there would be literally no possibility for the phenomenon called democracy. Though people would have plenty of spare time, there would be no spirit to benefit from it. Although Köymen described the 'urban utopia' as imaginary, he noted that even large cities such as London, New York, Moscow, Leningrad, Berlin, Vienna and Paris were attempting to reach this goal of materialism.

The negative aspects of city life were another target for Köymen. He argued that there was no financial security in cities, only the risk of hunger and unemployment. People's souls were being blinded as inhabitants of cities became 'distant from the tranquillity, quietness and beauty of nature'. Moral corruption was also becoming common since social control within the complex and crowded nature of the city was extremely limited. As family bonds and control had weakened, children were able to earn a living at an early age. Also the busy working style and noisy atmosphere of cities distorted 'spiritual and physical health'. City dwellers who were bound by financial and administrative ties were not always able to be 'independent and honest democratic citizens'. And, more importantly, he argued that class distinction in cities had decreased the power of many capable people and led to dangerous conflicts. In big cities expenses such as transport, water and sewerage, electricity, security and administrative services caused many unnecessary costs and 'miseries'.[39]

Juxtaposed with this portrayal of the city as a place of chaos and corruption was the utopian picture of village life as presented by the peasantists. Villages were considered genuine symbols of the noble, untouched, intelligent and pragmatic character of Turkish nationality. Peasants who lived in parts of Anatolia where there had been no occupation by foreign armies and virtually no contact with the outside world were seen as the genuine representatives of the Turkish race. They were regarded as not having been 'poisoned' by capitalist ideology. Moreover, since they faced natural conditions directly, the peasants were seen as a source of strong soldiers for the army, unlike pampered city youth. Believed to be the essential source of Turkish identity, villages should therefore benefit from the same rights and privileges as cities, including equal standards of living and learning opportunities.[40] In this context the Ottoman Empire's policy of 'favouring cities at the expense of villages' was criticised as a major reason for the loss of national culture in the Empire.[41] It was this peasantist ideology that would influence Istanbul's redevelopment programme over the next decade until the late 1940s.

Istanbul versus Ankara

A significant decision taken by Mustafa Kemal and his administration was the declaration of Ankara as the new capital city of Turkey on 13 October 1923. This was, above all, a strategic choice as Istanbul was under foreign occupation during the Turkish National War of Independence. In fact, the initial idea to relocate the Ottoman capital to Anatolia went back to the early 1910s. Following the Balkan wars and the subsequent defeat of the Empire by European armies, the Ottoman government had seriously considered moving its capital to central Anatolia. Konya, Kayseri and Kütahya—all important regional centres—were suggested but Ankara, interestingly, was not considered at this time.

Atatürk, while organising the national resistance movement, had shown some interest in Erzurum and Sivas, two cities located in Eastern Anatolia. These cities, however, were not close to the battlefronts of Western Anatolia and had poor communication links with Istanbul. For these reasons, Ankara came to the forefront as it had the advantage of being close to both the Ottoman capital and the battlefields and was connected to the railway. Therefore, Ankara became the de facto capital of the national resistance forces at an early stage. On 23 April 1920 the Turkish National Assembly was opened in Ankara to direct the national resistance forces and to host the Ankara government. Although the Ottoman sultan and his government were still recognised internationally, the national resistance movement created its own administration. From this time the Ankara government extended its powerbase and gradually took political control away from Istanbul. At the end of the Turkish National War of Independence the Ankara government, officially known as the 'Government of Grand Assembly of Turkey', conducted peace talks with the European states and signed the Treaty of Peace in Lausanne on 24 July 1923.[42]

The declaration of Ankara as the Turkish capital had a meaning beyond the geopolitical as it represented a strong symbol of the political and cultural preferences of the Republican regime. For Bernard Lewis, the new capital was 'symbolising and accentuating the changes that were taking place', whereas Istanbul was a city 'too intimately associated with the past'.[43] Ankara, like other purpose-built capitals, was a showcase for the new regime to illustrate its success and youthful vigour. In Republican eyes, Ankara became the symbolic heart of the new secular nation, in contrast to Istanbul which due to its sacred character was the centre of the Caliphate and the Sultanate.[44] According to the Kemalists, Ankara was the city of the future and Istanbul the city of the past. Istanbul exhibited the features of its imperial and dynastic traditions and had a cosmopolitan character. Its cul-de-sacs, crooked street patterns and timber buildings were all seen as symbols of the physical and social corruption and the degradation of the old Ottoman system. Ankara, with its modern buildings, wide boulevards, parks and, most importantly, its silhouette without minarets,[45] was considered the modern, secular hub of the new Turkish nation.

Nevertheless, the designation of Ankara as the new capital city was not an easy decision for the government. Istanbul had been the capital of the Ottoman Empire for almost 500 years. For this reason, many leading bureaucrats, intellectuals and even army officers, who had played significant roles in the national struggle, had strong emotional connections with the city. For them, the move to Ankara was temporary. They saw the eventual return of the seat of the new government to Istanbul, following the liberation of the city from occupation. In order to alter this expectation and to soften potential opposition within the National Assembly and from the wider public to the relocation of the capital to Ankara various tactical steps had to be taken. Firstly, immediately following the liberation of the former Ottoman capital from the occupying powers on 6 October 1923, Mustafa Kemal met with representatives of the Istanbul press in İzmit, a small town near Istanbul. In this meeting he explained the importance of selecting a geographically secure place as the capital of the new state. He stated that Istanbul's occupation showed that the seat of government should be located in a place out of the reach of enemy armies. The second tactical step came from İsmet Paşa (İnönü), Mustafa Kemal's right-hand man and the deputy for Malatya in the Assembly. On 9 October 1923 he submitted a proposed bill to the Assembly for the declaration of Ankara as the capital city of the new Turkish Republic, but also confirmed Istanbul as the official and permanent seat of the Caliphate. Although this promise was soon breached by the abolition of the Caliphate, until 1924 Turkey was a country with two capitals.

Ankara's status as the new capital city rapidly changed its urban and social character from that of a small provincial Anatolian town of about 25,000 people. Despite the significant cut in general expenditure after the 1929 Great Depression, the government maintained its commitment to the budget for the construction of Ankara and launched an extensive development programme to create its new capital city.[46] The Kemalist rulers took the same path as their Ottoman predecessors, and sought the assistance of foreign expertise. An international design competition was organised in 1927, culminating in the commission of a German planner Hermann Jansen to prepare a new city plan for Ankara.[47] Jansen's master plan, influenced by Camillo Sitte's planning principles, proposed major axes, public spaces and the preservation of the old citadel. In this plan the most significant characteristic of the new capital was its substantial public spaces, including large parks, entertainment venues, modern hotels and other outdoor recreational spaces. *Gençlik Parkı* (Youth Park), for example, was designed as a large urban park associated with an artificial lake and accommodating public recreational activities such as concerts, outside dining areas, performing arts and a children's swimming pool. It had special significance as a 'social school' intended to steer the nation towards acceptance of modern secular practices and social codes.[48] Other major public recreational venues developed in the 1930s were the 19 May Sport Stadium, *Atatürk Orman Çiftliği* (Atatürk Model Farm and Forest) and the Çubuk Dam picnic areas. Special meaning was attached to these areas as embodiments of 'the spirit of the Republic'. They also had an important symbolic function to represent the Republic's youth and its healthy nature.[49]

Whereas Jansen's plan aimed to establish the modern city form, the task of creating modern buildings in the new capital city was given to a group of European architects. These were the Austrian architects Clemenz Holzmeister, Wilhelm Schütte and Margarete Schütte-Lihotzky, the Swiss architect Ernst Egli and the German architects Bruno Taut and Martin Elsaesser. Together they were the most prominent figures in Republican architecture from the late 1920s until the early 1940s. The Ministry of Defence, the Headquarters of the Turkish Armed Forces, the Presidential Residence, the Ministry of Interior Affairs, the Ministry of Public Works, the Ministry of Commerce and the Grand National Assembly were the most significant works designed by Holzmeister. Egli designed the State Conservatorium of Music, the Higher Architectural Institute, the Commercial Lycée, the İsmet Paşa Girls' Institute and the Faculty of Political Science.[50]

Beyond its symbolic role as the 'heart of the nation', Ankara was also the nerve centre of Turkey. While the Kemalist regime tried to overthrow many past institutions, it also followed the well-worn path of its Ottoman predecessors and established a heavily centralised system of government. Turkey was divided into 74 *vilayet* (provinces) administered by a *vali* (governor).[51] Vilayets were divided into *kaza*s (counties) and were under the responsibility of another government appointee, the *kaymakam*. And the *nahiye*, the smallest administrative unit, was also governed by a *müdür* (director) appointed by Ankara. All administrative posts were linked to the Ministry of Interior Affairs, where all decisions were taken. While the Municipal Act required all cities to have an elected mayor and municipal council, the governor had a power of veto in situations where local decisions were contrary to central government policy. Also, the major cities—Istanbul, Ankara and İzmir—had a special administrative structure whereby the governor also served as the mayor. This hierarchical system gave Ankara a power that Istanbul had never attained as the capital of the Ottoman Empire for five centuries.

While Ankara was the focus of the government's attempt to create the 'heart of the nation', Istanbul lost all political privileges acquired over its 2,700-year history. The loss of Istanbul's administrative and governmental functions to Ankara was followed by a significant change in its demographic structure and a decline in its economic power. In line with policies designed to create a national bourgeoisie, many non-Muslim merchants and bankers who had dominated commercial activities in Istanbul left the city, thereby dramatically weakening its economic base.[52] In 1926 this highly charged ideological atmosphere saw the Post Office of Istanbul directed to return all letters addressed to Constantinople.[53] The Grande Rue de Pera, the most significant showpiece of cosmopolitan character in the city, was renamed İstiklâl (Independence) Street. By 1927 the city's population had declined to 690,857, half its pre-war size. Istanbul also became more homogenous, with the departure of its non-Muslim inhabitants. New Muslim immigrants had taken refuge in the city as a result of large territorial losses before and during the First World War. In 1885 Muslim inhabitants had represented 44 per cent of the city's population; by 1927 they formed 64 per cent of the population.

In this period Istanbul was neglected politically by the new government, as it was still considered the core centre for loyalists of the old regime. Growing opposition from the Istanbul press, particularly articles advocating the retention of the Caliphate, was seen as an immediate threat to the new system. The regime also had the psychological aim of extinguishing the hopes of bureaucrats, intellectuals and diplomatic missions who desperately looked forward to escaping the dust and dirt of the 'boring' central Anatolian town and returning to the beauties of Istanbul. An interesting indication of the extent of this neglect is that Atatürk did not visit Istanbul until 1927, although he had toured the entire Anatolian region and passed through the Bosphorus in the preceding years.

The declaration of Ankara as the new capital city was not well received in Istanbul. This decision not only injured the inhabitants emotionally, but also deepened the economic crisis which engulfed the city as a result of the great economic depression of the 1930s. The relocation of the capital meant unemployment for the tens of thousands of Ottoman bureaucrats who resided in the city.[54] Spending on public resources in Istanbul was cut and redirected to the development of Ankara and other Anatolian cities. The resources allocated to Istanbul in the first Five-Year National Development Plan 1934–39, for example, were very low in comparison to other Anatolian cities.[55] Rather than being used to create new industrial complexes, the limited investment funds were allocated, in most cases, to the rehabilitation of existing pre-Republican industrial plants, such as the Paşabahçe Glass and Bottle Factory.

The lack of sympathy for Istanbul, among the ruling elite of the regime, still had currency in the mid-1940s. Cemil Topuzlu, the former mayor of

Istanbul, records in his memoirs the depth of negative feeling for Istanbul held by the officials of the new government in Ankara:

> Unfortunately, Atatürk died soon after he started to deal with Istanbul's redevelopment. After this event things started to go badly in Ankara. Inappropriate opinions, short-sightedness and even the old enmity towards Istanbul reappeared. Some of the representatives [of the Grand National Assembly] and ministers who were born in Anatolia and who hated Istanbul claimed that there was no difference between the Anatolian cities and Istanbul, such a big and very significant city. They even made up the majority in the Assembly.[56]

An article published in *La Turquie Kemalsite* in 1943 represents similar feelings about Istanbul as those chronicled by Topuzlu. According to the article, a visitor who had spent a few days visiting the tourist sites of Istanbul was 'no better equipped than the stay-at-homes who get their ideas out of novels about the sultans'. As a result of the cosmopolitan social structure of the city, a visitor to Istanbul would probably eat 'Russian food', be guided by an 'Armenian courier' and get his political news from a 'Greek porter'. In order to understand contemporary Turkey and its future the best thing for a visitor to do, recommended the article, was to 'take the first train to Ankara'.[57]

Despite this resentment and neglect, there were still some piecemeal infrastructure works implemented in Istanbul in the 1920s, namely: a modern firefighting department established by Haydar Bey, the first *Şehremini* of Istanbul appointed by the Republican government; a new abattoir in Sütlüce on the northern bank of the Golden Horn; and a new 30-metre-wide road and tramline through the area devastated by the Fatih–Altımermer fire between Fatih and Edirnekapı. Moreover, a Dalmatian-born topographer, Jacques Pervititch, began to draw cadastral maps of the city for insurance purposes in the early 1920s and this task continued until his death in 1945. Although it only remained on paper, an urban planning scheme was developed by the German planner Carl Lörcher.

The most visible outcome of urban planning in this period was the reorganisation of Beyazıt Square. Various buildings were demolished to enlarge the space and an oval pool was constructed at the centre of this new square, making Beyazıt the most attractive place on the old Istanbul Peninsula. Another noteworthy work was the opening of a monument for commemoration of the Republic in Taksim in 1928. Designed by the Italian sculptor Pietro Canonica, with Giulio Mongeri who designed its landscape, the Republican Monument became one of the iconic places of the city.

Figure 22 Beyazıt Square redesigned in the 1930s

The status of Istanbul declined rapidly from that of the capital city of the Ottoman Empire to merely the largest city in the new Republic of Turkey. Istanbul lost most of its privileges and received no substantial public investment during the first decade of the Republic, but nevertheless it remained as Turkey's largest and most important cultural, economic and industrial centre. Istanbul alone contributed over one third of the total income tax payments to the National Treasury in 1950.[58] In Feroz Ahmad's words, 'Istanbul became the new Republic's New York while Ankara was its Washington'.[59]

Figure 23 Illuminated decorative pool in Beyazıt Square in the 1930s

Figure 24 Republican Monument designed by Canonica and Mongeri in Taksim

4
RESHAPING ISTANBUL UNDER KEMALIST PRINCIPLES 1933 – 1950

Redevelopment of Istanbul is not a challenging task for Atatürk, the real founder of our young Republic, the saver of Turkey from collapse, the founder of all civilised institutions, the creator of all and our most beloved leader... Istanbul should not be retained in its current ruined and confused state, and it will not be. Sooner or later it will be redeveloped and become the most modern city in the world... I would express my opinion without any hesitation that the great mastermind will soon give a prosperity to Istanbul and therefore confirm his reputation in urban history.

Cemil Topuzlu, 1937[1]

By the mid-1930s the implementation of the master plan for Ankara was underway, as well as the construction of various major public buildings and recreation projects designed by European architects. Istanbul, however, was not a city that could be deserted politically for a long period. With its economic and intellectual prominence, it was the showcase of the country. Istanbul was also Turkey's door to the world. The signature of the new regime would need to be carved in the soil of the biggest city of Turkey. The Republican government accordingly signalled its intention to reshape and rebuild Istanbul in line with the Kemalist reform agenda.

The government followed the same path in reshaping Istanbul as it had employed in Ankara, and organised an international urban design competition in 1933.[2] Following an extensive investigation, three European urban planners were invited to enter the competition, namely: Alfred Agache, Hermann Ehlgötz and Henri Prost.[3] However, Prost, who was then chief of the Planning Bureau of Paris, did not participate in the competition and another French planner, Jacques Henri Lambert, was invited on the recommendation of the French Embassy in Ankara. The three contestants came to Istanbul and stayed one month to prepare their proposals. They were provided with a general map of the city and were asked, without a specific brief, to prepare reports showing a range of planning options.

Agache, a French architect, urban planner and writer who had graduated in 1905 from the *École Nationale Supérieure des Beaux-Arts de Paris*, was the author of a prize-winning, but unexecuted, entry to the international competition for the design of Canberra, Australia, in 1912. Master plans for Dunkerque (1912), Creil (1924) and Poitiers (1928) were among the other major works prepared by Agache. In 1927 he was invited to prepare a master plan for Rio de Janeiro, then the capital of Brazil. This plan was completed in 1930 but, following a change of government, was not implemented. Lambert had worked on urban planning projects in New York and Chicago in the United States and was also one of Prost's deputies in Paris. Ehlgötz, a prominent urban planner in Germany, was a professor at the Department of Urban Planning in the *Technische Hochschule* in Berlin and a member of the Academy of Urban Planners in Germany. The master plan for the city of Essen in Germany was one of his most significant works.

Agache's project, *Grand Istanbul; Un Programme d'Urbanisation*, aimed to make Istanbul homogenous by linking its various precincts by major circulation highways.[4] His proposal focused on some significant issues, including zoning, road networks, transportation, railway stations, ports, airports, public transportation, hygiene, recreation and conservation of historic sites. He envisaged Istanbul as the largest economic centre in Turkey and the primary hub connecting Europe and the Middle East. His proposal comprised the construction of three bridges spanning the Golden Horn between the Istanbul Peninsula and the Beyoğlu district of the city, and the opening of large boulevards varying from 40 to 50 metres in width to connect the major residential, commercial and industrial quarters of Istanbul. While traffic and transportation plans were to be based generally on the automobile, he also proposed a rail network running under the Istanbul Peninsula. A central railway station, a port and a new commercial centre were proposed between Aksaray and Yenikapı on the shores of the Sea of Marmara. Agache also endorsed the preservation of the city's architectural heritage and archaeological potential. The definition of 'architectural heritage' in his vision, however, was limited to monumental buildings only. This was a typical approach shared by his contemporaries. He proposed clearing sites within the vicinity of the grand mosques and monuments and, with the exception of an area between Sultanahmet and Fatih, the entire Istanbul Peninsula was to be redesigned to accord with modernist principles. Particular attention was to be paid to the areas destroyed by fires.

In a similar way to Agache, Lambert saw Istanbul as one of the most important transit centres in the Middle East and estimated its future population at approximately 2.5 million.[5] His proposal contained three major themes: Istanbul of Industry; Istanbul of Culture; and Istanbul of Sport and Tourism. It included a major policy initiative to transfer port facilities from the Golden Horn to the shores of the Sea of Marmara. The 20-kilometre coastal belt between Kumkapı and west of Bakırköy was considered to be the most appropriate location. Lambert's plan proposed that a light industrial district be set up within the Istanbul Peninsula and that heavy industry be located outside the Istanbul Peninsula, with a 200-metre green buffer zone created to separate the heavy industrial area from the city. Yenikapı, with a proposed railway terminus, a port named *'La Porte de la Turquie'* (the Gate of Turkey) and a large public square named 'the Plaza of Turkey', was considered to be the new commercial hub of Istanbul. In common with the other competitors, Lambert included new boulevards to connect the major districts of Istanbul and prescribed major arteries of 44 metres in width and secondary roads of 24 metres in width. As proposed in the 1839 development policy and Auric's scheme of 1911, a littoral road alongside the Sea of Marmara was included in Lambert's proposal. He also contemplated the construction of new modern residential districts outside the city walls in Bakırköy and Yeşilköy. His recommendations for the historical sectors of Istanbul were similar to his fellow competitors, as they included the demolition of buildings within the proximity of the great mosques and monuments. Lambert also proposed a *jardin publique de la cité des arts* (public park) on the eastern side of the ancient Hippodrome between Hagia Sophia and Sultan Ahmet Mosque. The park was to be connected to the shores of the Sea of Marmara by a terraced transition. A sports centre in Yenibahçe, an archaeological museum in Sultanahmet and the extension of the University district in Beyazıt and Süleymaniye were other distinct features of Lambert's proposal.

Ehlgötz differed from the other competitors by emphasising the importance of preserving the historical character and natural beauty of the city. His report was accompanied by a total of 24 maps and seven photographs and focussed on economic principles, general circulation, zoning, new housing areas outside the city walls and the relocation of the port.[6] He stressed the importance of preserving monuments to retain and reinforce the city's artistic significance and recommended that monuments be interconnected by minor streets and separated from main roads. The protection of the city's silhouette as seen from the Golden Horn and the Sea of Marmara was underlined as critically important in his plan. Importance was also placed on the need for a smooth and sympathetic transition between the different city zones and on retaining and improving the existing road networks. Ehlgötz also included a coastal road alongside the Sea of Marmara between Sarayburnu and Yeşilköy, and recommended removing port facilities from old Istanbul and creating a new port on the Asian side of the Bosphorus at Haydarpaşa. Significantly, he foresaw the importance of establishing a legislative framework and recommended that the government prepare a general planning act for the whole country and a specific redevelopment act for the implementation of his proposals for Istanbul.

The competition jury set up a subcommittee to review the three proposals and eventually decided on Ehlgötz's proposal as the most realistic, appropriate and least intrusive for the historical and natural aspects of the city. The jury accepted the subcommittee's recommendations but the proposed plan was never implemented.[7]

Another noteworthy proposal was submitted in 1933 by the legendry Swiss-born architect Le Corbusier.[8] Le Corbusier's ideas were contrary to the proposals put forward by the candidates in the competition with respect to the historical character of Istanbul. While the contestants, with the exception of Ehlgötz, proposed large-scale boulevards, Le Corbusier advocated conserving the existing pattern and structure of Istanbul. He believed that the Istanbul Peninsula should be preserved, and that new development areas be created outside the Theodosian Walls towards the west. While the official response to Le Corbusier's application has not been found, in an interview published in *Arkitekt* in 1949 he was quoted as giving the following explanation as to why he was not appointed by the government:

> If I had not made the most strategic mistake of my life in the letter I wrote to Atatürk, I would be planning the most beautiful city of Istanbul, instead of my biggest competitor, Henri Prost. In this notorious letter, I foolishly suggested to the greatest revolutionary hero of a new nation to leave Istanbul as it was, in the dirt and dust of centuries.[9]

Martin Wagner, a prominent German architect, urban planner and theorist, was another important figure in Istanbul's urban planning during the 1930s. Following the urban design competition, Wagner was invited by the Municipality of Istanbul in 1935 to be a consultant to the newly established Directorate of Development and was appointed as an advisor for the Department of Public Works in 1937.[10] His primary interest was in the production of low-cost housing with acceptable social and hygienic standards. These standards were usually lacking in the speculative buildings that were typical of large nineteenth-century cities. As director of the Planning Department and Building Control Office of Berlin in 1926, he had focused on transforming Berlin into a vibrant metropolis and had little interest in aesthetic issues. Wagner's main concerns had been the city's increasing traffic and housing problems. As the National Socialists (Nazis) extended their power in the 1930s, Wagner, like many other German scholars, left Germany. He first resided in Turkey in 1935 and later migrated to the United States in 1938 on the advice of his close friend, Walter Gropius.

In Istanbul Wagner's main focus was solving major problems such as transportation, financial resources and the relationship of the city centre with its hinterland. His proposals were contained in a report to the Municipality of Istanbul and published in a series of articles in the architectural journal, *Arkitekt*.[11] Unlike the participants of the urban design competition, Wagner's analysis of urban problems was based on statistics and informed by the theoretical principles and practical experience he had gained from his previous work in Berlin. He therefore recommended a regional plan for the city and its hinterland drafted legislation for the implementation of the master plan, and prepared a number of other plans and proposals for the city.[12] Although these plans were never implemented, Wagner did contribute to the urban planning debate through his theoretical ideas and lectures at the universities.

The government's search for a foreign planner was an emotive issue among Turkish architects. Many writers of the period published articles in *Arkitekt* condemning the invitation to European architects and planners. For Turkish architects, Istanbul's planning works should not be left in the hands of foreign professionals who had little knowledge about the characteristics of the city and, in particular, the culture that formed its physical shape. Burhan Arif, for example, criticised the invitation to Ehlgötz, Agache and Lambert to prepare a plan for Istanbul:

> The planning of Istanbul is a universe of its own kind with distinguishing individual features. It would be a big mistake to liken it to a French, German or American one... The city of Istanbul has a unique aesthetic scale that no foreigner can perceive unless he becomes Oriental and knows, lives and works in its streets for a long period.[13]

The Prostian Years

The proposals to emerge from both the urban design competition and Wagner's plans in the end proved unacceptable to the government. Although official reasons were not given for the abandonment of Ehlgötz's and Le Corbusier's plans, it can be assumed that the preservation of the city's historical core and the limited and relatively minor alterations to the existing urban form were found to be contrary to Kemalist political ideology, which demanded a wholesale transformation of the former Ottoman capital. Wagner's statistical and analytical approaches, while detailed, were most likely seen as superfluous to the government's pragmatic policy to modernise the city as swiftly as possible. The government ended its search for the ideal plan by inviting the contribution of French urban planner Henri Prost. Prost, who had declined to participate in the urban design competition of 1933, accepted the offer to prepare a master plan for Istanbul, which was by then a decayed city that had lost almost half of its population, seen endless fires, been occupied by foreign armies and ignored by the new political regime.[14]

Prost had graduated from the *École Nationale Supérieure des Beaux-Arts de Paris* and had participated in a large number of city planning projects across Europe. He won the *Prix de Rome* in 1902 and studied at the French Institute at the Villa Medici in Rome between 1903 and 1907. From Rome, he visited Istanbul twice in 1904–05 and 1906–07 and worked on the preparation of surveys for Hagia Sophia and ancient Constantinople. Along with Agache and several other young architects, he participated in the master plan works for Paris under the supervision of Eugène Hénard. His first professional success as an urban designer was the award of first prize in the international design competition of 1910 for the city of Antwerp. Subsequently, at the invitation of the French military governor of Morocco, Marechal Lyautey, Prost prepared urban planning works for a number of French colonial cities in North Africa between 1913 and 1924, including Casablanca, Fez, Rabat, Meknes and Marrakech. He also participated in several urban design projects in the mid-1920s for the Côte d'Azur, including the cities of Toulon, Saint Tropez and Saint Raphael. In 1928 he returned to Paris as a member of a new urban planning committee. Under the guidance of Prost and Raoul Dautry, this committee prepared a master plan for Paris in 1934 which was approved in 1939.[15] For a short time between 1924 and 1925 Prost and René Danger also collaborated on the urban planning works for İzmir, located on the Aegean coast and Turkey's third largest city.

Prost arrived in Istanbul on 15 May 1936 and signed his contract on 11 June 1936. He remained in his post as the city's chief planner until 27 December 1950[16] and worked with three different governor and mayors, namely Muhittin Üstündağ (1928–38), Lütfi Kırdar (1938–49) and Fahrettin Kerim Gökay (1949–57). Prost never considered creating an overarching strategic plan for the entire metropolitan area, opting instead for a master plan for the Istanbul Peninsula and the Beyoğlu district and separate plans for the other parts of the city.[17] He categorised the goals of his master plan for the Istanbul Peninsula and Beyoğlu under six subheadings: clearance of unattractive buildings within the proximity of monuments; improvement of the old street network and opening of new boulevards; rehabilitation of old, poorly serviced neighbourhoods by the creation of hygienic housing and recreational areas; zoning; preservation of monumental buildings and sites and the natural beauties of the city; and preservation of Istanbul's silhouette from significant sight lines, including those from the Sea of Marmara, Golden Horn, Beyoğlu and the Asian shores.[18]

The lack of technical material such as accurate drawings and maps for Istanbul had always been raised as a significant concern by urban planners. Prost, however, considered that he had adequate drawings and photographic material to prepare his master plan.[19] Between 1936 and 1938 he compiled a total of 51 notes analysing the problems of the city for the information of government officials. The majority of these notes was translated into Turkish and published by the Municipality of Istanbul in 1938.[20] In addition to the notes, Prost also explained the projects in his letters to the governor and mayor and these form another significant source for understanding the spirit of Prost's plans and works.[21] Prost completed his master plan for the Istanbul Peninsula and Beyoğlu in 1937 and submitted it to the Municipality of Istanbul's General Assembly on 29 April 1938.[22] The plan was finally endorsed by the Ministry of Public Works on 30 June 1939.[23]

The Major Elements Proposed in Prost's Master Plan

The division of the city into industrial, commercial, residential and recreational zones and the establishment of an effective transportation system were the principal goals of Prost's master plan.[24] To achieve these goals the French urban designer recommended a group of radical measures that would significantly change Istanbul's urban morphology. On the Istanbul Peninsula his plan required the creation of a new urban pattern in accordance with modern design principles. This meant the erasure of traditional urban fabric that had existed for centuries, particularly in the western half of the peninsula. Even the Grand Bazaar would be encircled by large roads with new gates constructed at various locations. While the Theodosian Walls would be retained, the ramparts alongside the shores of the Sea of Marmara would only be kept locally where the planning of new neighbourhoods would permit. Additionally, only the most characteristic sections of the walls alongside the shores of the Golden Horn were to be retained. In Beyoğlu Prost's recommendations were even more extreme.

Figure 25 Prost's master plan for the Istanbul Peninsula as approved by the Ministry of Public Works on 30 May 1939

According to Prost's theory, the entire area bounded by the northern shores of the Golden Horn and Taksim should be demolished and rebuilt. As this option was not achievable due to costs and practicalities, he recommended the gradual transformation of the area by establishing new quarters in the empty spaces and demolishing the old quarters step-by-step.[25]

Prost placed considerable importance on establishing an uninterrupted traffic network throughout the city and, in the manner of Haussmann's plans for Paris, proposed several large boulevards and associated works such as viaducts, bridges and tunnels. He set out his reasons for regarding an effective transportation system as important:

> The roads that will regulate the traffic must be implemented immediately. These roads, which will be largely consistent with modern urban techniques, will rehabilitate the existing conditions radically. While the topography of the city will be navigated by viaducts or tunnels, numerous [unnecessary] level intersections will be eliminated and direct or large semicircular routes will be established. These proposed routes have been determined in order to minimise large property acquisitions, which may lead to unpredictable real estate speculations. These routes have been investigated so as not to disrupt the economic activities of neighbourhoods. With the completion of these roads, genuine inner city motorways will be in service on the left bank of the Golden Horn [Beyoğlu/Galata district] between Taksim Square and the bridges [Galata and Atatürk Bridges], and these motorways will pass over the low-priced houses. As there will be no need to stop over a considerable length of their routes, high-speed traffic can be established... The execution of these roads, which will form the major arteries of the city, will be followed by other works.[26]

Automobiles were envisaged as the major transportation mode in Prost's plan. Prost saw his master plan for Istanbul as even more modern than his plan for Paris as Istanbul would be dissected by major arterial roads designed for automobiles.[27] Although the full details of these roads were to be shown on later implementation plans, the master plan report indicated that they were to be constructed with up to 40-metre widths.[28] As a true believer in the automobile, Prost never saw rail transportation as a priority. He believed that the railways in Europe were in direct competition with automobiles, and that the latter were the transport mode of the future. Hence he proposed a major vehicular connection between Europe and Asia with a bridge over the Bosphorus.[29] Although his definite preference was the automobile, Prost's transportation plan still included an underground railway line connecting the Istanbul Peninsula to Beyoğlu passing over the Golden Horn.

The extension of Gazi (Atatürk) Boulevard to Unkapanı on the southern shores of the Golden Horn was the backbone of Prost's traffic plan.[30] This boulevard was planned as the main axis connecting the Istanbul Peninsula to Beyoğlu via Atatürk Bridge.[31] As previously noted, the first part of this 50-metre-wide road connecting Yenikapı to Aksaray was planned and partly executed in the late-Ottoman period on Auric's recommendation.[32] As evident in various documents—the *Municipal Bulletin* 1933,[33] the *City Guide* 1934[34] and cadastral maps prepared by Jacques Pervititch in 1936—the extension of this boulevard was planned well before the Prost era. However, the economic conditions at that time did not allow the execution of this costly work. Prost extended his maximum road width of 40 metres and designed the remaining parts of Atatürk Boulevard at a 50-metre width. Several major squares adorned with obelisks were included along the route of Atatürk Boulevard. The first square was to be opened in Şehzadebaşı, the second in Aksaray and, finally, a great square named Atatürk Esplanade was to be built on the shores of the Sea of Marmara to mark the termination of Atatürk Boulevard.[35]

Prost planned Atatürk Boulevard as a structural device to mark the natural division between the eastern and western parts of the Istanbul Peninsula. The former included the core commercial centre of Istanbul. Prost believed major interventions would harm these activities as they were considered vital for the functioning of the city. He therefore proposed major roads and new development areas for industrial, residential and commercial activities in the western portion of the peninsula.[36] His major transportation network in the Istanbul Peninsula included two principal arteries on an east–west axis to connect Aksaray to the outer sections of the city walls. The first boulevard was Millet Street bringing the Istanbul–Edirne motorway to the heart of the city. The second boulevard connected the proposed Olympic Stadium to the city centre through the proposed botanical garden in Yenibahçe. This avenue would have a total width of 60 metres including tree-lined pedestrian promenades on either side. These two major roads, together with Atatürk Boulevard, made Aksaray the most significant junction in the heart of the Istanbul Peninsula.

Prost followed the 1839 development policy and Auric's 1911 scheme by proposing two littoral roads: one along the shores of the Sea of Marmara in the south, and another on the Golden Horn in the north. The southern coastal road would be divided into three sections. The first would be a promenade connecting Galata Bridge to Yenikapı, adjacent to the Topkapı

Palace gardens. The aim was to create a place to 'appreciate the exceptional beauties of the Bosphorus'.[37] The second section was planned to connect the southern end of Atatürk Boulevard, where he proposed new port facilities and a train terminus at the western end of Yenikapı, to the airport in Yeşilköy and the outer suburbs in Florya district.[38] The littoral road on the southern shores of the Golden Horn would connect Eminönü to Unkapanı and then terminate in Eyüp, outside the city walls. The construction of this road would require the demolition of many buildings and ramparts along its route. The redevelopment of Eminönü included the creation of a public square, the demolition of 'parasitic' buildings in front of the Yeni Mosque, the demolition of commercial buildings to the west of Eminönü Square and the construction of a large road to connect Eminönü Square to Beyazıt. This road would also open up a vista of Süleymaniye Mosque from the Galata Bridge.[39]

An extensive road network in the Beyoğlu district was also proposed in the master plan. The reorganisation of Taksim Square was the major design element in the plan. Taksim Square was to be connected to the Istanbul Peninsula by two major roads crossing via the two bridges on the Golden Horn. The first road was to start from Atatürk Bridge and follow a parallel route to İstiklâl Street (formerly the Grande Rue de Pera) via Tepebaşı.[40] The second was designed to connect Galata Bridge to Taksim Square, and included more radical interventions such as extensive demolitions in Karaköy to create a square and the construction of tunnels and viaducts under and over the lower sections of Beyoğlu district.[41] Finally, Taksim Square was to be connected to Dolmabahçe and Kurtuluş by two new roads.

In addition to the roads which merged at Taksim Square, Prost proposed several other major roads to connect Karaköy Square to Tophane and Beşiktaş via Dolmabahçe. In a similar way to the coastal road on the southern bank of the Golden Horn, a littoral road alongside the northern bank was to be constructed to complete the industrial connection around the Golden Horn. His proposals for the port facilities and industrial areas of Istanbul required changes to the city's structure. Two principal ports, one in the European section at Yenikapı and another in Haydarpaşa on the Asian shores, were planned. Yenikapı, with a new railway terminus and ferry wharf, was envisaged as the new transportation hub of Istanbul. The existing port facilities at Galata would also be retained and connected to various sections of the city with newly opened large roads. Prost, however, did not support the extension of the existing port at Sarayburnu which was located at the easternmost end of the Istanbul Peninsula. He argued that the existing port should be reduced in capacity and considered temporary due to its superb location immediately below Topkapı Palace. His master plan, therefore, only allowed in this area single-storey docks constructed below a proposed promenade along the coast. On the Asian side, Haydarpaşa was seen as an ideal location to establish a major port as the Anatolian railways terminated there. New port facilities would also be opened further east along the shores of the Sea of Marmara at Tuzla and Pendik.

Perhaps the most controversial decision taken by Prost was designating the Golden Horn as the principal industrial zone. He saw the shores of the Golden Horn as the ideal location for industrial sites, and proposed heavy industry at the end of the gulf towards the west.[42] Prost was a typical representative of urban designers of his era whose decisions were generally driven by aesthetic concerns, and he did not foresee the significant consequences of his decision to open the low lying land in the Golden Horn to industrial development. This attitude is most vividly demonstrated in Prost's decision in relation to the Bosphorus where he suggested that coal depots in Kuruçeşme be relocated to other locations as they were diminishing the 'natural beauty' of the strait that connects the Sea of Marmara to the Black Sea.[43]

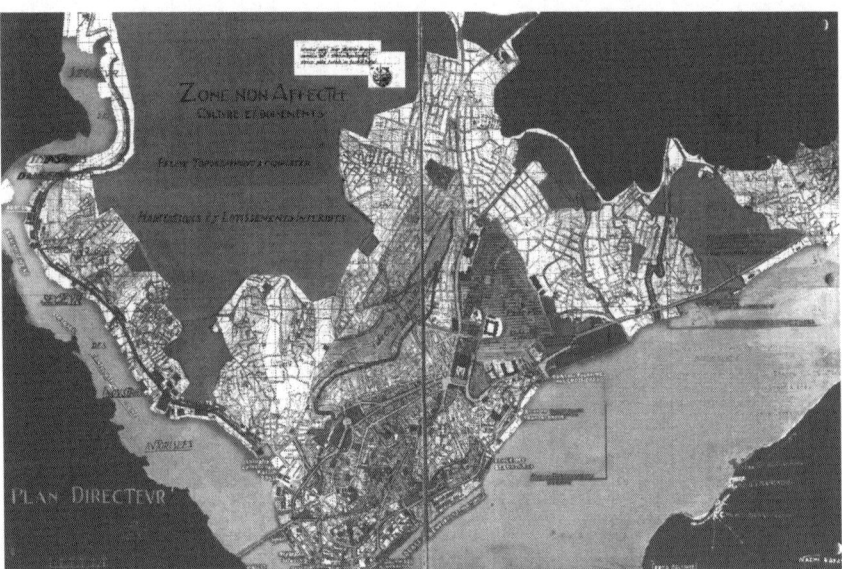

Figure 26 Prost's master plan for Beyoğlu as approved by the Ministry of Public Works on 30 May 1939

Figure 27 Prost's proposed roads in Beyoğlu connecting Taksim Square to Karaköy and associated viaducts and tunnels

Beyoğlu, Taksim, Maçka and Şişli were proposed as the major residential suburbs of the city. Prost also thought that new multistorey residential blocks surrounded by large roads would be in high demand and that new developments would follow this trend. To create more land for this purpose, he proposed to expropriate an old Armenian cemetery in Taksim.[44] Another area proposed for residential development in Prost's plan was located behind the proposed coastal road between Sarayburnu and Yedikule on the shores of the Sea of Marmara.[45]

The creation of new public spaces, such as parks, promenades, squares and children's playgrounds, was the other key feature of the master plan. Prost used the French term *espaces libres* (free spaces) in his original writings to describe the public open spaces,[46] and designed several parks and recreational areas in various sections of the city.[47] He proposed a botanical garden and zoo for the Yenibahçe region and an Olympic Park outside the city walls between Edirnekapı and Topkapı. Rejuvenation of the public beaches along both the Asian and European shores of the Sea of Marmara, and the construction of an archaeological park at the tip of the Istanbul Peninsula, together with several squares and promenades inside and outside the city walls, were the main provisions for public open space in his plan. Moreover Prost, in a similar way to Lambert, recommended a 500-metre green belt outside the city walls to act as a buffer zone.[48] In addition to the above recreation areas, Prost proposed several parks and open spaces in the Beyoğlu region. These works required the demolition of the old Artillery Barracks in Taksim, and included construction of a park and promenade, a park in Maçka, a sports stadium in Dolmabahçe and an open-air theatre between Taksim and Maçka.

The reorganisation of Sultanahmet Square and its connection to Sirkeci and Eminönü were other important proposals in Prost's plan. Sultanahmet Square was to be designed as a place for official celebrations and military parades on national days. His aim was to recover the remnants of the ancient Hippodrome and to reorganise the square to better interpret its past. Buildings at the southern end of the square were to be demolished to open up vistas to the Sea of Marmara. This work would mean the demolition of three tombed annexes of Sultan Ahmet Mosque and the removal of the Trade School. Prost considered that Sultanahmet Square, with its monuments of the Greek, Roman, Byzantine and Ottoman periods, should also be adorned with monuments of the young Turkish Republic and be renamed the *Büyük Cumhuriyet Meydanı* (Great Republic Square). He proposed a colossal monument for this purpose at the southern end of the old Hippodrome. He recommended the demolition of the Title and Cadastral Office Building and the construction in its place of a large platform and public seating. Finally, Prost's plan proposed the construction of a 30-metre-wide road connecting Sultanahmet Square to Sirkeci.[49]

The Implementation of the Master Plan

Prost's master plan was embraced by both the government and the municipality. It was introduced to the Municipal Assembly by the governor and mayor, Üstündağ, in a special meeting on 28 April 1938. The assembly accepted the master plan unanimously and with great enthusiasm. After a century-long delay, Istanbul was finally to have large avenues, parks, promenades, public squares, sporting complexes and theatres similar to those of contemporary European cities. And these works had been proposed by a celebrated European urban designer.

Prost's contract was renewed in order to allow him to prepare detailed implementation plans.[50] He accepted the offer and prepared a master plan for the Asian side of Istanbul in 1940, a beautification project for Büyükada and a master plan for Eyüp district in 1941. These plans were accompanied by a large number of implementation plans for various parts of the city.[51] Prost also prepared several pieces of draft legislation in relation to land use, planning controls, conservation of coastlines on the Asian side of Istanbul, industrial activities in the Golden Horn and expropriation of land.[52]

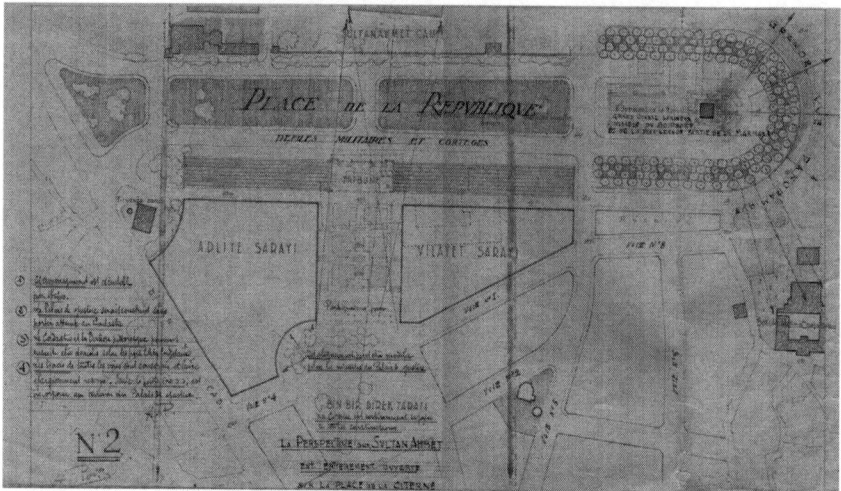

Figure 28 Prost's proposal for the Republican Square in Sultanahmet with a deliberate spatial arrangement highlighting the old Hippodrome. The gigantic Republican Monument is placed in the centre of the sphendone which is regenerated with landscape elements.

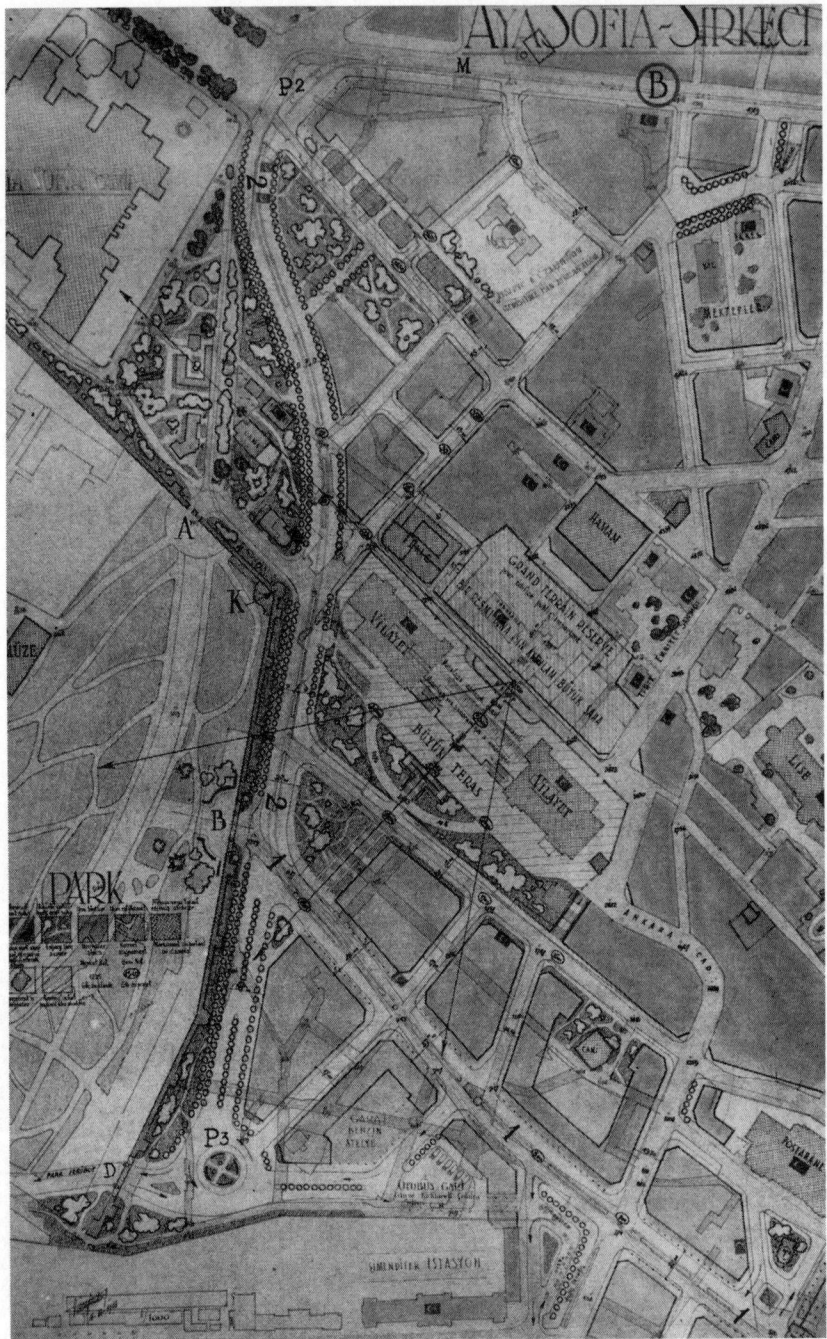

Figure 29 A proposed 30-metre-wide road connecting Sirkeci to Sultanahmet

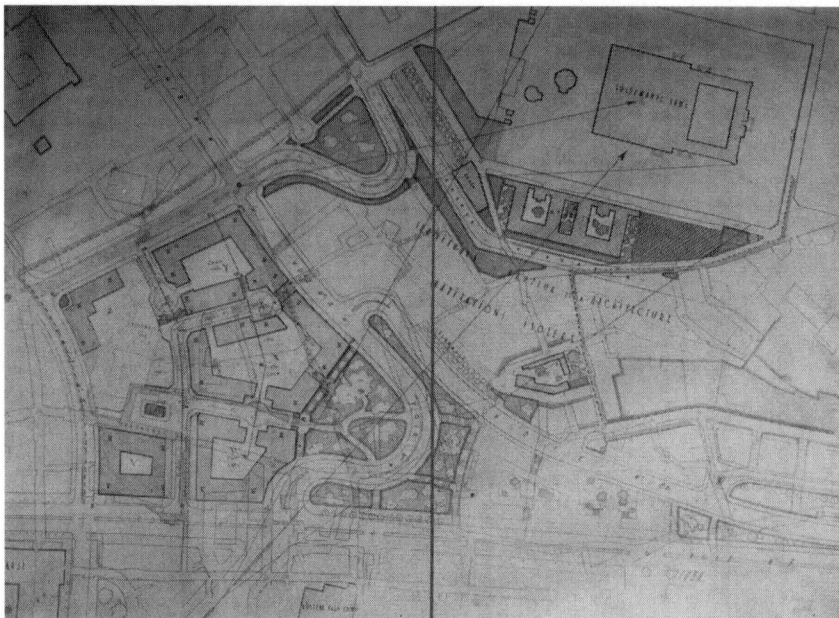

Figure 30 Prost's proposed road linking Eminönü to Süleymaniye

Despite his long-term service, the provisions of his master plan were only partially implemented. With the exception of several roads, parks and demolitions, most of the planned works did not materialise. There are several probable reasons as to why Prost's plan stalled. The first was financial difficulties due to the Second World War.[53] The majority of the works prescribed in the master plan were costly projects, and neither the Municipality of Istanbul nor the government was able to finance them during wartime economic conditions. Lütfi Kırdar, the governor and mayor of Istanbul, explained the reasons for the delays in a press conference in 1945:

> The war turned life and the order of the whole world upside down. The countries that did not enter the war were also deeply affected by this six-year-old tragedy… In this context, naturally, the city of Istanbul was also adversely affected by the war. In the beginning of the last month of 1938, when I was appointed as the Governor and Mayor of Istanbul, we had to either postpone or partially execute the works in the city, which is the largest in the homeland and the most beautiful in the world. For this reason, I am sure you understand that I feel the largest anxiety and grief.[54]

Secondly, the preliminary and unfinished nature of the master plan also added to difficulties concerning its implementation. Documents reveal that some of the proposed roads were neither well designed nor feasible. In particular, the topography of the city was not always considered, which meant that the construction of some of the roads would have required extensive and unnecessary demolitions that were often difficult to justify and somewhat unrealistic. Also, the scant documentation and poor quality drawings that formed the basis for construction suggest that many of the projects were still in rudimentary form and were almost hypothetical in conception. These aspects of the plan were also noted by the Municipality of Istanbul three years after the master plan was approved, and in 1942 Prost was asked to review his road proposals between Eminönü–Sirkeci, Sirkeci–Sarayburnu, Sirkeci–Sultanahmet, Taksim–Tepebaşı and Karaköy–Galatasaray–Taksim in terms of their compliance with the Building and Road Act.[55] Another noteworthy shortcoming of the plan was its lack of solid statistical data and analysis. For example, during his 14-year term as principal planner, Prost did not have a basic calculation method for estimating the future population of Istanbul. And, even more importantly, although his master plan was based primarily on an extensive road network, there was no data to justify the demand for transport infrastructure in the city. In fact, the only statistical data contained in his master plan report was the number of barges in the Golden Horn.[56]

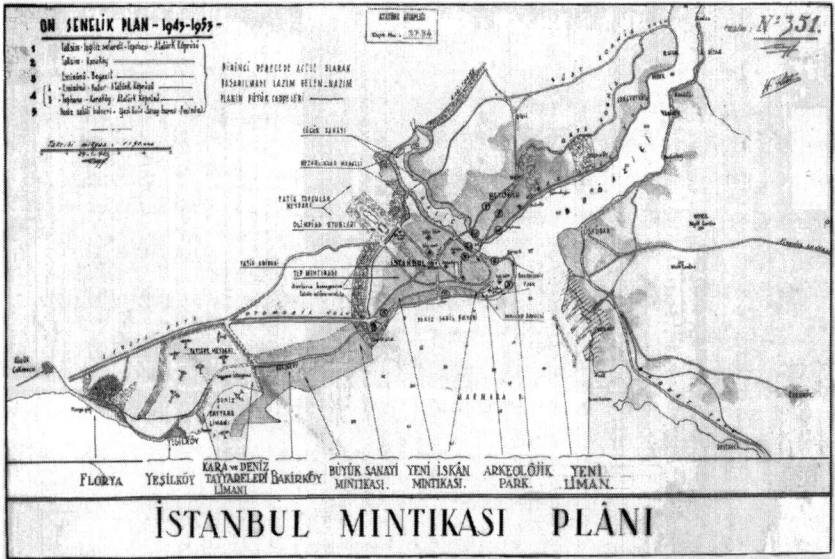

Figure 31 A map showing the major works proposed for completion according to Prost's master plan between 1943 and 1953

The delay and piecemeal implementation of the works also dismayed Prost. Towards the end of the 1940s he began to complain about the government's ignorance of his specific requests for the implementation of his projects and its general lack of support for the master plan. As previously mentioned, Prost submitted a draft planning act in 1936 and subsequently proposed several amendments in relation to the implementation of the provisions of the master plan. But neither the draft act nor his subsequent requests were taken into consideration by the government. After several warnings, Prost delivered his ultimatum in 1948:

> The municipality should now understand that the development plans on a scale of 1:1,000 or 1:2,000 are two different phases of the implementation of a development programme for the city... During my absence between 29 June and 4 December 1947 the Bureau of Redevelopment put the Regulation of Buildings and Roads into action without considering the basic principles of health standards. My proposal for an act in 1942 regarding this matter, however, was not taken into consideration... This proposal, similar to the others, did not work at all. All these reports were referred to the commission, but at the end of the day they were abandoned and remained in a deep drawer.[57]

The following lines show Prost's disappointment in the government's lack of support for his legislative framework:

> It is very disappointing to see that all the efforts made [on the draft act] have been forgotten. As I mentioned in my letter to the Minister for Internal Affairs dated 15 April 1937, because my previous proposals have not been taken into consideration, today the implementation of the master plan of Istanbul is impossible... If the legislative measures are not taken simultaneously, certainly no redevelopment plan can be implemented.[58]

The wartime economic conditions and technical deficiencies of Prost's plan contributed to the piecemeal approach towards its implementation. On the Istanbul Peninsula only a small number of works could be executed. Firstly, Eminönü Square was opened with the major aims of regularising the traffic flow and liberating Yeni Mosque from the 'parasitic' buildings in its close proximity. Although the demolitions were undertaken, the new building blocks were not constructed, resulting in the creation of a large space devoid of architectural and other urban design elements.[59] Nevertheless, it was promoted in the official propaganda materials published by the municipality as a great success in the name of modernisation. Other works completed included the demolitions around the Sirkeci and Beyazıt districts, a road connecting Cağaloğlu to Ayasofya and the partial extension of the Istanbul–Edirne Motorway towards the inner section of the city walls between Topkapı and Şehremini. However, apart from the first section, the road not did proceed any further.

Yet the most important project executed on the Istanbul Peninsula was the extension of Atatürk Boulevard. The work was completed in two phases. The first section between Saraçhane to Unkapanı was constructed in 1941–42 with a length of 1,100 metres and a width of 44 metres, as originally proposed by Auric in 1912. This section passed through the areas damaged by the 1922 Çırçır and Vefa fires and did not require major demolitions. The second section of the boulevard was constructed in 1943–44 and was 555 metres in length and 50 metres in width. Its construction, however, resulted in large expropriations and demolitions as the area was occupied by residential neighbourhoods.[60] Atatürk Boulevard was the largest road ever built in Istanbul and, together with Atatürk Bridge, it remained the only major route connecting the Istanbul Peninsula to Beyoğlu until 1973 when a third bridge was built across the inner Golden Horn.

Figure 32 The void created in Eminönü after the demolitions c.1940s

Figure 33 Eminönü and Galata Bridge after the demolitions c.1940s

Figure 34 Atatürk Boulevard from Unkapanı to Saraçhane, late-1940s

Figure 35 Atatürk Boulevard, between Aksaray and Saraçhane, late-1940s

Figure 36 Atatürk Boulevard between Saraçhane and Unkapanı

Figure 37 Artillery Barracks in Taksim before their demolition, late-1930s

Figure 38 Taksim Square, mid-1940s

In contrast to the limited number of works executed on the Istanbul Peninsula, several major works were completed across the Golden Horn. The first section of one of the two major arteries connecting the Istanbul Peninsula to Taksim Square was constructed from Atatürk Bridge to Şişhane. The upper sections of this road were not executed but, following extensive demolitions, a square was created at Şişhane where a road connecting the shores of the Golden Horn terminated. A new road was also constructed between Kasımpaşa on the northern shore of the Golden Horn and Şişli.

The reorganisation of Taksim Square was the centrepiece of Prost's master plan. The Artillery Barracks, which had been built in the late-Ottoman period, were demolished and a public promenade was constructed and named after İsmet İnönü who was elected the president of Turkey after Atatürk's death in 1938. A municipal casino was built in the vicinity of the promenade, and the cemetery and parks in this area were removed and replaced by apartment blocks and the new Radio House. The *İnönü Gezisi* (İnönü Promenade) was established on a site with an area of 26,000 square metres, and was specifically planned as a walking route with grassed areas, flowerbeds, magnolias, trees, seating benches and kiosks for concerts of the Municipal Philharmonic Orchestra. This promenade is one of the successful, perhaps the most successful, works of Prost's master plan as it reflects the secular and modern character of the young Turkish Republic.

Figure 39 Taksim Square and the Republican Monument, mid-1940s

Figure 40 İnönü Promenade, c. 1940s

The İnönü Promenade was complemented with the construction of Maçka Park, which was known as Park No. 2 in Prost's master plan. To complete this public venue, an open-air theatre and a sports stadium were constructed in 1947.[61] Dolmabahçe Mosque was temporarily turned into a naval museum and its environs were shaped into a new square and quay for ceremonial arrivals from the sea. The roads on either side of the Bosphorus were renovated and partially enlarged. The groves in Yıldız and Emirgan were designed as public recreation areas.

On the Anatolian side, a large square was constructed in Üsküdar. The opening of this square required the demolition of many buildings yet, in a similar way to Eminönü Square, the space created did not go beyond being a void surrounded by monumental Ottoman mosques and vernacular buildings since no planning activities followed the demolitions. Other noteworthy works executed in this period on the Asian side of Istanbul were the construction of a new road between Üsküdar and Kısıklı and the upgrading of some of the main existing roads in Kadıköy, Göztepe and Bostancı districts.

Why Prost?

Today it remains an open question as to why Prost's master plan did not go beyond a partially completed beautification project and why the government appointed Prost in the first place. He was a well-known urban designer, having held a prestigious position in Paris. Prost also had a sound knowledge of Turkey due to his student days in Istanbul and his time spent working as an advisor for the master plan works in İzmir. Perhaps most influential of all was his work in North Africa where he had introduced Western planning principles to Islamic cities. It was this skill that was likely to have been highly valued by the Republican government.

Prost was appointed at a time when the government had consolidated its power under the auspices of a single-party regime and had intensified its secular reforms. It was in this political climate that Prost was asked to reshape the old capital. He was well aware of the scale of the task. Many of his writings during his stay in Istanbul are full of rhetoric concerning his understanding of, and sympathy for, Kemalist ideology. For example, in one of his articles he describes Atatürk as follows:

> A man, a military-staffer, and a couple of his friends quickly established an army of peasants and women. He came as a hurricane from the northern mountains of Turkey and defeated the enemy. That general was the great Atatürk. Then he came to Istanbul to negotiate with the Allies about their withdrawal. He drew new frontiers for Turkey

and established the Republic of Turkey. Ankara became the capital of the government. Istanbul lost its role as a great imperial centre, but remained as the primary harbour of the new Turkey. Reforms followed one another. The new government abandoned the policy of sovereignty of the Sultan which had been observed in the Muslim world from India to Morocco. He [Atatürk] strictly banned the wearing of religious costumes, no matter of which religion. The Turkish language has been experiencing a deep revolution. The Arabic and Persian words have been abandoned, the Arabic script has been replaced with the Latin alphabet… And, finally, the result of the revolution was that Atatürk removed the veil of women and strictly banned its use forever. The effects of this last reform on Istanbul's urban redevelopment are great indeed. Turkish women do not want their old houses with *kafes* anymore. Because of financial and other technical difficulties, some of them look for apartments equipped with lifts, central heating and hot water in every season, while others construct magnificent villas within large gardens along the shores of the Sea of Marmara and the Bosphorus.[62]

Prost's proposals were consistent with the government's overall secular and modernising policies. The parks and promenades in his plan, for example, envisaged men and women participating equally in social and recreational activities. In his parks men and women could freely enjoy a mixed social life, which would never have been possible in a traditional *mahalle*.[63] Prost's large boulevards were superimposed on the traditional urban fabric and were deliberately designed to break the traditional pattern of Islamic social life. When Prost started to draw up his master plan for Istanbul the total number of private motorcars, as calculated by Wagner, was only 959.[64] It is reasonable to argue then that rather than being a traffic plan, the opening of the gigantic 'Haussmannian' boulevards was the design motif of Prost's modernisation project.

Prost's consistent support for the Kemalist project is also evident in his efforts to highlight the Greco-Roman character of the city. He repeatedly emphasised the importance of the conservation of the city's cultural and national heritage and described historical sites and monuments, such as Hagia Sophia, as 'universal cultural heritage' belonging to 'humanity'.[65] Although he emphasised the heritage significance of the major Ottoman monuments, Greco-Roman heritage prevailed with the conservation and promotion of antique and Byzantine characteristics being given a privileged position in his master plan. His proposals for the conservation of the Theodosian Walls, the application of a construction ban within a 500-metre zone outside the walls, the construction of an archaeological park at Sarayburnu, the regeneration of the antique Hippodrome and the reinstatement of the ancient Forum Tauri in Beyazıt with the archaeological excavation of the antique triumphal arch were all major elements of his design approach.

Further questions can be posed as to why Prost was so ineffective in implementing his ideas? Why did he not foresee the extent of future population growth? And why was this deficiency not raised by the government as an issue during his 14-year term in office? In answering these questions it should be remembered that Prost's plan was developed at a time when peasantist ideology was central to the Republican policy agenda of retaining the agrarian demographic structure of the country and preventing mass migration from rural areas to the cities. Therefore, there was no urgent need to address population pressures in cities such as Istanbul. This could provide a plausible explanation for the lack of important details such as population forecasts in Prost's master plan.[66]

The Early Postwar Years

While not directly participating in the Second World War, Turkey suffered because much of its limited economic resource base was diverted to defence, so preventing essential investment in social and economic infrastructure.[67] Economic difficulties ensued, requiring reforms to the country's political structure that saw it embark on a multiparty democratic system of government. This forced the government to make significant changes to the economic and social policy platform which caused the first cracks in the long-standing peasantist pro-agrarian position.

The economic hardship was felt mostly in the country where 80 per cent of the population lived. The peasants remained in extreme poverty despite the official propaganda which portrayed an ideal image of village life.[68] Medieval methods employed in agriculture, combined with the lack of machinery and crude irrigation technology, meant that production was almost wholly dependent on the vagaries of the weather.[69] Severe droughts in 1945 brought a sharp decline in agricultural production when the harvest was reduced to one third of the average yields recorded over the previous five years. Such economic hardships were made worse by the extraordinary wartime conditions which saw the tithe reinvoked in 1943. Known as the *Ayniyat Vergisi* (Payment-in-kind Tax), it forced peasants to pay the equivalent of 10 per cent of their agricultural produce to the government.[70]

Poorly maintained roads added to the problems by isolating many country villages during the long winter months when electricity supply was almost nonexistent. An estimate put the electrification rate at ten out of 40,000 villages in 1953.[71] This stark reality of village poverty was brought to the forefront of Turkish society in Mahmut Makal's sensational 1950 novel, *Bizim Köy* (Our Village). Makal, a teacher himself at a village institute in Central Anatolia, vividly portrayed the appalling living conditions whereby peasants lacked even the most basic services such as running water, sewerage, electricity and rudimentary medicine. Hence the reality of village life was far removed from the idyllic image presented in the official Republican propaganda with its empty rhetoric and high-minded principles of modernism and secularism.[72] These bitter living conditions, coupled with officious tax enforcement and ill-treatment of the peasantry by gendarmes, made the government very unpopular, even hated, by the majority of the Turkish population.[73]

Despite the modest improvements in living conditions, cities also suffered in the aftermath of the war with shortages of basic goods and services. Istanbul was the first to feel the effects. While upgrades were made to the Silahtarağa power plant, which was constructed in 1914 and was the sole electricity supply to Istanbul, there was still a severe electricity shortage. Public transport was another area badly affected by the wartime conditions. For example, the Municipality of Istanbul ordered 23 new buses from the US and Britain but due to the war only nine new buses were delivered. The solution was to convert 15 lorries into buses. In a similar way, Istanbul Tunnel could not be operated for a period of 118 days in 1941 because of the lack of spare parts.[74]

Hyperinflation in the 1940s, together with heavy-handed and inequitable bureaucratic controls on prices and profit margins, led to deep discontent within urban populations, particularly among civil servants, bureaucrats and the richer business class who were the strongest supporters of the Kemalist regime.[75] The *Milli Korunma Kanunu* (National Protection Act) of 1940 gave the government complete control of the national economy during the war years[76] and the *Varlık Vergisi* (Capital Levy) of 1942 imposed a wealth tax on non-Muslim businessmen and large farm owners to finance expenditure on defence, with local authorities assessing and determining the application of this tax.[77] These general economic emergency measures and the Capital Levy, in particular, profoundly altered the structure of Istanbul's economy as many non-Muslim merchants and businessmen emigrated from the city after the war. This opened new opportunities to Turkish businessmen in Istanbul's commercial activities.[78]

Turkey's international relations also changed following the victory of the Western democracies over the single-party dictatorships in Germany, Italy and Japan. Turkey, after its successful neutrality, finally declared war on Germany and Japan on 23 February 1945 in order to qualify for an invitation to the founding conference of the United Nations in San Francisco.[79] This opened a new chapter in the long journey of Turkish modernisation with Turkey establishing a firm alliance with Western countries—particularly the United States—under the threat of Soviet Russia.[80]

The first criticisms of the single-party political system emerged from these complex events where the absence of a political opposition to the ruling RPP was widely seen as a deficiency in the Turkish polity. In fact, it was President İnönü, the *Milli Şef* (National Chief) and permanent chairman of the RPP, who raised this issue in his presidential speech to the National Assembly on 1 November 1945 when he declared his willingness to make major political changes to bring Turkey into line with Western democratic systems of government.[81]

Political opposition first crystallized within the ruling RPP during discussions on the Charter of the United Nations in the Grand National Assembly. Adnan Menderes, the RPP's deputy for Aydın, gave a speech to the assembly emphasising that Turkey, by signing the charter, was engaged in bringing genuine democracy to its political system.[82] Celâl Bayar, Atatürk's former prime minister, together with Fuat Köprülü, a celebrated Turkish professor of history and literature, Refik Koraltan, a strong supporter of Atatürk and one of the former presidents of the *İstiklâl Mahkemeleri* (Tribunal of Independence),[83] and Menderes himself presented a joint motion on 7 June 1945 calling for more freedom and the modification of the unconstitutional and dictatorial character of the Republican regime. The RPP Group discussed the proposal but did not approve it, leading Menderes and Köprülü to publish articles critical of the government's overall policies in an independent newspaper, an act considered a breach of party discipline. Both deputies were subsequently expelled from the RPP. Bayar and Koraltan also left the RPP and together with other defectors established the Democrat Party (DP) on 7 January 1946.[84]

The first multiparty election was held in 1946 and delivered an overwhelming victory to the RPP with 395 seats out of a possible 465.[85] Although the DP had the edge in the cities, the results from the countryside, where the RPP had strict control over ballots, was very disappointing. And in Istanbul, where the DP had expected a good outcome, the election results were announced after a three-day delay causing rumours that they were rigged in favour of the RPP. Eventually, the final results were declared and the DP won 18 seats out of 27 in Istanbul.[86]

Although the 1946 election did not bring a major change to the political make up of the National Assembly, it nevertheless sent a strong message to the ruling elites that urgent changes were needed to the political system. Hence a series of reforms was introduced between 1946 and 1950 to integrate Turkey into the postwar international political and economic system. As a result the existing economic model based on absolute state control of the means of production was abandoned in favour of a market-based economy.[87] This led to a realignment of the currency in 1946 which saw the Turkish lira devalued by 117 per cent against the US dollar, and a more open policy developed in relation to imports.

These economic reforms forged closer political ties with the United States—the chief aim being to protect Turkey against the imminent threat of communism.[88] A famous political slogan, 'Making Turkey a little America in its region', which is often attributed to the DP, was actually first voiced by the RPP's deputy prime minister in 1949.[89] Turkey then became the first case study for the Twentieth Century Fund, an American foundation established to investigate how American financial resources and technical skills might be used to assist other countries in developing their living standards. Turkish-American cooperation also brought a group of American military and technical experts to the country who found the economy 'chaotic' and 'archaic' with limited 'half-baked' industries. Turkey initially received a US$100 million grant from the United States for military purposes in 1947, in accordance with the Truman Doctrine which was proclaimed by the US president, Harry Truman, to prevent Turkey and Greece from falling under the influence of Soviet Russia. In July 1948 Turkey formally became a member of both the Organisation for European Economic Co-operation and the International Monetary Fund, and was included in the European Recovery Programme, which was drafted to facilitate the implementation of American aid under the famous Marshall Plan.[90] Turkey's goal for this recovery programme was to expand agricultural productivity in order to supply crops to Western European countries.[91] Hence the modernisation of agriculture and establishment of an effective transportation network to increase accessibility to rural areas became the two principal economic aims of the Marshall Plan in Turkey.

A special instrument known as the Turkish–American Co-operative Program was established to deal with transportation problems in Turkey. In November 1948 an American mission of eight engineers led by H. E. Hilts from the American Public Roads Administration came to Turkey to assist in the planning and construction of a national highway system. The mission completed a detailed survey of Turkish highways in February 1948.[92] An agreement was signed between the Turkish Ministry of Public Works and the Public Roads Group of the American Aid Mission on 20 April 1948.[93] This agreement effectively ended Turkey's established pro-railway transportation policies.[94] According to Kasım Gülek, Minister of Public Works, this agreement would not only bring 'Middle Europe and [the] Balkans nearer to the Middle East' but also reduce the United States' 'own burden in opposing [the] Communist danger in Europe'.[95]

The agreement provided for a long-term cooperative highway improvement programme and a central semi-autonomous administration known as the *Karayolları Genel Müdürlüğü* (General Directorate of Highways) under the Ministry of Public Works[96] The directorate was to play a critical role in the redevelopment of Istanbul in the 1950s. This has always attracted criticism from Turkish architectural historians who have seen the directorate as the 'Trojan Horse' for Menderes' zealous redevelopment programme. In other words, they contend that Menderes did not consult with the 'appropriate expertise' (understood to mean 'architects') and carried out all the works on the advice given by the engineers and bureaucrats of the directorate.[97]

Another significant impact of Western economic aid was the rapid mechanisation of agriculture. Samples of American tractors and other agricultural machinery arrived at Istanbul Port on 4 May 1949. In the ensuing couple of years the number of tractors in Turkey's countryside increased dramatically.[98] Modern farming techniques changed the demographic pattern of the countryside, as the reduced demand for farm labour triggered significant migration from rural areas to the big cities. Istanbul, for example, experienced a net population increase of 47 per cent between 1945 and 1955.[99] The result was the collapse of the 'peasantist utopia' created by Kemalist intellectuals in the mid-1930s. The estimated population of Ankara projected as 300,000 by 1980 in Jansen's plan, for example, was reached by 1950 with more than 75 per cent of the population being born outside the city.[100] In this climate the village institutes, which were a key part of Kemalist ideology, bore the brunt of criticism from Republican officials because they were seen to be harbouring communist nests. From 1947 they lost their distinctive political status.[101]

Istanbul's rapid population increase also brought the shortcomings of Prost's master plan into sharp focus. While the city had experienced some piecemeal beautification projects, there were no plans for the accommodation of the new immigrants who began to flood into the city after the Second World War. Insufficient residential building stock exacerbated the illegal use of public lands for shanty houses, particularly in the areas outside the city walls such as Kazlıçeşme and Zeytinburnu. This became one of Istanbul's long-standing urban problems with the shanty buildings being described as the *gecekondu* (literally 'built-at-night'). These conditions led Cemil Topuzlu, who was twice mayor of Istanbul during the late-Ottoman period, to propose a commission of international urban designers and economists to review Prost's plan.[102] This signalled the oncoming demise of Prost's master plan.

The above economic and political developments were accompanied by a series of radical socio-cultural changes. In 1947 a group of delegates at the Seventh Congress of the RPP argued that although secularism had brought great benefits, its strict interpretation and disregard for religious traditions had brought with it deterioration in the moral values of society. Because the delegates knew that the anti-religious policies would eventually cost them seats in the forthcoming elections, they convinced the party congress to relax the rigid control over religious affairs. Religious education by private individuals was permitted outside the public school system and later incorporated into the curriculum of primary schools on a voluntary basis. Other changes included the opening of a Faculty of Theology at Ankara University in 1949. The public were permitted to visit the tombs of Ottoman sultans and other sacred dignitaries and foreign exchange was made available for pilgrimages to Mecca. People who had ended their marriages to members of the ruling Ottoman dynasty were also allowed to re-enter Turkey by the permission of the Ministerial Cabinet.[103]

This liberal policy agenda was extended to the press, universities and professional associations. Amendments were made to the Press Law to allow greater freedom and to end the strict financial requirements which forced newspapers to enter into bonds to obtain their licences. Although still financially dependent on the national budget, universities were given autonomy over their internal affairs and administration. And the law governing associations in relation to their administrative affairs was amended to pass control from the government to the courts.[104]

The second multiparty election was held on 14 May 1950. This time, however, the conditions were significantly different to those in 1946. The harsh economic conditions had hardened people's antipathy to the government, even with its less autocratic face, enabling the DP to establish a strong support base. The DP rhetoric employed the slogan, '*Yeter Söz Milletindir*' ('Enough, the nation has the word') and the party went on to gain 53.4 per cent of the total votes with the RPP achieving 39.8 per cent, thus delivering 396 seats to the Democrats, 68 seats to the Republicans, seven to independents and one to the National Party with 15 seats remaining vacant. Following the by-elections in September 1951 the composition of the Assembly was 411 DP seats against 61 RPP seats.[105] This was an outstanding result given that the Turkish electoral system in the late-1940s was geared to keep the RPP in power. The Grand National Assembly elected Celâl Bayar as the president, who then appointed Adnan Menderes as the prime minister. The first Democrat government was announced on 22 May 1950 with the DP continuing its success by winning the municipal elections held on 3 September 1950 where it took 560 of the total 600 municipalities. The party also won a psychological victory against the RPP in Istanbul by winning all seats in the Municipal Assembly. In October 1950 it further consolidated its electoral dominance by taking 55 of the 67 provinces in the provincial elections. After 27 years in power, the RPP was removed from office. A new era was opened in Turkish political history in which Istanbul would assume again its role as Turkey's most prominent and influential city.

5

ISTANBUL UNDER DEMOCRAT PARTY ADMINISTRATION 1950–1955

> *In many respects, the Ninth Grand National Assembly will have a very important place in our history. For the first time in our history, as a result of a full and free expression of the national will, this distinguished Assembly has come to a position where it can shape the nation's destiny.*
>
> Adnan Menderes, Grand National Assembly, 29 May 1950

The elections of 1950 not only marked the end of the early Republican period, but ushered in a series of liberal economic and social changes that were to radically shape Istanbul's urban form. For the first time in Turkish history the mass of society was given the opportunity to express its preferences in the political arena. In contrast to the RPP's autocratic face, which reflected its political structure based on an alliance between the military and bureaucratic elite of the centre and traditional notables in the countryside, the DP came to represent the 'peripheral' stratum of Turkish society.[1] The DP was attractive to all main opposition groups, regardless of their different expectations, interests or cultural traditions. Support came from the broad strata of society, including the urban poor, religious groups, the commercial bourgeoisie, workers, landlords and, surprisingly, communists who had been excluded from the political system by the single-party regime.[2] The Turkish intelligentsia, which had found the RPP 'too rigid and monopolistic in its control of state institutions', also supported the DP.[3]

The support of rural populations was particularly noteworthy. From its very early days the DP was able to gain the absolute support of the countryside, and it gradually became the favoured political vehicle for rural people to voice their interests in the political arena. Menderes, in his speech to the National Assembly in 1945 while still deputy of the RPP, had harshly criticised the peasantist polices of the Kemalist regime. He called them 'inspirations of Nazi Germany's *Erbhof* regulations' and believed 'the setting up [of] unbreakable barriers between the village and the city' would mean 'the continuation of the country's backwardness'.[4] While Menderes agreed that the living conditions of the peasantry should be improved, he was in direct opposition to the former RPP policies by arguing that this should be done without the prerequisite of keeping the great mass of peasants in their villages. The DP's policy continued along this path throughout its ten years in office, as the party aimed to expunge the disparity between the village and the city.

Inclusion of the peripheral stratum of the population in Turkey's political and social context also changed the elite-driven, 100-year-old modernity project. One significant indication of this change can be found in the varied socio-cultural character of the representatives sitting in the National Assembly. The DP's deputies were generally younger and more provincial, with backgrounds in commerce and law and strong roots in their electorates. This social makeup was very different to that of the military–bureaucratic deputies of the former Republican administration.[5] The diversity of political representation was also echoed in the demographic mix of Istanbul's Municipal Assembly where the elected deputies comprised a wide group of representatives, including those belonging to non-Muslim minorities who had suffered under the RPP's infamous Capital Levy in the 1940s.

Ending the separation between the 'periphery' and the elites was a major point of contention between DP and Kemalist circles. '*Taşralı Politikacılar*' ('Politicians of the Countryside') had been the main slogan used by Republicans to disgrace the new high-profile politicians of the Democrat administration. Metin Toker, a journalist and political opponent of the DP and son-in-law of İnönü, described that time in his memoirs: 'The elections of the 14 May brought some unusual people to Ankara as deputies... Most of them had no life experience. There were a lot of *taşralı avukatlar* (provincial solicitors) among them'.[6] Interpreting the *Taşralı Politikacılar* slogan in a wider perspective, modern architectural historians who vehemently criticise Menderes' urban redevelopment projects have given it a significant place in their assessments.[7]

The Economic Miracle and Liberal Tendencies

A rapid and largely uncoordinated boom in the Turkish economy was significant in the DP period, particularly in the early 1950s. The international politics of the postwar era provided an unprecedented opportunity for the Democrat government to expand the economy. In the early years of the Democrat government between 1950 and 1953, Turkey achieved an exceptional 13 per cent growth rate in its economy. Turkey's integration into the world capitalist system had already begun before the DP came to power, yet its incorporation into the Western world was intensified in the 1950s, not only economically but also in terms of its defence and foreign relationships.[8]

In other words, the international atmosphere of the Cold War period allowed Menderes to use Turkey's new strategic importance as a lever to obtain foreign aid from the United States and Western Europe.[9] Turkish–American relationships were intensified as Turkey became a member of NATO in 1952,[10] with the DP leaders adopting the RPP's slogan of the late-1940s, 'Making Turkey a little America in its region', together with another political motto, 'Creating one millionaire per neighbourhood'.[11]

The DP saw agriculture as the real engine of the Turkish economy and facilitated major technological advances in the countryside. The government made the interests of farmers paramount in importance for the first time, and these pro-farmer policies continued until the end of its term.[12] Menderes, a large farm owner himself, provided cheap credit to farmers and subsidised agricultural products.[13] Following the implementation of large-scale irrigation projects, Turkey saw a spectacular increase in its total cultivated land area from 16 million hectares in 1948 to 25.3 million hectares in 1960.[14] This increase in arable land required mechanisation and the total number of tractors in Turkish villages increased from 10,227 in 1950 to 42,136 in 1960.[15] These improvements transformed Turkey into a major grain exporter by 1953.[16]

Other remarkable infrastructure improvements occurred in road construction in the 1950s. As mentioned above, American technical and financial assistance saw Turkey witness a boom in road making, with the total length of hard-surfaced roads increasing from 930 kilometres in 1948 to about 7,345 kilometres by 1961. This substantially reduced travel time between the major cities.[17] The total travel time between Istanbul and Ankara, for example, was reduced from 13 hours in 1950 to 6.5 hours in 1962. At the same time the total number of motor vehicles on Turkey's roads rose from 20,231 in 1948 to 102,806 in 1960.[18] The impact of significant improvements in the road network, as well as the mechanisation of agriculture, was the creation of a direct link between the majority of the Anatolian peasantry and the outside world for the first time.[19]

Significant improvements also took place in energy production where several dams were constructed increasing the total electricity production from 790 million kWh in 1950 to 1,402 million kWh in 1954, reaching 2,815 million kWh by 1960.[20] The average annual production of crude oil increased from 30,000 tons during the pre-1950 period, rose to 179,000 tons in 1954 and then peaked at 373,000 tons in 1959. Total demand for fuel in this decade increased from 445,000 tons in 1950 to 1,270,000 tons in 1959.[21] Istanbul was the main recipient of all these improvements with the total number of workers in the industry increasing fourfold in ten years. Fuel consumption tripled and electricity supply more than doubled over a six-year period. And this infrastructure investment resulted in rapid urbanisation, with a 50 per cent population increase in Istanbul over a ten-year period to reach more than 1.5 million in 1960.[22]

Progress in the economic sector was accompanied by remarkable advancements in other areas of social need. Primary schools, for example, increased from 17,428 in 1950 to 24,398 in 1960 and secondary schools from 493 to 744 in the same period. A real boom, however, occurred in the circulation figures for the press over the decade, with the number of daily newspapers increasing from 72 to 566 and the total daily circulation growing from 300,000 to 1,411,000.[23] The average number of published books, which was approximately 2,600 per year between 1936 and 1950, increased to over 4,000 per year at the end of the 1950s.[24]

The liberal political atmosphere created by the DP and the improvements in the economy in its early years brought about changes in religious life. The pre-1950 policy of relaxing regulations governing religious activities was further accelerated by allowing religious groups to express their ideas in the political system for the first time since 1923. Religious loyalties, which had remained unaffected by the strict secularist policy of the Kemalists, resurfaced under the relaxed DP administration.[25] The reforms mainly consisted of symbolic acts, such as ceasing the ban on the recital of *ezan* (call to prayer) in Arabic and allowing religious programmes to be broadcast on the radio, both of which were very popular with the vast stratum of Turkish society. In addition, the number of mosques built during the DP period increased dramatically; the total number of mosques constructed between 1950 and 1960 was approximately 15,000. Special schools were established in seven cities in 1951 for the education of Islamic clergy and their number increased to 16 schools in 1955.

Despite this palpable relaxation in religious affairs and support for religious institutions, the DP did not allow any fundamental change to the essentially secular character of the state.[26] Political demands from Islamist groups were not answered and strict measures were taken against reactionary activities, including the severe punishment of leaders of those groups. The DP even passed a bill to protect the memory of Atatürk in 1951.[27]

The Democrats also increased their popularity by opening up social and cultural life to ordinary Turkish citizens. For example, the government reduced the period of compulsory military service, passed a liberal Amnesty Law that lifted the restrictions on Turkish citizens travelling abroad and, more importantly, provided wider freedom to the press by amending some of the authoritarian clauses in the Press Law.²⁸ Investments in industry and infrastructure and the rapid growth in agricultural productivity, together with the liberal political atmosphere and freedom in religious life, delivered another victory to the DP in the election of 1954.²⁹

The DP often used freedom of religious expression as an important propaganda tool in its urban redevelopment policies for Istanbul. Both Menderes and Governor Fahrettin Kerim Gökay focussed on the city's Ottoman past in their speeches, which underlined the importance of Istanbul throughout its history. The opening of the mausoleums of the Ottoman sultans to the public and the restoration of Ottoman monuments were representative of the steps taken by the DP to emphasise the Ottoman and Islamic character of the city. Pictures of restored mosques and other Ottoman monuments and graphic illustrations showing the number of restorations were all part of the official propaganda of the Municipality of Istanbul.

These policies and other symbolic acts helped Menderes to increase his popularity and to make him a hero in the eyes of ordinary people. Myths were created that represented him visiting tombs of Islamic and Ottoman fabled characters on his white horse at dawn. The white horse in this context symbolised Sultan Mehmed II the Conqueror who rode into Constantinople in 1453. Menderes used these symbols in his propaganda speeches to promote the redevelopment of Istanbul and described his planning initiatives as the second conquest of the city.³⁰

Istanbul During the Early DP Period

Although it had lost all its administrative functions during the early Republican years, Istanbul was still the major intellectual, economic and social hub of Turkish life. Ankara presented Turkey's bureaucratic, national, planned and secular face, while Istanbul symbolised its cosmopolitan, spontaneous, religiously oriented and international face. In this sense the Republican administration's intention to create a new national centre in Ankara could not overcome Istanbul's pre-eminent position as the cultural and economic magnet of Turkish society. Furthermore, the monumental administrative buildings, large boulevards, geometrically planned parks and monuments of Ankara, at least in the eyes of certain strata of society, could not compete with the richness of Istanbul's medieval character, its Ottoman architecture and natural beauty.³¹ For many intellectuals, the best part of Ankara was still the road back to Istanbul.³²

Turkey's new role in postwar international politics also brought Istanbul back into international prominence as one of the most important commercial,

Figure 41 Menderes visiting Ottoman sultans' tomb

political and cultural centres in the eastern Mediterranean region. It also realigned Turkey's geo-political position as a bridge between East and West and helped Istanbul to regain its prominent status as a large and rich port city of the region and a gateway to Europe. Furthermore, Istanbul was ideally situated to monitor Soviet naval movements from the Black Sea to the Mediterranean, an important task assigned to Turkey as a member of NATO.

Istanbul's importance was given further impetus because the DP used the city to display Turkish cultural achievements to the rest of the country. From its very early days the DP was aware of Istanbul's importance and was cognisant that any investment in Istanbul would have a significant impact on public opinion. Menderes, therefore, launched his candidature for the 1950 general elections from Istanbul rather than from his home town of Aydın.[33] It was also Menderes himself who underlined the importance of Istanbul on the night of the elections. In the words of one of his political colleagues:

> We were all together and were tracking the results of the elections. It was very late, the dawn was almost breaking. A postman arrived and knocked at the door. He brought a note saying, 'Fuat Köprülü is calling Menderes from the headquarters [of the DP]. We are leading in Turkey and have taken power. I kiss from your eyes'.[34] All our friends who

were waiting in nervous anticipation became very happy. There was an explosion of joy. At that point Menderes silenced us saying, 'Hold on a minute, please find that postman and ask him to find Köprülü in Ankara. He should find out about the results in Istanbul ... It appears we have come to power, but if we haven't won the elections in Istanbul, our power without it would not even count as half the power'.[35]

Hence the *İstanbul'un imarı* (the redevelopment of Istanbul) became one of the primary targets of the DP administration from its very early days in power. It blamed the previous Republican administrations for neglecting Istanbul for 27 years and believed it was time to return the city to its glorious past. Beliefs such as these were voiced repeatedly in the speeches of DP representatives. Ahmet Hamdi Başar, a Democrat member for Istanbul in the National Assembly, portrayed the city in this way: 'Following the relocation of the governmental centre of Turkey to Ankara, Istanbul, similar to a drought mill, became an abandoned, neglected and heartbreaking city'.[36]

The DP's municipal programme for the elections of 3 September 1950 also voiced precisely this outlook. Samet Ağaoğlu, the spokesman and minister of state in Menderes' cabinet, portrayed this political posture as follows:

> Initially, Istanbul was neglected with an unreasonably antagonistic attitude... While many institutions were relocated to Ankara—without considering whether they had to be moved as a matter of necessity—Istanbul was neglected. That is why the urban renewal works implemented in Istanbul until 1938 achieved very little... The city had been left without roads, water and lighting. The cleaning works had been appalling. The inhabitants of Istanbul, the most intellectual city in our country, did not have an opportunity to select their mayor. Public transportation, electric and gas services were in the hands of foreigners... From the end of 1938 importance was given to Istanbul's redevelopment. Unfortunately, after a short while, the Second World War began. The government suspended the process because of the war. The renewal plan was not applied.[37]

In addition to the rhetoric of neglect, the separation of the governorship from the mayorship and the creation of the Municipality of Istanbul as an independent authority were two major initiatives promised by Ağaoğlu.[38] Tourism was selected as the key policy objective for the city. The DP also promised that municipal services would be provided equally across the various districts of Istanbul—particularly the provision of hygiene and health services to every person in every corner of the city. New legislation would be developed to facilitate the modern infrastructure services through a more open, responsive and transparent municipal administration. In short, the DP decided to reshape Istanbul in accordance with the changing dynamics of postwar international and national politics of the 1950s.[39]

Decommissioning Prost

Undoubtedly, the most important decision taken by the incoming DP administration was the removal of Prost as the chief planner of Istanbul in the late-1950s. Prost was placed at the centre of the debate after the DP's victory in the municipal elections and his plans were discussed extensively in political circles and the press.[40] The Municipal Assembly established a commission to review Prost's master plan and the feasibility of its implementation at a meeting on 5 December 1950.[41] The commission prepared and submitted its report to the Municipal Assembly on 26 December 1950. The report focussed on the incomplete nature of the master plan after a 14-year period. This caused deep concern and disappointment to the councillors of the assembly and, eventually, played a key part in the termination of Prost's contract. Most members of the assembly claimed that although Prost was commissioned for a period of three years only, he had failed to complete his tasks despite his contract being extended to a total of 11 years. For this reason, the members argued that extending his contract further would not bring any favourable outcome for the city.[42]

The assembly's second major concern was Prost's character. Many councillors felt that he was open to manipulation by politicians, in particular Lütfi Kırdar, the former governor and mayor of Istanbul. Some members even speculated that Prost had lost his professional authority by acting on directions given by the governor and other state officials. An example of this criticism can be found in reference to Maçka Park (Park No.2 in Prost's master plan) where it was believed that the main reason for the park's creation was to increase the value of a nearby land parcel owned by Governor Kırdar.[43] The creation of Maçka Park, according to some councillors, also required a modification to the plan resulting in an unnecessary increase in costs. Similarly, the expropriation of a piece of public land in the Taşlık area and its transfer to President İnönü was criticised by the assembly as inappropriate.[44]

Prost's contribution to Turkish architecture and urban planning was another matter of concern. Several members of the assembly claimed that despite his long term of service, Prost did not educate any young Turkish professionals to participate in the redevelopment of Istanbul.[45] The members believed that he had essentially completed his task and that it was time to employ young Turkish architects and urban planners who could plan the city more appropriately according to Turkish social and aesthetic values. Overall, the assembly found Prost's plans intruded on the 'architectural and natural beauty' of Istanbul.[46]

The assembly allowed Prost to speak before making its decision on his contract. In reality, however, it was not an invitation but a response to a request made by Prost himself. The French urban planner requested an opportunity to address the assembly as to why he could not successfully implement the provisions of his master plan and how bureaucratic barriers had prevented him from doing so. Despite the overwhelmingly negative feelings towards Prost, some members argued that another extension was warranted to allow him to complete his task. The principal argument made in favour of Prost was that he was not the only person responsible for the inaction as this problem was endemic to the former Republican regime. Eventually, Prost was given a chance to address the issues in the assembly.[47]

In response to the above criticisms, Prost complained about the lack of a special legislative framework for the implementation of his master plan. He argued that although he had requested a modification to the existing Building, Roads and Acquisition Act of 1937, the government had not taken his request into account and that this was the main reason why his master plan did not achieve the desired outcomes.[48] In fact, Prost had already published the reasons for the delay and difficulties of the urban renewal of Istanbul in his report of 1948. This report, which was published by the Municipality of Istanbul under the DP administration in 1951, blamed the delays on the lack of essential technical staff and legislation.[49] Prost also reiterated his views that the lack of a legislative framework and inadequate financial resources had caused the delays in implementing his master plan in a newspaper interview before he spoke at the Municipal Assembly. It is clear in the emotive language he used in this interview to where he pointed the blame for his disappointment and he expressed his view of the 'laziness' of the previous governments:

> Instead of retirees, I requested new personnel. They have sent 15 or 20 architects from Ankara who are active but do not know the streets of Istanbul yet… There has been talk about the reshaping of a city such as Istanbul. But there is a lack of essential legislation on this matter. It is necessary to respond to the people whose houses and lands will be expropriated. Nobody has taken this point into consideration. I have made plans for two cities up until now. The first one was Casablanca which now has a population of 600,000. The property owners were incorporated within the redevelopment of the city and therefore the

task was easier there... Although the plan [for Istanbul] has been made for a 50-year period, the municipality has been asking me to implement it within five years. We are implementing the plan, creating squares and parks. But after a while you see that there is a building erected in the middle of the planned sites out of nowhere... As you know I am the Director of the Architectural School of Paris. I must also manage there. I will stay and serve should my contract be extended. But I should not be asked stupid questions such as 'How tall should Ahmed Efendi's chimney be?'[50]

The assembly asked Prost to explain one of his earlier reports prepared in 1940 in which he recommended the allocation of a land parcel in Taşlık to President İnönü. Prost argued that during the general planning work for Maçka Park he learnt that President İnönü had a small site near the proposed park and he thought that it would be appropriate to give some additional land to the president as the small parcel of land he owned was not worthy of the President of Turkey.[51] Given the highly charged political climate of the time, which was founded on anti-RPP and İnönü rhetoric, this was a critical mistake that dramatically changed the atmosphere of the meeting. Members who had initially supported the renewal of his contract changed their opinion, claiming that Prost had lost his expert authority in the face of political pressure. This left the assembly in no doubt that his contract should not be renewed. It is noteworthy that only three of the total 32 members voted for an extension. This marked the end of the Prost era in Istanbul. Atatürk's urban designer was unceremoniously removed by a democratic decision of the Municipal Assembly of Istanbul.[52]

After Prost: the Interim Revision Commission

Prost's effective dismissal gave a long awaited opportunity to Turkish architects and planners who had been excluded from the process since the very early days of the Republican period. First a congress was organised by the governor and mayor of Istanbul in 1952. It was to comprise professionals from several institutions, including the Municipality of Istanbul, the universities and professional organisations such as the Chamber of Trade and Industry. A report submitted by two DP deputies to the organising committee's meeting on 23 November 1951 severely criticised the previous RPP administration for its neglect of Istanbul. They also criticised the lack of a detailed redevelopment programme. The deputies claimed that previous governments had made a 'big mistake by appointing an urban designer [Prost] without a detailed programme being prepared beforehand'.[53]

The municipality responded by setting up an interim commission, the *Revizyon Komisyonu* (Revision Commission) to carry out a general review of Prost's master plan and other implementation plans prepared in the 1940s.[54] Its main task was to investigate the applicability of the plans in relation to economics, planning and urban morphology. The commission included representatives from several official institutions and universities: Kemal Ahmet Aru from the Istanbul Technical University; Cevat Erbel and Mithat Yenen from the *İller Bankası* (Bank of Provinces); Mukbil Gökdoğan from the *Türk Yüksek Mühendisleri Birliği* (Turkish Union of Engineers); Muhittin Güven from the *Türk Yüksek Mimarlar Birliği* (Turkish Union of Architects); Mehmed Ali Handan from the Fine Arts Academy; and Behçet Ünsal from the Technical School. The Municipality of Istanbul was also represented in the commission by architects Ertuğrul Menteşe and Faruk Akçer and, as an observer, Seyfi Arkan.[55]

The commission's report, entitled the *Revizyon Komisyonu Raporu* 1951 (Report of the Revision Commission), reviewed many documents, including Prost's master plan report, his notes, drawings and other related material. The major criticism of Prost's plan was based on the lack of essential data and analytical studies. The commission found the master plan extremely superficial, focussing on beautification and ornamentation rather than on research and statistical studies, investigations into population growth, zoning, transportation, housing, public health, education, industrial sites, geological and meteorological data and statutory development provisions. The majority of the roads and squares proposed by Prost were considered inapplicable and unrealistic as they failed to account for the city's topography. The commission was particularly concerned with the proposed viaducts, tunnels and inner city motorways, as well as with the quality of the plans and other materials. It also commented on the structure and logical order of the master plan report and the disorganised notes and poor quality preliminary drawings which omitted essential data and dimensions.[56] The commission, however, recommended the continuation of ongoing works in accordance with Prost's plan until an adequate master plan could be prepared. The report finished by recommending that the municipality create a permanent team to carry out future urban renewal projects.[57]

The Permanent Commission

The *İstanbul Şehir İmar Planı Daimi Komisyonu* (Permanent Commission for Istanbul's Master Plan) also known as *Müşavirler Heyeti* (the Board of Advisors) was established in 1952. The commission's major task was to advise on the planning process for the master plan and to collaborate with the Directorate of Development at the Municipality of Istanbul. The permanent commission was formed by members of the former interim commission: Aru, Erbel and Gökdoğan. Emin Onat, a professor of architecture at Istanbul Technical University also participated in the *Müşavirler Heyeti*.

The commission prepared two reports on the progress of the planning works in February and June 1953.[58] It continued the work of the interim commission and highlighted the omission of a detailed map of the city showing existing conditions and the lack of analytical studies. The *Müşavirler Heyeti* commissioned its own analytical works and investigations into population distribution, industrial sites, parks and recreation areas, transportation and circulation, as well as preparing local master plans and detailed maps of Istanbul.

While the new plan was being produced by Turkish planners, the commission wanted to test their progress by consulting a foreign expert. Sir Patrick Abercrombie, a renowned English urban designer and the author of the Greater London Plan in the last years of the Second World War, was invited in 1954 to advise the *Müşavirler Heyeti*. Abercrombie stayed in Istanbul for ten days and prepared a report for the governor. His report emphasised the importance of a detailed survey and up-to-date maps of the city, and generally considered the progress of the *Müşavirler Heyeti* to be successful.[59]

The studies carried out by the interim and permanent commissions concluded with the production of a new master plan for Istanbul. The plan contained two parts: *Beyoğlu Ciheti* (Beyoğlu Side)[60] and *İstanbul Ciheti* (Istanbul Side).[61] Although the drawings associated with these master plans are now lost, the reports still provide sufficient information to understand their underlying rationale and scope. Additionally, the correspondence between the Municipality of Istanbul and other government and non-government agencies shows that the proposed works were coordinated and that consultation had taken place with all relevant authorities and institutions.[62]

Remarkably, the commission's new master plan generally followed the fundamental principles of Prost's plan, even with the additional statistical data and analytical calculations. The retention of the existing port in Salıpazarı, the construction of a new port in Yedikule, the establishment of a rail terminus in Yenikapı, the building of industrial estates in the Golden Horn area, as well as the creation of additional industrial sites along the Pendik–Tuzla belt, were all similar to the initiatives proposed by Prost.[63] And even the proposed road scheme reflected Prost's plan, although modifying it to a minor extent. The extension of the Istanbul–Edirne Motorway to the centre of the city, the opening of littoral roads alongside the Sea of Marmara and the Golden Horn and the enlargement of the road between Aksaray and Sultanahmet were among other proposals previously advocated by Prost. In the Beyoğlu district the plan proposed a 30–metre-wide boulevard between Karaköy and Azapkapı and a 22–metre-wide street between Karaköy and Tophane. The latter street was to be extended to Beşiktaş and then to Bebek. New buildings of up to eight floors were to be constructed on either side of the new avenues. In a similar way to Prost, the commission proposed expropriations and demolitions in Karaköy to construct a new square and the construction of a third bridge connecting the Istanbul Peninsula to the Galata district over the Golden Horn. The existing Tarlabaşı Street was to be enlarged to establish a new traffic artery between Taksim Square and Atatürk Bridge over the Golden Horn. In Taksim Square the old water reservoirs were to be demolished and replaced by a new multistorey building.

Istanbul, for the first time in its history, had master plans that had been prepared by a group of professional experts. More importantly, these plans had been reviewed extensively and amended in line with recommendations made by the Municipal Assembly, other central government agencies and professional organisations such as the Chamber of Commerce and Chamber of Industry. This approach was very different to that of the preceding era when Prost held all responsibility and prepared his scheme without any participation by unofficial professional organisations.

All these plans, however, did not bring any material change to Istanbul in the first part of the 1950s. Apart from the preparation of some large-scale infrastructure projects, such as a suspended bridge over the Bosphorus and a public transportation scheme designed by a French firm[64] which never left the drawing board, the most noteworthy outcome of the early DP period was the construction of the Hilton Hotel and the Municipal Palace, both of which strongly express postwar international modern design principles.[65] The other noteworthy change in Istanbul in the early 1950s was the design of the first garden city suburb in the upper sections of Beşiktaş. The project was first initiated in the late-1940s in a joint venture by Istanbul Municipality and the state-owned *Emlak Kredi Bankası* (Real Estate Bank). Named after Ottoman marines, Levent Houses comprised a total of 1,347 dwellings constructed at various stages between 1948 and 1958.

By 1955, four years after Prost's departure, no single noteworthy development had occurred in the city. At the same time Istanbul's population had continued to increase rapidly, the number of cars on its streets had increased ten-fold and the lack of adequate housing for new immigrants had resulted in mushrooming *gecekondu*s on the outskirts of the city.

6

ISTANBUL IN MENDERES' HANDS
1956–1960

Istanbul's redevelopment is a story of a triumphal parade. We will conquer Istanbul one more time. Not only Istanbul, we will also reconquer Ankara and all other cities.

Menderes, 26 February 1957[1]

Istanbul was redeveloped before and after Menderes. Today it is still being redeveloped and this will certainly continue. But it will not be possible to erase his stamp on this city, perhaps for centuries. It will not be possible to the degree that shortly after his death one of his strongest enemies in the press could not stop himself from saying: 'We should take him from his graveyard to finish the uncompleted streets and works, and then we should put him back again'.

Samet Ağaoğlu, DP front-bencher 1950–60[2]

Istanbul in the second half of the 1950s saw the most radical redevelopment projects in its history. The Democrat government made the city's redevelopment a top priority, and channelled major funds and resources towards this goal. In fact, Prime Minister Menderes personally supervised the redevelopment works, spending most of his time in Istanbul during the last four years of the Democrat government from 1956 to 1960. This period saw the demolition of thousands of buildings, the expropriation of many properties and the construction of gigantic boulevards, both within and outside the Istanbul Peninsula. These works largely shaped modern Istanbul into what it is today. Indeed, the redevelopment of Istanbul was the leitmotif of the Menderes years.

The DP's redevelopment plan came about as the government began to struggle with major economic problems in the second half of the 1950s. The positive and progressive political and social atmosphere in Turkey during the early years of the DP administration was to change abruptly when the phenomenal development in agriculture came to an end in 1954 as a result of decreased international demand and declining prices in international markets after the end of the Korean War. This changing market, coupled with unfavourable climatic conditions, saw economic growth fall from an extraordinary rate of 13 per cent per annum to 4 per cent and the total public debt more than double in the five years to 1960. Furthermore, the decline in foreign economic aid and insufficient foreign investment led to a sharp downturn in the Turkish economy, resulting in a severe shortage of consumer goods and the emergence of black markets in the big cities.[3]

In response to these economic problems, the government adopted an autocratic position and reversed its liberal policy agenda to one of centralised control. Although the DP went on to win the 1957 elections, albeit with a reduced majority, its extreme partisanship and profound intolerance of political rivals brought an end to its alliance with the middle class intelligentsia. The severe opposition from the RPP, who saw everything the DP did as wrong, also fuelled political tensions which led the government to impose stringent measures against any opposition, including the press. State radio, for example, was banned for use by the opposition party and a press law was passed restricting the independence of the mass media. Increasing violation of democratic rights and loss of individual liberties further alienated the government from a broad stratum of society.[4]

During this political malaise one significant incident occurred in September 1955 that deeply affected Istanbul, both physically and demographically. On the night of 6 September a riot started in the city against the Greek minority after stories appeared in newspapers stating that Atatürk's house in Thessaloniki had been bombed by Greek nationalists. During the riot, which continued into the following day, many shops and properties belonging to non-Muslim inhabitants of the city were looted and burned. Properties owned by Greeks were especially targeted with some Turkish properties also looted. The riot seems to have been sparked by a government supported public demonstration against the Greek plans in Cyprus. The protest, however, had quickly escalated beyond control with devastating consequences. As a result of these riots, Istanbul lost the last remaining vestiges of its cosmopolitan character, as many Greeks who no longer felt themselves secure left the city.

Increasing public discontent laid the basis for the rival Kemalist elite to vent its anger against the Democrat government. It was a fight for the retention of power. The economic and social policies of the Democrat government created a new urban middle class who gradually extended their power in Turkish politics. The Republican elite, who had benefited from the economic polices of the singe-party regime, saw the members of this new middle class as economically corrupt and socially reactionary.[5] Moreover, they saw the DP's liberal policy agenda and its wider freedoms in religious life as the nucleus of reactionary religious fever and populist Islam.[6]

The military was also deeply troubled by DP policies which caused a deep division with the government. This relationship had been turbulent since the very early days of the DP. The first serious warning of things to come emerged immediately after the 1950 elections when some army officers offered a plan to İsmet İnönü to conduct a coup against the DP accusing them of communist activities. Although the plan was not successful (İnönü refused it), the hostility against the DP grew deeper especially among lower ranking officers whose contact with Western armies through NATO had made them aware of the comparative backwardness of the Turkish army. Like the civil elites, many army officers saw the DP as undermining the fundamental secularist principles and constitutional foundations of the Turkish state. All this political and economic malaise finally ended in a military coup d'état on 27 May 1960.

Following the coup the Great National Assembly was closed and all political parties suspended. The president, prime minister, other ministers in the cabinet, all DP deputies in the National Assembly and party representatives in the cities and towns were arrested. The *Milli Birlik Komitesi* (National Unity Committee) was then formed to govern the country and it appointed a special tribunal, the *Yüksek Adalet Divanı* (High Court of Justice), to try the former government members and DP politicians. The trials began on 14 October 1960 on the island of Yassıada in the Sea of Marmara. Pre-trial investigations were carried out by a special committee known as the *Yüksek Soruşturma Kurulu* (Higher Investigation Commission) which comprised 31 members selected by the military junta. Nineteen different cases were opened against the DP administration.[7] The first cases selected were the most sensational, with the explicit intention to discredit Menderes and the government in the eyes of the public. The Dog Case, for example, charged president, Bayar, with forcing the zoo to buy a dog, which was then given to him as a gift from the King of Afghanistan. Another was the Baby Case in which Menderes was accused of ordering the murder of a child he fathered with Aydan Ayhan, a famous Turkish opera star. The prosecutor failed to prove this charge, but the issue attracted wide newspaper coverage as the former prime minister was married with three children.

The trials ended on 15 September 1961 with 15 members of the DP, including Bayar and Menderes, being sentenced to death. Charges were brought not only against those officials charged with corruption, crime or specific political misdeeds, but also against almost the entire Democrat membership of the Grand National Assembly. Many other DP members, bureaucrats and officials were sentenced to life imprisonment. The National Unity Committee approved the execution of Menderes, Hasan Polatkan (Minister for Finance) and Fatin Rüştü Zorlu (Minister for Foreign Affairs). The sentences of the other accused men were commuted to life imprisonment. Bayar's sentence was also commuted to life imprisonment because of his advanced age. Polatkan and Zorlu were executed by hanging immediately after the trials on 16 September 1961 on the island of İmralı, to the south of Yassıada. Menderes, after an unsuccessful suicide attempt, was hanged on 17 September 1961 on the same island.[8]

The so-called *İstimlâk Yolsuzluğu Davası* (Case of Corrupt Expropriation), more commonly known as the *İmar Davası* (Case of Redevelopment), was one of the 19 cases brought against Menderes and the Democrat administration. Menderes, together with nine other former officials including the governors and mayors of Istanbul between 1957 and 1960,[9] was accused of four principal crimes: unlawful expropriation of private properties for the redevelopment of Istanbul without proper compensation and with forcibly signed releases from citizens; coercion of several governmental agencies, such as the *İşçi Sigortaları Kurumu* (Workers' Insurance Agency), to purchase land parcels alongside the newly constructed boulevards; unlawful demolition of the *Zirai Donatım Kurumu* (Agricultural Equipment Agency) buildings in Beşiktaş; and corruption in relation to the Ataköy Residential Complex.[10] The expropriation of 317 properties formed the centrepiece of the accusation by the chief prosecutor, who blamed Menderes and some bureaucrats of the Municipality of Istanbul for forcing the owners of these properties to sign releases without proper compensation. Menderes, above all others, was personally blamed for conducting the urban redevelopment programme irresponsibly by using the government's resources inappropriately and carrying out expropriations illegally. According to the prosecutor, Menderes declared himself 'the chief architect of the country' and 'the second conqueror' of the city. He demanded the death penalty for Menderes and the other five accused men.[11] The trial was held between 17 April and 3 June 1961 in 13 sessions. A total of 37 witnesses, most of them public servants who worked for the Municipality of Istanbul, were called throughout the trial. Menderes, Dilâver Argun, the former director-general of the Ministry of Internal Affairs, and Kemal Aygün, a former mayor, were found guilty on the first set of charges.[12]

While the trial had been set up ostensibly to investigate corrupt expropriations and unfair use of public resources, it can be seen from the tone of the chief prosecutor's words that much of the criticism concerned inappropriate and unprofessional approvals for redevelopment projects. Every opportunity was used to discredit Menderes and his administration. This included articles in daily newspapers, copies of Menderes' personal speeches and the uncorroborated testimonies of witnesses.[13] For example, the chief prosecutor, Ömer Altay Egesel, made the following indictment during the case:

> The honourable Chair and other respected members of the High Court of Justice:
>
> The city of Istanbul is a pearl of the world which is a favour of God to the Turkish nation because of its historical aspects, role in the life of the Turkish state and civilisation, its privileged condition as the capital city of the Turkish state for approximately five centuries, its national beauties and its strategic and economic connection between the two continents.
>
> It is impossible to imagine a person in the Turkish homeland who does not keep a warm love for Istanbul in his or her heart. Istanbul is loved by all Turks, with its unique character that makes the whole world envious. It is such a beloved city that it shines with its past, its historical character, its beauty and the countless memories which honour and make a nation proud.
>
> It is impossible to ignore the historical character of this city that was given to the Islamic world and the Turkish nation by the brave soldiers of Sultan Fatih [the Conqueror] 500 years ago. While the last period of the Eastern Roman Empire, which was called Byzantium, had been dying out within the ramparts of Istanbul, the Turkish sword and the Turkish shell opened the doors of these walls along with a new historical era. Here, in a new judicial case, we have good reason to mention Istanbul's historical identity and monuments because what gives Istanbul its unique character is the fact that it has accommodated those historical monuments in its bosom, as well as its natural beauties. There is no sacrifice that the Turkish nation cannot realise for Istanbul, which is coloured by the deepest beauty of the world on its shores and has made proud not only the Turkish civilisation but also the civilisation of the world with its great mosques, medreses and palaces on every hill. However, this sacrifice can only be realised and understood by being willing to make Istanbul more attractive and something to be even

more proud of. In this respect, it is absolutely essential to differentiate between this case which is called the Expropriation Case and the idea of the redevelopment and beautification of Istanbul.

While we accuse Menderes, the chief defendant of this case, of ignoring his primary duties as the prime minister and of acting as a needless chief architect for Istanbul, we do not want to be seen talking about a subject that is not in our domain. Yet the special qualities of Istanbul and its status in our common values force us to talk in this way to a certain extent…

Even if it had not been for a trial, we would still blame Menderes, the fallen prime minister of the fallen government, for the demolition of neighbourhoods such as Direklerarası and Şehzadebaşı for which we are still mourning, for the mentality that damaged some of Sinan's eternal works with dynamite blocks, for the demolition of the *yalı*s [waterfront residences alongside the Bosphorus] and fountains that had enabled us to visualise Istanbul's mythical atmosphere and life. Because there is an eternal and historic beauty at every corner of Istanbul, such that Nedim[14] would sacrifice an angel for every stone of it, it would have been necessary to consider an architectural approach that is illuminated by artistic spirits that enjoy history, literature, architecture and fine arts rather than a general redevelopment project. Adnan Menderes, who we refute even on this point, does not agree with us on the redevelopment of Istanbul. Furthermore, it cannot be claimed that he has any idea on this matter at all… In our opinion Menderes did not really want to redevelop Istanbul, but he used it as a pretext to excuse his long visits in Istanbul. He pretended that he was busy dealing with the redevelopment of Istanbul, however, with such a will he caused the destruction of Istanbul and its residents.[15]

Today the records of the Yassıada trials, together with the memoirs of politicians, journalists and other witnesses of the era, remain as one of the most significant, but at the same time untouched, sources of information about the DP's urban redevelopment projects in Istanbul. Chief Prosecutor Egesel's accusation against Menderes and statements made by Menderes and the other defendants, as well as testimonials made by witnesses, provide valuable material evidence for analysing and assessing several unanswered questions about the scope of the works and the true nature of Menderes' role in Istanbul's redevelopment. A close inspection of the minutes of the tribunal can help answer two critical questions: firstly, who was responsible for the urban redevelopment? And secondly, was there adequate technical preparation and documentation available before the works started? Although it is difficult to be absolutely certain of the answers to these questions due to the extraordinarily biased nature of the trials, the Yassıada archive is a rich source of information for understanding the role of the prime minister and the planning documentation available at the time.[16]

Istanbul in the Mid-1950s

Istanbul continued to grow throughout the first half of the 1950s. Immigration to the big cities, fuelled by the mechanisation of agricultural production and rapid economic growth, dramatically increased the city's population. Between 1950 and 1955 the population rose by 285,000 to reach 1.2 million.[17] The population pressure significantly increased the number of *gecekondu*s on the outskirts of the city. Concomitant with this population influx was an increased number of motor vehicles on Istanbul's streets. For example, vehicle ownership rose dramatically from 1,971 in 1944 to 20,868 in 1955, resulting in major traffic congestion.[18] Public transport in the city was also very poor. The average speed of the inadequate tram network was only seven kilometres per hour.[19] This led to the emergence of a pragmatic solution in the form of a new mode of public transport: the *dolmuş*, a shared taxi travelling a set route at a fixed price. By 1955 over 20 per cent of all public transport in Istanbul was based on the *dolmuş*.[20]

Under these drastic conditions the first signs of redevelopment came in the autumn of 1956. Although the demolitions had started months before, Menderes made the official announcement of his redevelopment programme in a press conference on 23 September. In his speech he drew a general picture of the aims of his urban redevelopment programme and, while acknowledging previous attempts to redevelop the city under the former Republican administration, highlighted the economic achievements of the Democrat government during its five years in power. Menderes believed there was an obvious difference between the 'power of the state before and during' his term in office. He accepted that works were not completed in the past because of financial difficulties. Yet as the economy developed, he saw no excuse for his government to postpone the redevelopment of Istanbul. He also provided assurances on the rights of property owners, and asserted that the government had learned from the mistakes made in the redevelopment of Ankara.[21]

Menderes' redevelopment programme, above all, was based on the idea of opening up large boulevards throughout Istanbul. In common with many politicians of the postwar era, he was much influenced by the magic of highways.[22] Hence he proposed several major arteries both within and outside the Istanbul Peninsula to connect the major commercial centres and encircle the shores of the Sea of Marmara and the Golden Horn. He outlined the major aims of his urban renewal programme as: reducing traffic congestion; regularising existing street patterns; demolishing buildings in the vicinity of the grand mosques; opening large avenues; and increasing Istanbul's attractiveness for foreign visitors.

Menderes first pointed to the traffic problems of Istanbul and how it was important to welcome travellers from Europe via a highway from Yeşilköy Airport and lead them to the city by a first-class road, and so prevent both friend and foe from entering Istanbul through areas that resembled a backward medieval town. He stated that the problematic junctions in Aksaray, Beyazıt, Eminönü, Karaköy, Tophane and Taksim, where there was traffic congestion at all hours of the day, were to be reorganised and the squares renovated. The roads that connected these squares to each other and constituted the skeleton of the city were also to be improved. The city was to be connected from suburb to suburb by equally perfect roads. Karaköy Square was to be enlarged and connected with Beşiktaş and then with the Bosphorus over Salıpazarı. Beşiktaş Square was to be enlarged and connected to Yıldız by a new boulevard. The Galata Bridge was to be reoriented to keep the axis of the new square. A new littoral road was to be constructed between Eminönü and Florya, and Yenikapı was to be turned into a new recreation district. The construction of this road would make the shores of the Sea of Marmara accessible to all residents of Istanbul. Eyüp was to be organised and connected to the city centre by three or four different roads. And, finally, a new road of 30-metres width was to be constructed between Üsküdar and Beykoz along the Asian shores of the Bosphorus.

Even some detailed works were announced at the prime minister's press conference. An 18-storey modern building, for example, was to be constructed at the site of the metro in Galata. The areas from the Atatürk Bridge to Şehzadebaşı were to be expropriated, and a modern complex called the *Manifaturacılar Çarşısı* (a modern shopping complex for textile merchants) was to be constructed. The cleaning of the surroundings of Süleymaniye Mosque was to be completed before the 400th anniversary of its construction in 1957. Çırağan Palace was to be converted into a hotel that was 'grander than its equivalents in Europe'.

The *gecekondu* problem, according to Menderes, was caused by insufficient land release. Therefore, the government would solve this problem by increasing the amount of land released for new residential areas. The support of the central government was another important point addressed by the prime minister. He highlighted the importance of coordination amongst the relevant governmental offices concerned with Istanbul's redevelopment. After addressing the criticisms raised by the opposition regarding the general economical conditions, Menderes finished his press conference by giving a timeframe of 1958 for the results of this new redevelopment programme.[23]

Reactions to the Urban Redevelopment Programme

The reaction in the press to the prime minister's press conference to officially launch the DP's urban redevelopment programme was overwhelmingly positive. All newspapers, regardless of their political persuasion, widely welcomed the demolition of old buildings and the opening of large boulevards and squares. Sensational headlines such as, 'Istanbul will be the most modern city of the Middle East in the near future', 'A total of 1.5 billion will be spent for the redevelopment of Istanbul', and 'Beyazıt Mosque will be brought into light with its all grandeur' provided front-page celebrations of the urban redevelopment programme. 'Liberating' the great Ottoman masterpieces from 'ugly' and 'primitive' structures and giving the city a 'European appearance' were major themes used in the daily newspapers.[24]

This unconditional support for the demolitions was not only limited to the headlines of major newspapers, but was shared by many writers and intellectuals. A brief review of the writings of newspaper columnists and commentators clearly reveals the level of appreciation and approval for Menderes' urban renewal programme among the educated stratum of society. The urban renewal of Istanbul was promoted and celebrated with great enthusiasm by writers and intellectuals in the name of solving traffic problems and beautifying monuments. Şevket Rado, a well-known writer, newspaper columnist and publisher, saluted the demolitions by comparing Paris with Istanbul:

> Paris, today, is the city that has the largest streets and squares of the world. How could it happen that the scale of the current traffic could be foreseen years ago and such large boulevards were opened? This is a matter of having the ability to see the future… The city of Istanbul is also one of the biggest cities of the world. However, in terms of its roads and squares under the current traffic conditions, it is also first amongst the most backward cities… In this respect, Istanbul's luck turned around just a couple of months ago.[25]

In another article Rado celebrated the demolition of timber houses around the mosques:

Again, there is one redevelopment work among others that will help to bring one of our beautiful and unique monuments into the light. I would like to mention the efforts being made to clear the surroundings of Süleymaniye Mosque. Undoubtedly, Süleymaniye is not only one of the most spectacular monuments in Istanbul but in all of our country. But the parasitic buildings that have been surrounding it for ages hide its beauty from our eyes… The cleaning away of timber buildings in its surroundings through the opening of the magnificent 70–metre-wide road from Atatürk Boulevard will show us the façade of Süleymaniye Mosque, which has not been seen by the Turks for ages. It will be the most respectful act made towards the mosque since its construction 400 years ago.[26]

Even the DP's political opponents were very supportive. According to Metin Toker, a leading pro-Republican political commentator of the era, DP politicians had more foresight and grander visions than their Republican rivals when promoting major projects such as a suspended bridge over the Bosphorus and the underground rail proposal.[27] The problem for the DP's political opponents, however, was not the redevelopment per se but its implementation. Indeed, the DP was the object of some jealousy. According to the former president, İnönü, the redevelopment of cities was a 'good thing' yet the DP was too slow in implementing Istanbul's urban renewal programme, as they had only just started the work six years after firing Prost.

Support for redevelopment also came from within architectural circles, particularly at the early stages of the redevelopment works. According to Zeki Sayar, the editor of *Arkitekt* and a former councillor of the Municipality of Istanbul, the municipality's limited budget and experience made the central government's support for Istanbul's redevelopment indispensable. He further voiced his appreciation of Menderes' urban renewal programme by making a remarkable comparison between the programme and the previous works carried out by Cemil Topuzlu, the legendary mayor of Istanbul in the early twentieth century:

> In recent times the inhabitants of Istanbul have been witnessing urban renewal activity that they have never seen or been familiar with before. Since the mayorship of Cemil Paşa [Topuzlu] the streets of Istanbul have not seen such rapid and broad enlargement or demolition activities. This activity is proof of a radical change in the mentality of the Istanbul Municipality: acceptance of the impossibility of planning without demolition. Finally, the conversion of Karaköy Street into a square and

the enlargement of the Karaköy–Bebek coastal road are events that make every city dweller happy. At the beginning of the redevelopment of Istanbul it is impossible, as a city dweller, not to appreciate the change that has occurred in the bureaucratic and procedural mentality. To witness such intense demolition activity after only one month arouses our gratitude and, at the same time, our astonishment.[28]

The redevelopment programme also attracted support from academics. For example, Sıddık Sami Onar, a professor of administrative law at Istanbul University who was given the task of drawing up a new constitution after the 1960 military coup and, indeed, created a formula to legalise the military coup according to the constitution, voiced a sympathetic attitude to the redevelopment works in the 1950s.[29] In an article advocating the role and responsibilities of the central government over local governments in the redevelopment of cities, Onar showed the level of his support for the demolition of the fish market in Eminönü by calling it a *Vak'a-i Hayriye* (Benevolent Event) [30] in the history of urban redevelopment in Turkey. According to Onar, the redevelopment works in Turkey's biggest cities could only happen because of the 'energetic initiatives of some statesmen'.[31] Ironically, the central government's involvement in the redevelopment programme was used against Menderes at the Yassıada trials.

Financing the redevelopment programme was a contentious matter and it had been used repeatedly against the DP by both its political opponents and architectural critics. Between 1956 and 1960 the Municipality of Istanbul's budget was increased dramatically to fund the demolitions and the construction of new roads. According to the municipality's promotional publication, the expenditure over the seven years of DP administration was 4.5 times greater than the total spent on demolition and road construction over the 27-year Republican period.[32] Similarly, the money spent on expropriations was 13 times more than that spent for the same purpose over the entire Republican period.[33] The government also canalised all the available resources of different official agencies towards the redevelopment of Istanbul. Many of the construction works, for example, were supervised by engineers from the Directorate of Highways using their own machinery, while many other demolitions and works were carried out by equipment and manpower supplied by the army. The *İşçi Sigortaları Kurumu* (Workers' Insurance Company) and the *Emekli Sandığı* (Pension Fund for Public Servants) provided much needed financial support by purchasing many lots around newly created boulevards and roads.

Figure 42 Demolitions executed in the west of Eminönü to construct the littoral road (Ragıp Gümüşpala Street) along the southern bank of the Golden Horn

Thousands of vernacular buildings, as well as some Ottoman and Byzantine monuments, were sacrificed in the name of modernisation to solve the traffic problems of the city. According to the testimonies of the witnesses in the Yassıada trials, who were mostly technical personnel of the municipality, the expropriations were carried out in a 'smooth manner' and in line with the municipality's modest budget until the prime minister's press conference in September 1956.[34] After this date, claimed many witnesses and defenders, the volume of expropriations increased dramatically to the extent that the municipality could no longer make the payments to building and site owners. In order to overcome this problem, and to continue the redevelopment programme, the government introduced the *rızaen feragât* (voluntary renunciation) formula. This saw agreements made with property owners to surrender their properties without the usual upfront payment of compensation. Most of the agreements, according to witnesses at the trials, were obtained by coercion whereby municipal officials intimidated property owners.[35]

It is difficult to estimate the total number of buildings demolished during Menderes' redevelopment programme as conflicting figures have been published in several sources. Some scholars put the number of buildings demolished during the Democrat period at 7,289.[36] Menderes himself provided some statistics in his monthly press conference of March 1957 and confirmed that a total of 5,540 properties had been expropriated since the beginning of the redevelopment programme.[37] In the Yassıada trials he later stated that the total number of properties expropriated was between 8,000 and 10,000.[38] The municipality records the number of total expropriations in about 1957 as 5,479.[39] Governor and mayor, Mümtaz Tarhan, provided a more detailed figure in his defence during the Yassıada trials and confirmed that the total number of expropriations between 1956 and 1960 was 5,720.[40] However, it should be noted that the total number of expropriations given in the municipality's book and by Tarhan included vacant lands and small agricultural parcels.[41] While it is difficult to estimate exactly how many buildings were demolished, it can be argued that a total of approximately 5,000 buildings was demolished.

New Roads in Istanbul

In a similar way to the previous proposals—namely, the 1839 development policy, André Auric's scheme and Henri Prost's master plan—the DP's programme included the connection of major commercial and administrative centres of the city by large streets running in an east–west direction. The construction of Ordu Street, together with Millet and Vatan streets, was the backbone of the urban redevelopment programme. These roads, together with Atatürk Boulevard, made Aksaray a significant junction in the centre of the Istanbul Peninsula. The intention was to extend the newly constructed parts of the Istanbul–Edirne Motorway (between Küçükçekmece and Topkapı) to the city centre.

The first part of this road completed the axis of Sultanahmet–Beyazıt–Aksaray. The eastern section between Sultanahmet and Çemberlitaş (Divanyolu) was constructed between 1869 and 1872 under the *Islahat-ı Turuk Komisyonu*. The construction of the western end of this road between Beyazıt and Aksaray began in the late-Ottoman period under the directorship of the French engineer Auric. The road was further developed and opened as a 30-metre wide boulevard in the early 1930s. The only unexecuted section of the road was in Beyazıt and it formed a bottleneck between the eastern part of Laleli and the end of Divanyolu in Çemberlitaş. Prost proposed a road extension at this location in 1944 but, like many of his proposals, it was not carried out. The adjustments made to the alignment towards Aksaray resulted in the complete demolition of several building blocks. Many residential buildings and shops were sacrificed for the sake of a straight connection between the two ends of this artery.

Figure 43 Enlarged Aksaray and Ordu Street towards Beyazıt, early 1960s

Some Ottoman monuments were also destroyed during the street enlargements. In particular, the demolition of a substantial portion of the Simkeşhane (former Imperial Mint and workshop for spinners of silver threads), constructed in the eighteenth century, and the *Han* of Hasan Paşa, constructed in 1747, was one of the most controversial decisions taken by the municipality. The eighteenth-century baroque Laleli Mosque and its annexe were also modified during the road construction, with the demolition of the courtyard and its reconstruction behind the original alignment. Because the levels of the entry were changed as a result of the roadworks, stairs were added between the entry gate and the courtyard of the mosque. The reconstructed walls, however, were demolished at a later date and replaced with a group of shops. The Ragıp Paşa Library was another significant Ottoman building that was adversely affected by the roadworks. During the works the façade of the library was lowered by 1.5 metres as a result of the raised level of the road.

The 50-metre-wide Millet Street (today renamed Turgut Özal Boulevard) was the second section of the route that connected the Istanbul–Edirne Motorway to the city centre. Topkapı, being the gate in the Theodosian Walls through which the Ottoman troops first entered the city in 1453, was chosen as the endpoint of the motorway. Millet Street was also one

Figure 44 Junction of Vatan and Millet streets in Aksaray, early 1960s

of the major boulevards proposed in Prost's master plan. However, with the exception of some enlargements made at nearby Aksaray and the partial construction of the boulevard at the western end near Topkapı, this project was not implemented during the 1940s.

Vatan Street, renamed Adnan Menderes Boulevard in the 1980s, was the other principal road that connected the city walls to Aksaray. Prost originally planned this road as a link through the proposed botanical park and the zoo in Yenibahçe Valley. The road was to serve the proposed, but unbuilt, Olympic Stadium outside the city walls. Vatan Street was opened in 1957 as an important element of the urban redevelopment programme and, with a width of 60 metres and eight traffic lanes, it was the widest boulevard ever built in Turkey. This same area, which was originally reserved for Park No.1 in Prost's master plan, was subdivided into smaller lots and distributed among several government agencies, including the Workers' Insurance Agency, the Police Department and the Municipality of Istanbul.

The DP's urban redevelopment programme also included the creation of two major littoral roads encircling the Istanbul Peninsula. Both roads were first proposed in the 1839 development policy and then in Auric's scheme and further detailed in Prost's master plan of 1937. These roads were also included in the 1955 *Müşavirler Heyeti* plan. Kennedy Street, the coastal road connecting Sirkeci to Florya along the shores of the Sea of Marmara, was the largest landfill project in Turkey. It was intended as a four-lane boulevard of 30-metres width, with the first section starting at the central railway station in Sirkeci and terminating in Yenikapı. The second section of the road ran through Yedikule and terminated at Yeşilköy.

Kennedy Street changed Istanbul's urban image quite radically. Parts of the city walls along the ramparts were demolished, which significantly changed the city's silhouette from the Sea of Marmara and altered the picturesque landscape once formed by the ancient Byzantine walls. It also reinforced the separation of the city from the sea, a process which had started during the reign of Sultan Abdülaziz when the construction of the railway alongside the inner walls had partly severed the waterfront link.

The second littoral road, named Ragıp Gümüşpala Street, connected Eminönü to Unkapanı. This street was planned as the extension of Kennedy Street from Sirkeci to Atatürk Boulevard along the southern bank of the Golden Horn. The area was a maze of narrow streets that specialised in commercial buildings, ports and markets and had been the major commercial centre of the city since its foundation. Ragıp Gümüşpala Street was planned

Figure 45 The western end of Millet Street where it transects Theodosian Walls in Topkapı, early 1960s

Figure 46 An aerial view of Vatan, Millet and Ordu streets and Atatürk Boulevard, early 1960s

to be 50 metres in width with a total of eight traffic lanes. Both sides of the road were to be provided with modern office blocks and docks. The old ramparts, fish market, fruit and vegetable market constructed in the 1940s and many other traditional buildings were to be demolished to enable the area to be redesigned according to modern urbanist principles. New commercial buildings were proposed alongside the newly opened boulevard.[42] Although the road was opened, the proposed office blocks on either side were never constructed, with the exception of the Snack Market and the headquarters of the Istanbul Chamber of Commerce.

While the Istanbul Peninsula was redesigned with large boulevards, other parts of the city were also on the DP administration's redevelopment agenda. The opening of Karaköy Square, on the opposite side of the Galata Bridge, was one of the major projects carried out in the Beyoğlu district. The traffic congestion in Karaköy Square had been a problem since the late-1930s. Although the existing road connecting Karaköy to Dolmabahçe was slightly enlarged in the 1940s, the major demolitions recommended in Prost's master plan were delayed and could only now be carried out. A new road

Figure 47 Barbaros Boulevard connecting Beşiktas to Levent, early 1960s

was constructed to connect Karaköy to Dolmabahçe via Salıpazarı on the western bank of the Bosphorus. Beşiktaş Square was enlarged and the roads connecting the neighbourhoods along the European side of the Bosphorus were widened. Karaköy Square was also connected to Atatürk Bridge by a large road on the northern bank of the Golden Horn through Perşembe Pazarı. The road network in this part of Istanbul included a large boulevard as the principal design feature. It was located between Beşiktaş and the newly constructed garden suburb of Levent, and was named after the legendary sixteenth-century Ottoman figure, Admiral Barbaros. This road was also extended to Ayazağa and then to İstinye on the upper shore of the Bosphorus. On the Anatolian side, a large avenue, Bağdat Street, connecting Kadıköy to Bostancı and a motorway between Haydarpaşa and Pendik were the major works executed in this period.

Menderes' Role in Urban Redevelopment

Menderes played the key role in Istanbul's urban redevelopment in the second half of the 1950s. As project coordinator, he personally directed most of the works. From the commencement of the operations he spent most of his time in Istanbul's Park Hotel and in his office

Figure 48 Littoral road (Kennedy Street) encircling the Istanbul Peninsula along the shores of the Sea of Marmara, early 1960s

in the municipality.[43] He was even kept informed about the progress of the works while on official visits to foreign countries.[44] The whole municipality was under the control of Menderes. Following an argument, Menderes accused the governor and mayor, Fahrettin Kerim Gökay, of sabotaging the works and removed him from office. He then established a team in the municipality and appointed Dilâver Argun as the permanent undersecretary responsible for the coordination of redevelopment matters.

However, Menderes' interests in Istanbul were deeply felt and not just a matter of political expediency, as is widely believed today. Evidence

from the memoirs of his close friends shows that the redevelopment of Istanbul had always been a matter of great consequence to Menderes since the DP's early days in power. Mükerrem Sarol writes:

> In the last week of August we went to Istanbul together. The derelict condition of the historic city caused him a deep sadness. It was impossible to afford the necessities with the limited budget of the municipality. Its roads were perplexing, the primitive infrastructure, such as sewerage and gas, was far from satisfactory when measured against what is required for a rapidly growing industry and population. The danger of shanty

houses was reaching a level that could threaten the social life of Istanbul. Families were flowing into Istanbul from Anatolia. It had become impossible to provide water and electricity adequately. The historic monuments were derelict and abandoned to collapse. The city walls had not seen any restoration since the period of Fatih [Mehmed II the Conqueror]... While we were inspecting these places Menderes told me, 'I assure you I feel shame and pain that we don't appreciate the value of these beautiful monuments in the spiritual presence of our ancestors'... Whenever we walked through the streets of Istanbul the matter of redevelopment was becoming clearer and more definite in his mind.[45]

During the redevelopment works Menderes was regularly briefed by the governor and mayors, architects and other technical personnel when inspecting the sites. This mostly occurred in the very early mornings when he gave directives to the engineers and workers.[46] According to Argun's testimony in the trials, Menderes had regular daily meetings with the high-ranking municipal staff and technical experts and discussed the projects and models with them. His personal interest and active participation in the execution of the works became a constant theme, both in daily newspapers and official propaganda. Photographs showing him at meetings and site visits together with his advisors were published extensively in the press.

Samet Ağaoğlu, one of Menderes' closest friends and a minister in the DP cabinet, wrote of the prime minister's enthusiasm:

Menderes' excitement for the development of Turkey was expanding to include the reconstruction of Istanbul. A brand new Istanbul... He had established a team with both Turkish and foreign, young and experienced architects. He was consulting with all of them and inspecting the models as if a child playing with toys. He was having long discussions about the width of streets, recreation areas, the routes of new bridges and roads, regularised and infilled areas. Menderes created a mysterious feeling in me regarding the redevelopment of Istanbul. It seemed that the old and backward Istanbul, with its dirty and crooked streets, marked with burnt places and with rubbish along its coasts, wanted revenge on the European Beyoğlu. From time to time this ambition led him to impetuous acts, but he made a great effort to create an Istanbul that is 100 per cent different to the Istanbul of the 1950s, and which today is appreciated by both his friends and enemies.[47]

The memoirs of witnesses also provide several interesting accounts about Menderes' involvement in the execution of the urban renewal works.

Menderes' statements, such as 'I want to see Süleymaniye Mosque from this point' or 'I want to see the sea from this street', and his directives to the engineers are the most interesting parts of the eyewitness accounts of the operations.[48] Witnesses often adorned their accounts of the prime minister's involvement with apocryphal stories: 'One day while Menderes was visiting a construction site a fly perched on his nose and when he repelled the fly by his hand the engineers around him understood that the Prime Minister wanted to demolish all old buildings on that site'.[49] Such accounts were even used against Menderes in the Yassıada trials:

> While Menderes was inspecting the construction sites with his technical personnel in his automobile, he suddenly had an attack of hiccups and began to generate noise, 'hık, hık, hık…' Yet the engineers misunderstood him as ordering, 'yık, yık, yık…' [demolish, demolish, demolish]. And eventually one street was demolished entirely.[50]

Stories such as these were even published in the international press. *Time* magazine, for example, published an article in 1957 about the redevelopment of Istanbul under the colourful headline, 'Benevolent Bomber'. According to the reporter, 'Istanbul's face lifting' was costing US$1 million a day and 10,000 buildings were being 'Menderazed' in a week. Menderes' personal passion is sometimes conveyed in mystical tones: 'On business in Baghdad recently, Menderes jumped out of bed in the middle of the night to send a cable announcing, "Have decided to tear down [the] house opposite [the] Spice Bazaar on Eminönü Square. Proceed with expropriation". Or, 'One night he spent five hours in the sidecar of a motorcycle supervising the construction of a new superparkway that will stretch from Beyazid Square to Emperor Theodosius' 5th century wall'.[51]

Nevertheless, this intense involvement and enthusiasm for urban planning put Menderes at the centre of controversy. Today he is believed to have been 'embraced by a strong passion for redeveloping the city' in his fifth year in power.[52] In the eyes of many academics Menderes, who was seriously influenced by what he saw in the Iranian capital Tehran, is held personally responsible for the demolition of many historical buildings and for much of the destruction of Istanbul's historical character.[53] According to this common view, the difficulties in the general economy and Menderes' decreasing popularity, especially among middle-class city dwellers and intellectuals, led him to demonstrate his effective administration through urban redevelopment projects.[54] A principal criticism is that Menderes did not listen to those with real expertise, but was influenced predominantly by a group of architects and academics who were politically close to the DP, as well as by engineers of the General Directorate of Highways.[55]

Figure 49 Menderes, together with Mayor Gökay and other officials, inspecting a model representing a new bridge over the Golden Horn

Menderes' personal involvement was also criticised by the chief prosecutor in the Yassıada trials:

> We asked a question to Menderes during the trial, because he was the Prime Minister of Turkey while he was dealing with the redevelopment of Istanbul. In accordance with our Constitution, he was the Chief of the Cabinet. Undoubtedly his duties as a prime minister are clear to everybody. As a prime minister he is supposed to run the general policies of the State and to ensure that the ministers in his Cabinet work in harmony. You must have noticed that he did not answer this question. Because, again, the rights, duties and elements of the municipalities have been clearly defined by laws under the Constitution. Perhaps the fallen Prime Minister could have been in a position of monitoring some activities in the municipalities. Nevertheless, neither the Constitution nor the other relevant acts allow him as a prime minister to leave his primary responsibilities and to devote himself to specific matters related to a city. Yet Adnan Menderes' understanding of the law is completely

contrary to ours. He thinks his desires are equivalent to the law, and for this reason we see that he can even lie without any hesitation.[56]

The reason for his involvement, according to the chief prosecutor, was Menderes' wish to stay in Istanbul rather than Ankara. His extensive residences in the Park Hotel became an object of accusation:

> Above we have mentioned that Adnan Menderes wanted to spend his time in Istanbul and that's why he dealt with the redevelopment of Istanbul. He wanted to mask his real aim with a lie. Because he wanted to reside in Istanbul, he settled down in the Park Hotel which was financed by the discretionary fund. It would continue like that for months and years. This residence [in the hotel] by itself would cost millions for the country. Yet he would follow a path to hide his irresponsibility with a plan which is nowhere near the truth.[57]

As well as Menderes' personal interests and involvement, his declaration that the redevelopment of Istanbul was a matter for government was also criticised by the court. According to the chief prosecutor, who used very emotive language in his indictment, Menderes was simply a 'liar' when he declared that the redevelopment of Istanbul was a matter of government as there was no such decision taken in the Ministerial Cabinet and, therefore, the matter could not be considered government business.[58]

Menderes, in his defence, refuted the above claims and argued that Istanbul's population had increased dramatically in ten years and that the municipality was unable to deal with the redevelopment of the city due to its limited budget. According to Menderes, the redevelopment programme would not have been possible without the definite support and involvement of the government.[59]

It is interesting to note that Menderes in his defence accepted his personal responsibility and was aware of the small details of the redevelopment programme. His usage of technical language and planning jargon in his speeches at the court also showed his deep involvement in the planning works. For example:

> I think it was the Botanical Institute building that was blocking the view of Süleymaniye Mosque from the north-west direction. With its clumsy and cubic architecture, it prevented the scene of Süleymaniye from being visible, and was attached to it as an ugly shadow... I think one or two floors on top of the Botanical Institute were removed and buildings were cleared in its proximity.[60]

Menderes strongly denied the accusation of illegal expropriations and demolitions, and claimed that he, as a prime minister, was not aware of technical and legal details of the works. When defending himself he said: 'For example, when I ordered the Deputy Mayor to demolish that building, I don't remember him advising me that its procedure had not been completed and there was a legal restriction on demolition'.[61]

Planned Works or Ad Hoc Development?

The lack of detailed documentation before and during the construction stage of the projects is another matter vehemently criticised in modern academic circles.[62] It is generally believed that Menderes carried out the execution of the urban renewal of Istanbul without having adequately prepared plans and other essential documents. According to many modern critics, works started throughout the city with neither a 'programme' nor a 'construction plan' and the redevelopment of the city was an 'ad hoc' and 'unplanned' process.[63] As time was important, the architects and engineers did not intend to make detailed plans and mostly decided the works on an ad hoc basis at the construction sites, thus turning Istanbul into a 'sketching paper'.[64]

The lack of detailed plans was also raised in articles published in the architectural journals of the period. It is very interesting to note that the celebrative tone of Sayar, the editor of *Arkitekt*, during the early days of Menderes' redevelopment programme was to change noticeably. His later articles published in *Arkitekt* criticised the urban redevelopment works for their lack of adequate preparation and detailed programming and for their uncoordinated implementation. According to Sayar, the Directory of Redevelopment of the Municipality of Istanbul was caught without any preparation for such a large project. He also argued that as a result of this deficiency, control over projects passed from the urban planners and architects to the bureaucrats.[65] In another article published in *Arkitekt* he criticised the demolitions in the historical parts of the city, particularly those carried out in Beyazıt Square and Beşiktaş:

> The last experiences have showed that the redevelopment is an issue of time. Despite the expropriations and demolitions that have been carried out to date, there is no regularised view of our city. Naturally, there could not be. All demolished streets and squares have brought worse ones and new shapelessness.[66]

Menderes' response to such critics appeared in a magazine published by the Municipality of Istanbul. According to the prime minister, all redevelopment plans were being carried out in accordance with a 'definite plan and programme' and were prepared with the appropriate expertise. It was not possible to imagine the government carrying out unplanned and arbitrary works in a city which was under the 'world's intellectual consideration'. Not one single step of the redevelopment works was carried out without a plan. However, according to the prime minister, as the work was of a large volume, it might cause such misinterpretations.[67]

The lack of essential documentation was also extensively criticised in the Yassıada trials. The chief prosecutor accused Menderes of conducting the urban redevelopment of Istanbul without a plan. According to the prosecutor, 'If Menderes had had the slightest idea about the redevelopment of Istanbul, Istanbul wouldn't have been a mess within such a short time as three or four years'.[68] The prosecutor's indictment held Menderes responsible for all works. Cabinet members, governors, mayors and some high-ranking officials were accused of failing to advise on unlawful orders and illegal works. With the exception of Aygün, all other defendants refuted the accusations and argued that Menderes was personally responsible for the demolitions, expropriations and administration of the works.[69] Even the governor and mayor, Gökay, who was one of the strongest supporters of Menderes before he was dismissed and who had offered him an honorary mayorship for his support for the redevelopment of Istanbul, blamed the prime minister.[70] In his written testimony to the trial Gökay accused Menderes of starting works without adequate funds to support the redevelopment programme.[71] Gökay's testimony was shared by other defendants and witnesses who claimed that up until 1956 all works had been carried out in accordance with the regulations and municipal budget. However, after the prime minister's opening press conference all power passed to Menderes, and he then personally directed the officials and supervised the works.[72] Witnesses at the trial also contributed to the claim concerning the lack of essential documentation.[73]

Menderes denied all accusations and claimed that the share of the expenditure for the redevelopment works from the general budget of the Municipality of Istanbul was not sufficient to carry out such a costly project:

> As the Prime Minister, I have paid attention and made all efforts to complete at least the first stage of the works. Why is Istanbul so important? Because it is located in the best possible place in the country and is connected to all regions, cities and towns with roads and railways... Its population was under one million in 1950, but today it's over two million. This means the population of Istanbul doubled in ten years. On the other hand, the number of transportation

vehicles increased four or five times... Who would be responsible for the completion of the works? Of course, the municipality. But how? The traffic problems on the one hand and the increased population on the other made it impossible. On the other hand every year tens of thousands buildings are constructed...The money allocated by the municipality for the redevelopment of Istanbul in 1955 and 1956 was only TL 3 million... It was unrealistic and impossible. With only that much money the municipality had to put the redevelopment aside as it was not in a position to carry out routine building approvals and to control the city's enlargement... The municipality was carrying out the redevelopment works with its own budget of TL 3 million. It would have meant leaving Istanbul alone with its problems. [74]

He also denied that there was no adequate plan to carry out the redevelopment:

And it has been claimed that there was no plan for the redevelopment works. Prost worked for 10 to 12 years. His colleagues are still there. Firstly, if there was no plan how did the municipality grant 8,000 to 10,000 development approvals per year? Secondly, the municipality previously carried out some redevelopment works, though they were limited. Examples are the enlargement of Eminönü Square, Bayıldım Street and Exhibition Palace and its environs. As we know, these are the redevelopment works made in previous periods. If we now think that there was no plan to guide Istanbul's redevelopment, how were these works given approvals? Of course, Prost undertook some works and prepared plans. These plans were applied in some regions, and some of them are still being implemented. I mean that before our redevelopment programme started, these plans were in action... What did Prost do in this country in twelve years?... Prost was invited two years ago; he came to Istanbul and inspected the works. He expressed his gratitude for the works. Both Turkish and foreign experts were employed for the works... This means the works were not executed without planning. The planning works have been carried out for 20 or 25 years, and they [the plans] have been reviewed, modified and implemented... As Kemal Aygün said, Istanbul was chosen as the city of the year in 1959 by the International Urban Planning Foundation. The Mayor was invited [to the ceremony]. There were many architects, famous planners and even statesmen from all over the world and they showed their interests.[75]

The available documents suggest that Menderes' redevelopment did not appear as a sudden decision and that he knew what he was doing in the redevelopment works. As noted earlier, he provided very detailed descriptions of the works in his speech to the press in September 1956 when he launched his programme. Not only detailed descriptions of the major roads constructed as part of the DP's redevelopment, but also some small-scale works such as the construction of a modern shopping complex for textile merchants (*Manifaturacılar Çarşısı*) were announced by the prime minister in this press conference. Also, the speeches of the governor and mayor, Gökay, and the writings of some official bureaucrats indicate that the urban renewal programme was a principal policy long before the prime minister's announcement. Gökay often mentioned the progress of the *Müşavirler Heyeti* in his speeches and his press conferences.[76] The prime minister was also briefed by members of the *Müşavirler Heyeti* during his visits to Istanbul long before the works commenced. Between 1951 and 1956 the daily newspapers regularly provided detailed information on the progress of the works. Furthermore, an article published in *Arkitekt* by the head of the Planning Bureau of the Municipality of Istanbul, Ertuğrul Menteşe, ten months before the prime minister's press conference officially launched the redevelopment programme, provided detailed information about the phasing of the works.[77]

A detailed reading of Menteşe's article shows that the plan prepared by the *Müşavirler Heyeti* was substantially the same as the urban redevelopment programme implemented between 1956 and 1960. Menteşe, who was the representative of the municipality on the 1951 Revision Commission, described the general outlook of the proposed programme and the roads to be built as part of Menderes' operations. A schematic map showing the proposed roads, various plans and pictures of models were also published in his article. Menteşe concluded by supporting the role of the central government in the urban redevelopment programme.

Another significant indication that Menderes' urban renewal was not solely a spontaneous and unprogrammed action was the preparation of a legislative framework prior to the commencement of works. The first legislative step came as early as 1951 with the establishment of the *Gayrimenkul Eski Eserler ve Anıtlar Yüksek Kurulu* (High Council of Immovable Heritage Items and Monuments) under the Ministry of Education. Although some provisions for the conservation of monuments and historic sites were always included in various acts of Turkish legislation, this specific act empowered the council as a consent authority for heritage buildings and sites. This was followed by the issue of a specific regulation called *Gayrimenkul Eski Eserler ve Anıtlar Yüksek Kurulu Talimatnamesi* (Regulation for the High Council of Immovable Heritage Items and Monuments) on 10 May 1952.[78] In terms of the legislative reforms that directly impacted on Istanbul's redevelopment, the first step was the introduction of a new *İmar Kanunu* (Redevelopment Act) in 1956. This law allowed the municipalities to enforce planning controls not only within the boundaries of their local government areas but also in the peripheral districts encircling the core municipal areas. The new act required each municipality to prepare detailed planning control instruments. In 1956 the Municipality of Istanbul also issued the *İstanbul İmar Talimatnamesi* (Istanbul Redevelopment Regulation). And, finally, a new expropriation act was passed in the parliament in the very same year. This act superseded approximately 50 planning control instruments and allowed greater flexibility in land expropriations. It was these planning control instruments that gave Menderes the legal mandate to commence his major redevelopment programme in Istanbul.

The works were carried out in accordance with the revised master plans and in consultation with foreign experts invited by the government. The technical aspects of Menderes' redevelopment were conducted by four different offices. The first office was established under a German professor, Hans Högg, who had previously prepared plans for Hanover and Munich. Högg knew Istanbul as he had worked on castles along the Bosphorus and in the Dardanelles for the doctoral study that he completed in the early 1930s. He came to Istanbul in August 1956 at the invitation of the municipality and stayed in the city for 20 days. Initially, he prepared a 55-page report and discussed his proposal with Governor Gökay in Germany.[79] Högg inspected the 1956 master plan prepared by the *Müşavirler Heyeti* and made some recommendations before the plan was referred to the Municipal Assembly for approval.[80] He was then subsequently appointed as an advisor to the Municipality of Istanbul and given responsibility for preparing implementation plans based on the works done by the *Müşavirler Heyeti*.[81] According to Högg, Istanbul was undergoing a similar experience to that addressed by Baron Haussmann in Paris during the reign of Napoleon III. He believed that the city needed 'perfect tourist attractions' and that large roads were necessary for the establishment of modern traffic systems.[82] Considering the rapid population increase, Högg suggested construction of a road network, together with the necessary infrastructure works. He estimated the city's maximum population capacity to be 3.5 million.[83]

The second office was established under the municipality's Directorate of Redevelopment. This office had approximately 30 to 40 technical personnel, mostly architects and engineers. The third office was set up under the Directorate of Highways to coordinate the directorate's technical support to the municipality for Istanbul's redevelopment.

And, finally, a new office to carry out planning works for Istanbul was established in 1958 under the *İller Bankası* (Bank of Provinces), an affiliate under the Ministry of Public Works which was established to assist municipalities in project preparation and execution of large infrastructure works. This agency was separated from the approval process. Cevat Erbel was appointed as the director of the new office. He worked with Mithat Yenen and Faruk Akçer from the Directorate of Redevelopment of the Municipality of Istanbul. An Italian professor in urban planning, Luigi Piccinato, was also appointed to the bank's planning section as a consultant.[84] Piccinato first came to Istanbul in January 1957 and subsequently submitted a short report to the prime minister about his overall comments on Istanbul's redevelopment.[85] According to Piccinato, the latest redevelopment works had 'awakened a sleeping city'. The Italian urban planner considered that although its redevelopment was difficult due to its historical character, Istanbul had three major advantages: firstly, its geographic location; secondly, its modern legislative framework; and, thirdly, the prime minister's great plans for the city.[86] The major aim of the Bank of Provinces' office was to support the urban renewal programme of the Municipality of Istanbul and to update the master plan for the greater region prepared by Prost and revised by the *Müşavirler Heyeti*. This group also prepared an inventory of building types and other socio-economic data collected by the *Müşavirler Heyeti*. A bridge project over the Bosphorus prepared by an American firm was also introduced into the master plan by the Bank of Provinces' group.[87]

Although Menderes was personally conducting the whole redevelopment programme, the Municipality of Istanbul's Assembly actively participated in the discussions. Many decisions including the invitation of foreign expertise, implementation of the roads and modification to the plans were all extensively discussed and approved in the assembly. As the urban renewal programme intensified and the expropriations and demolitions progressed, the first criticisms began to be voiced by the councillors. Some members of the assembly complained about the lack of coordination and the independent role of Högg and the 21 members of the *İstişare Heyeti* (Advisory Board), which had been established to control the works under the governor's office.[88] They also raised issues of legal matters relating to land expropriations and argued that some demolitions had adversely affected property owners.

Another key government agency involved in the redevelopment of Istanbul was the High Council of Immovable Heritage Items and Monuments. A careful examination of the records shows that many works that included demolitions of heritage buildings were referred to the council for approval. For example, the most controversial demolitions of the Menderes' redevelopment, the Simkeşhane and the *Han* of Hasanpaşa, were sent to the council in July 1952 as part of a proposal to demolish the nearby *Hamam* of Beyazıt. The council initially did not approve the demolition of the *Hamam* and requested further investigations, including a design competition for the production of a local development plan for the area including the Simkeşhane and the *Han* of Hasanpaşa.[89] The municipality prepared a further scheme in June 1955 and submitted it to the council for approval. The new scheme proposed to retain the *Hamam* of Beyazıt and to demolish the front sections of both the *Şimkeşhane* and the *Han* of Hasanpaşa by up to 12 metres. The council unanimously approved these demolitions at its meeting on 15 July 1955, and requested measured drawings and designs for the new facades following the demolitions of the front sections.[90] The progression of the demolitions near the Simkeşhane and the *Han* of Hasan Paşa provoked objections from several agencies, including the Chamber of Architects and the Turkish Historical Society, which forced the council to review its decision.[91] A long and vitriolic debate then ensued, with the proponents for demolition securing approval on 14 July 1956.[92] The municipality then applied for the removal of the majority of the remaining sections of the Simkeşhane. The council also approved its demolition in July 1957.[93] Investigations of the archives also show that the municipality and the Directorate of Highways worked cooperatively with the council, which later approved the construction of the Sirkeci–Florya coastal road (Kennedy Street).[94]

Despite the vigorous debate on whether or not the works were guided by adequate plans and professional expertise, by 1960 Istanbul finally had its long awaited large avenues. Apart from the large boulevards, one of the other significant outcomes of the Democrat period in Istanbul was the emergence of postwar International Style architecture. As noted previously, the most significant examples of this new architecture were the Hilton Hotel designed by Skidmore Owings and Merrill with the collaboration of the renowned Turkish architect, Sedad Hakkı Eldem, in 1951–55 and the Municipal Palace designed by Nevzat Erol in 1953. This trend continued, with many large-scale buildings constructed in this style throughout the 1950s. Perhaps the most significant outcome of this trend was the introduction of residential apartment buildings with a reinforced concrete structure and facades with large glazed surfaces. The most elaborate example of this new trend in residential architecture was the new housing complex built in the former *Baruthane* (Gunpowder House) near Bakırköy on the coast of the Sea of Marmara. Designed by a group of Turkish architects under the supervision of Piccinato and Menteşe, the Ataköy housing complex became a model for similar complexes built in the following decades in various parts of Istanbul. The changes in legislation to enable flat ownership combined with the advantages of the new architecture resulted in a boom in residential blocks in every corner of the city.[95] All the roads constructed by the DP administration and the buildings designed in accordance with international architectural styles paved the way for Istanbul's future redevelopment over the next four decades.

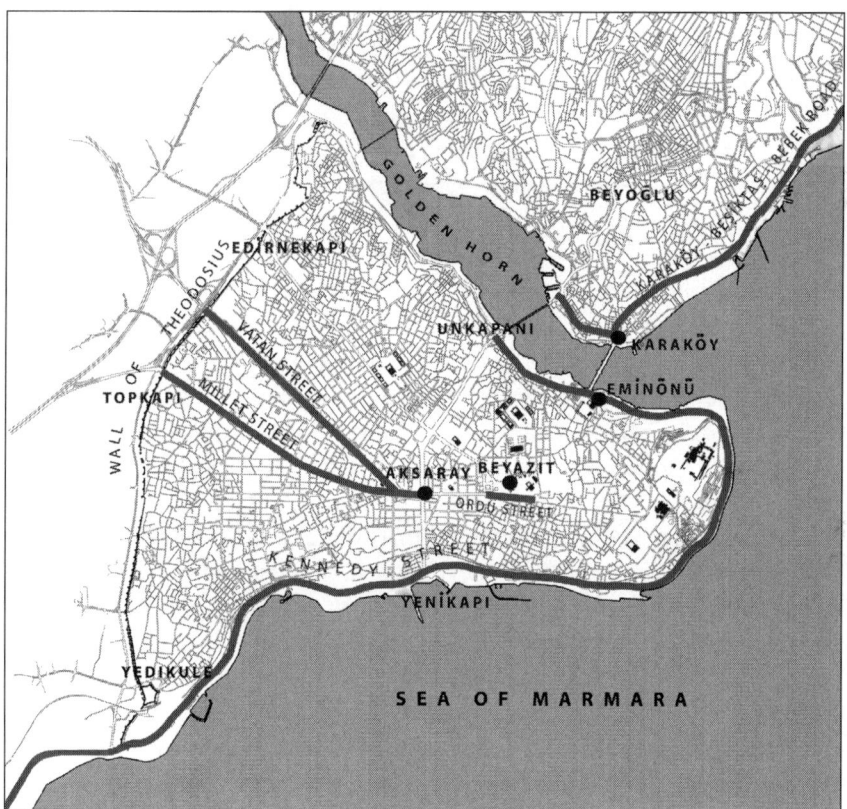

Figure 50 Major roads constructed between 1956 and 1960 in the Istanbul Peninsula and Beyoğlu

CONCLUSION

By May 1960, when the ruling Democrat Party was overthrown by a military coup d'état, Istanbul had finally succeeded in getting its large boulevards through the ambitious and progressive policies of prime minister, Adnan Menderes. The boulevards and regularisation works had been envisaged for almost 150 years from Tatarcık Abdullah Efendi's first embryonic ideas for improving the urban form to the subsequent attempts by Ottoman and Republican administrations to solve the city's chronic urban problems.

Menderes is, without doubt, the most controversial figure in this long journey towards the transformation of Istanbul into a modern metropolis. Ambition and dedication during the last four years of his life catapulted Menderes to the centre of the debate about the urban renewal programme. Today, many modern architectural critics portray him as the person solely responsible for much of the destruction of Istanbul's architectural and cultural heritage. And it is generally believed that Menderes' motives for Istanbul's redevelopment were political, the principal purpose being to camouflage deficiencies in his government's economic management. Menderes is also accused of implementing projects on an ad hoc basis without appropriate consultation with qualified planning expertise.

From a shallow historical perspective this picture of the Menderes years presents a plausible explanation for Istanbul's unprecedented change. It is a truism that Menderes was actively involved in the coordination of projects and that he personally directed many of the works. It is equally true that these same works had a dramatic impact on the city's urban structure, and form, and that some of them were crudely executed without due regard for the protection of the legitimate rights of property owners.

However, a careful reappraisal of the Menderes years presents a very different picture. Firstly, it must be emphasised that Menderes was not the 'inventor' of large roads for Istanbul. There is a long history showing that the majority of the roads he constructed were foreshadowed during the last decades of the Ottoman Empire and the early Republican period. Indeed, a careful examination of the development proposals of the nineteenth and early twentieth centuries clearly illustrates the significant legacy of earlier planning proposals for Istanbul inherited by Menderes. This fact is beyond mere speculation as many of the proposed works, although largely not implemented in the earlier periods, were conceptually similar to the works executed in the late-1950s. For example, the opening of Vatan and Millet streets and the construction of littoral avenues along the shores of the Sea of Marmara, the Golden Horn and the Bosphorus were all significant design schemes prepared in the last days of the Ottoman Empire that were to later appear in Prost's master plan.

Another widely held assumption is that Menderes' road scheme was far more grandiose than Prost's plan and that the actual road constructions implemented by his traffic engineers were two to three times larger than those envisaged by Prost. Archival documents, however, show this to be incorrect, as the opening of very large boulevards in the Istanbul Peninsula was first proposed by Auric and then later adopted by Prost. Atatürk Boulevard, with its 50-metre width slicing Istanbul Peninsula into two parts, vividly demonstrates this point, as do many of the other large boulevards proposed in Prost's plan. This provides strong evidence that Menderes gave effect to the century-long dreams of both Ottoman and Republican rulers who passionately tried to modernise Istanbul's urban infrastructure.

Prost's role in the redevelopment of Istanbul must also be revisited. Many modern accounts present him as an urban planner with sensitivity and respect for the historical character of the city. In this context, he has been somewhat immune from criticism. While it is true that Prost proposed conserving Ottoman architectural masterpieces and retaining and regenerating Istanbul's Greco-Roman heritage, many of his proposals, if implemented, would have had a destructive impact on the traditional character of Istanbul. Hence it could be said that Menderes' redevelopment programme was more modest than the French urban designer's radical solutions. In fact, Prost's plan would have brought new urban areas to the western portion of the Istanbul Peninsula, opened large roads connecting Eminönü Square to Süleymaniye, encircled the Grand Bazaar with motorways, converted the *Sandal Bedesteni* into an underground station and created new residential neighbourhoods on the shores of the Sea of Marmara. All these changes would have tranformed Istanbul's urban landscape into an irrevocable assemblage of modernist urban forms interspersed with monumental historic buildings.

Reflecting on the past, it is reasonable to see both Prost's urban design proposals and Menderes' grand road projects as severe interventions to address the city's problems with little regard for its heritage. While this position has some validity, it must be remembered that the concept of heritage in the 1930s, 1940s and 1950s had limited meaning, not only in Turkey but also internationally. From this viewpoint, the ideas of both Prost and Menderes concerning the opening-up of areas surrounding the large mosques and other monuments were fairly consistent with the general principles of heritage conservation at the time. The conservation of vernacular heritage was not well known then and, more importantly, the fire-prone timber dwellings of Istanbul had been seen as grimy and archaic in the eyes of both ordinary residents and elites since the late-Ottoman period. By the time of Menderes' redevelopment programme in the mid-1950s, most residential areas on the historic Istanbul Peninsula had appeared as a result of the spontaneous actions of owners to rebuild their properties following devastating fires. Most quarters of the city still lacked fully operating sewerage systems, proper roads and an acceptable level of building standards. Many redundant buildings had been occupied by immigrants because the 'well-to-do' population of Istanbul had already moved to modern apartments in other parts of the city.

From the available archival evidence, several important findings come to light about the Menderes period. The first is that the DP's redevelopment programme was, in fact, based on plans. While it is correct to say that detailed cartographical material and blueprint plans illustrating the spatial configuration of the desired urban form in great precision—a popular urban design approach in postwar Europe in the 1940s and 1950s—were not always available and that some decisions were made on site, the evidence does not support the position that the redevelopment programme was carried out without an overall master plan that included appropriate technical detail, especially in relation to roads. The major roads constructed in this period were based on a master plan first prepared by Prost and later detailed by the Revision Commission. Although the implementation of the plan indicates some adjustments were made, the underlying principles of the earlier plans were retained in Menderes' programme. And, even more importantly, it should be noted that a 20-year planning process originating with Prost's initiative in the mid-1930s had failed to come to fruition as an alternative scheme.

Secondly, the urban redevelopment programme sponsored by the DP was not a single-handed process directed by the prime minister, but a collaborative process with considerable input from many Turkish and foreign professionals. Menderes' personal enthusiasm and direct involvement in many of the works cannot be denied. However, a careful re-examination of the archival material shows conclusively that he consulted widely with architects, engineers and planners and with relevant government agencies including the High Council of Immovable Heritage Items and Monuments.

And, thirdly, the DP's programme was based on specific legislation passed to legitimise the works prior to implementation. It should also be noted here that a lack of legislative power was a formidable barrier to implementing Prost's plans, and one of which he continually complained. In this sense, Vico's view that 'history repeats itself' has some credence in relation to Istanbul's modernisation given the almost constant appearance and reappearance of various city plans with similar content throughout the late-Ottoman, early Republican and DP administrations.

This cyclical description of history, however, cannot fully explain the influence of the specific events of the 1950s and the complex politics surrounding them. There are distinct differences between the initiatives of the DP period and the earlier periods in relation to the prevailing political and social conditions. For example, the Ottoman administration was certainly influenced by modernist principles due to the need to reverse the Empire's declining military and economic power. The plans, however, were conceptual only and did not go beyond embryonic ideas, largely because of the bleak economic conditions in the Empire on the eve of the First World War.

Similar modernisation plans for the city were placed on the political agenda during the Republican period, but for very different reasons. The concept of modernisation at this time was more revolutionary in nature. The Kemalists fervently propounded the transformation of Turkey's Islamic heritage to align the country more closely with the modern European states. The removal of the Arabic alphabet and the Caliphate, the introduction of Western social mores with respect to dress standards and the recognition of women's right to use and enjoy parks and public spaces were considered modern new values that should be promoted through city planning principles and practices. Hence not only the urban fabric of Ottoman Istanbul had to be transformed, but also its symbolic identity and meaning. Prost's appointment is especially interesting because his competitors offered more comprehensive, innovative and ambitious plans. Yet the government decided to appoint Prost based on his reputation and, particularly, his planning experience in the French mandated traditional Islamic cities of North Africa.

Prost's cultural landscape in Istanbul and his association with the Kemalist rulers could be described as encompassing the rhetoric of progress and development spiced with the conservatism of agrarian utopianism in the countryside. While the few examples of his completed works, which indeed gave Istanbul properly designed squares and parks, were promoted by the government as triumphs of modernisation, there was a strong undertone that their impact on the built environment was modest and predominantly cosmetic.

The truth, however, was that after the Second World War the city's population was growing out of control, despite the peasantist rhetoric and educational programmes that sought to contain it. Prost's reluctance to use statistical information to provide forecasts for the demand of services such as transport and housing has led to a perception that his contribution to correcting the city's problems failed. Despite the regime's anti-urban bias, Prost, as an experienced urban designer, should have been able to foresee that Istanbul would regain its prominent political and economic status and that a significant population influx was inevitable. It is also noteworthy that even if implemented in a rudimentary form, Prost's plan could not have coped with the population increases foreseen by Wagner and Lambert. From this perspective, his appointment can be seen as a lost opportunity to establish a master plan that was capable of responding to long-term demographic change.

Although the Menderes administration adopted past planning initiatives, its approach was very different to its Ottoman and Republican predecessors in that the DP administration cast the modernisation programme in a much larger social and political context. Menderes essentially saw Istanbul as an international city inextricably linked with the postwar world economy and sitting at a strategic point between East and West. The implementation of the planning and redevelopment programmes during the DP years was due, in a large part, to the impact of the Second World War and especially to the economic aid that flowed into Europe generally, and Turkey specifically, through the Marshall Plan and other financial assistance programmes. It was this money that allowed the Menderes administration to embark on its large-scale redevelopment programme. Menderes' urban renewal programme was also a direct reaction to Istanbul's population boom. Significant economic aid for the mechanisation of agriculture had reduced the demand for labour and forced many former agricultural workers into the major cities such as Istanbul. This structural economic change created an urgent need to accommodate the increasing number of people migrating to the city.

Istanbul's urban redevelopment in the 1950s was not unique. Similar schemes incorporating major road building projects were repeated in many postwar cities because of the mass production of more affordable motorcars and the need to accommodate them in the urban landscape. The car was seen as the liberator of the people, unshackling them from rigid public transport timetables and allowing them to travel at will. Regrettably, the popularity of the motorcar brought with it the destruction of tram and train services which today has led to chronic traffic congestion problems and air and noise pollution.

Today many architectural and urban historians still adopt a negative attitude towards Menderes, reflecting the narrow and selective view of history generally propounded by Turkey's intelligentsia. This view of history fails to fully appreciate the need to see Menderes' involvement in the city's urban redevelopment in a wider historical context. In this sense, it can be argued that any political leader during the early postwar period who faced the special circumstances and problems of the time and who had access to foreign economic aid would have responded to these problems in much the same way as the Menderes did. And, although the specifics of the plans may well have been very different, change would have taken place regardless of the political leanings of the government or the personality traits of its leader.

There were also distinct differences between the early Republican and Democrat governments. Prost, for example, prepared and tried to implement his plan under an authoritarian single-party rule with little transparency and public accountability. He had no obligation other than to explain his proposal to the regime's elites such as the governors and mayors, ministers, prime minister and president. For this reason, Prost's plan generally remained unknown to the public until it was approved and partially implemented.

The redevelopment plans for Istanbul during the Democrat governments of the 1950s proceeded in a very different political atmosphere. The amendments to Prost's plan that were carried out by the Revision Commission were subject to full public exposure through the Turkish media and the press conferences of the governor and mayors and other state officials. Reports of the progress and implementation of the works were also published extensively in architectural journals and newspapers.

The limitation of the 'linear method of history' is also worth mentioning. It cannot adequately account for specific phenomena and events in one particular period and simultaneously reflect the influence of relevant historical events that occurred in earlier periods. This study confirms this position by showing how a complex array of social, economic and political phenomena that occurred in the late-Ottoman and Republican periods of the city's history influenced the urban plans for Istanbul during the 1950s. Dwelling too much on the actual physical changes to the city distorts the historical lens unless proper reference is made to the social, political and economic context in which these changes occurred. In this respect, the perceived roles played by many of the important figures identified by contemporary architectural historiography, for example Moltke, Arnodin, Prost and Menderes, are couched too narrowly and restrict a more considered understanding of their true role in the overall history of the city's redevelopment.

In trying to come to terms with the polemics concerning Menderes' role in Istanbul's urban history, one should ask the following critical question: have any alternative schemes been prepared since 1960? The short answer to this question is 'no'. Despite several later attempts, no effective master plan was put in place to overcome the shortcomings of Prost's and the later Revision Commission's plans. At the time of the military coup d'état in 1960, Istanbul's population had reached approximately two million people. Today the city with its population of over 13 million people is still struggling with similar problems, but at a much greater level.

Retrospectively, the boulevards opened in the 1950s present a poor policy choice because they fuelled land speculation in the city's historic quarters and induced further demand for car travel to the city, which added to the environmental costs associated with pollution. Also, the road constructions of the 1950s have not been able to cope with the ever increasing traffic load which has led the municipality to introduce piecemeal solutions, such as transforming significant squares on the Istanbul Peninsula into junctions and constructing tunnels and viaducts for motorcars. The rapidly increasing population has also caught the government and municipality off guard as there are no proper plans in place to generate sufficient land release. This is causing new *gecekondu* quarters to mushroom on the city's outskirts.

Perhaps the most noteworthy project of the twentieth century to originate in the late-Ottoman period and find its way into the plans of the early Republican and Democrat periods was the construction of the Bosphorus Bridge in 1973. Other uncompleted works in Prost's and the Revision Commission's plans—the Tarlabaşı Boulevard in the Beyoğlu district and the extension of littoral roads along the Golden Horn to the end of the gulf— were carried out in the 1980s by another ambitious political personality, Bedrettin Dalan, the mayor of Istanbul from 1984 to 1989. This period also saw Istanbul gain a second bridge over the Bosphorus constructed in 1988, the demolition of industrial sites and many buildings along the shores of the Golden Horn and the construction of new roads along the European side of the Bosphorus.

Since the late-1980s, Istanbul has embarked upon a new phase of development with the intensive construction of high-rise office towers. The liberal economic policies introduced from the 1980s, coupled with intensified integration of the national economy into a world economic order, have made Istanbul one of the most sought after and attractive places for international investment. Such developments have also brought innovative projects to Istanbul from some of the world's most renowned architects. Zaha Hadid's master plan for Kartal on the Asian side and the Ken Yeang proposal for Küçükçekmece on the European side were both innovative proposals for the megacity that never left the drawing board. In this respect, they owe their heritage to late-nineteenth-century projects for Ottoman Istanbul. On the other hand, the most notable project of this period is an underwater railway tube linking the Asian and European shores of the Bosphorus. Unlike other unrealised proposals the railway tube, which is due for completion in 2013, is located at the spot proposed by Arnodin for his transporter bridge more than a century before.

On the eve of the 2011 general elections, Istanbul was clearly on the political agenda. In particular, the projects proposed by Prime Minister Recep Tayyip Erdoğan—which became known as the 'Crazy Projects'—recalled the Menderes' ambition. An interesting project here is the opening of a new water channel between the Black Sea and the Sea of Marmara parallel to the Bosphorus on the west side of the city. Erdoğan, who previously served as mayor of the city between 1994 and 1998, claimed this project would not only provide an alternative for naval traffic to the Bosphorus, but also offer new land releases to allow expansion of the city in the west. Another project is the reorganisation of Taksim Square. This proposal will see the whole road network placed underground allowing the creation of a gigantic pedestrian square and the reconstruction of the former Artillery Barracks which were demolished by Prost's plan in the early 1940s. The most recent proposal, however, is the construction of a third suspension bridge over the Bosphorus at the entrance to the Black Sea. The bridge, which is designed to carry both vehicular and railway traffic, will push the city's expansion to the north with unfortunate adverse impacts on the last remaining green areas of the city. While these projects have created synergy and excitement, they have also attracted strong public criticism because of their lack of transparency and accountability.

While the current debates about Crazy Projects are ongoing, the city continues to regenerate itself with little planning guidance. Almost every day a new office tower or mega-scale shopping mall is presented in the newspapers, giving the city a Singaporean character and worsening the already hectic traffic congestion. The dramatic increase in land values has pushed the limits of an already inadequate planning control system to the extent that it has led to illicit development, even including skyscrapers, that detracts from the city's environmental and aesthetic amenity. All this rush for development and frenzied economic activity surely recalls the ghosts of Prost and Menderes as they walk the streets of Istanbul thinking about and pondering over their ambitious plans for a great city to connect the continents of Europe and Asia.

NOTES

Introduction

1. Şevket Süreyya Aydemir, *Menderes'in Dramı* (Istanbul, 2007), p.489.
2. Influential writers on Istanbul's urban planning during the DP period are Doğan Kuban, Burak Boysan, İlhan Tekeli and İpek Akpınar. Texts include: Doğan Kuban, *Kent ve Mimarlık Üzerine İstanbul Yazıları* (Istanbul, 1998) and *Istanbul an Urban History: Byzantion, Constantinopolis, Istanbul* (Istanbul, 1996); İlhan Tekeli, 'İcabında plan', *İstanbul* 4 (1993), pp.32–4 and *Modernite Aşılırken Kent Planlaması* (Ankara, 2001), pp.77–82; Burak Boysan, 'Politik hummanın silinmeyen izleri: Halkla ilişkiler stratejisi olarak İstanbul'un imarı', *İstanbul* 4 (1993), pp.84–9; and İpek Akpınar, 'The rebuilding of Istanbul after the plan of Henri Prost, 1937–1960: From secularisation to Turkish modernisation', PhD thesis, Bartlett School of Graduate Studies, University College London, 2003. Also one of the most complete historical accounts of Istanbul's planning history after the establishment of the Turkish republic was given in: Niyazi Duranay, Ersen Gürsel and Somer Ural, 'Cumhuriyetten bu yana İstanbul planlaması', *Mimarlık* 7 (1972), pp.65–109.
3. A further noteworthy point is that while Menderes has been severely criticised by architectural historians, Prost, Atatürk's urban planner, has not attracted such criticism. Modern Turkish historiography shows a very tolerant attitude to Prost, despite the substantial influence of his plans on Menderes' redevelopment programme. It is interesting to note, on the other hand, that Islamic conservative circles have tended to portray Prost as the person most responsible for destroying much of the city's Ottoman heritage, calling him an 'Imported Nero': İrfan Özfatura, 'Depremlerin yapamadığını H. Prost yaptı!, "İthal Neron" İstanbul'da"', *Tarih ve Düşünce* 49 (2004), pp.12–18.
4. As noted by Erik Zürcher, in order to be a 'valid instrument', periodisation must have an 'explanatory value'. Periodisations can be unlimited in number, but they can only help if they allow the historian to segregate the 'stream of events' or phenomena to make important developments identifiable. Periodisation should also reflect the actual developments of the period under description and should not be considered as a 'wholly inductive process': Erik J. Zürcher, *Turkey; A Modern History* (London, 2004), p.1.

5. Sir John Summerson crystallised the changing role of the architectural historian in the creation of a new urban history during the early 1960s. As an architectural historian, he described the history of the city as an 'artefact' or 'the history of the fabrics of the city'. According to Summerson, 'the main issue, all the time, is tangible substance, the stuff of the city' and 'the physical mass of marble, bricks and mortar, steel and concrete, tarmac and rubble, metal conduits and rails'. The urban historian, he argued, should use the social, economic and political aspects of the history to understand the 'artefact'. In other words, the social life should not be ignored but instead integrated with studies of the physical form so as to provide a more comprehensive understanding of the history of the city. But Summerson also emphasised that the social, political and economic aspects of cities should not dominate at the expense of its physical form: John Summerson, 'Urban forms' in Oscar Handlin and John E. Burchard (eds), *The Historian and the City* (Cambridge, 1963), pp.165–76.

Chapter 1

1. Charles MacFarlane, *Turkey and Its Destiny: The Results of Journeys made in 1847 and 1848 to Examine into the State of That Country* (London, 1850), vol.1 p.104–5.
2. Traditionally, the name 'İstanbul' defined the walled city of old Constantinople. The other parts of the city including Galata, Eyüp and Üsküdar were occasionally called 'İstanbul'. The present use of the name 'İstanbul' describes the whole metropolitan area of the city. In this book the old city of Istanbul is described as 'Istanbul Peninsula' or 'the walled city of Istanbul' or 'Dersaadet' in accordance with the context.
3. For detailed reading about Istanbul's re-population after the conquest: Halil İnalcık, 'The policy of Mehmed II towards the Greek population of Istanbul and the Byzantine buildings of the city', *Dumbarton Oaks Papers*, 23 (1969–1970), pp.229–49.
4. Halil İnalcık, 'Istanbul', *Encyclopaedia of Islam*, vol.4, p.241. See also Halil İnalcık, *Volume 1: 1300–1600* of H. İnalcık and D. Quataert (eds) *An Economic and Social History of the Ottoman Empire:* (Cambridge, 1994), pp. 209–16.
5. İnalcık: *An Economic and Social History,* pp.212–4.
6. İnalcık: 'The policy of Mehmed II', p.246. The first name of the city was, 'Byzantion', and derived from the name of the founder of the city, Byzas, in the seventh century BC. From 330 AD the official name of the city was 'Constantinupolis', and it remained in use (in the form of 'Constantinople') until the first quarter of the twentieth century. The word 'Konstantiniyye' was also used by the Ottomans in various imperial decrees and stamped upon coins. The present day official form of 'İstanbul' first appeared in the fourteenth century (in various spellings such as 'İstinbol', 'İstanbol', 'İstimboli', 'Stimboli' and 'Stambol'). In addition to these names, the city, in line with the common Islamic chancery usage, had a large number of epithets and salutary titles such as '*Payithat-ı Saltanat*' (Seat of the Sovereignty), '*Dersaadet*' (Gate of Felicity) or '*Âsitane*' (Court of the Sultan). For detailed reading: Necdet Sakaoğlu, 'İstanbul'un adları', *Dünden*

Bugüne İstanbul Ansiklopedisi, vol.4, pp.253–6.
7. İnalcık: 'The policy of Mehmed II', p.237.
8. The first Ottoman palace constructed soon after the conquest was located in Forum Tauri in the centre of the city. After the construction of the Topkapı Palace the former palace was allocated to other members of the ruling family. For detailed reading: Mustafa Cezar, *Osmanlı Başkenti İstanbul* (Istanbul, 2002), pp.50–61.
9. İnalcık: 'Istanbul', p.226.
10. For detailed reading for *Kapalı Çarşı*: Mustafa Cezar, *Tipik Yapılariyle Osmanlı Şehirciliğinde Çarşı ve Klasik Dönem İmar Sistemi* (Istanbul, 1985), pp.127–59.
11. Today the road between Sultanahmet Square and Çemberlitaş is called 'Divanyolu'. The exact extent of this major thoroughfare during the Ottoman era is not known. For detailed reading about Divanyolu and its development throughout history: Maurice Cerasi, et. al., *The Istanbul Divanyolu: A Case Study in Ottoman Urbanity and Architecture* (Würzburg, 2004).
12. There are no certain figures showing the exact number of inhabitants of the city. Even the official Ottoman registers, the most reliable sources, did not include the various strata of Istanbul's population who were exempt from tax such as women, children, the military class and some other segments of society. They can give an overall figure for the population of the city between the fifteenth and mid-nineteenth centuries when more regular and reliable censuses began to be executed. Although some historical sources state Istanbul's population in the seventeenth century to be as much as 1.2 million, such estimations seem to be exaggerated. Considering most of the houses had one or two storeys, Istanbul's overall population (including Galata) in the sixteenth and seventeenth centuries was about 300,000. For more detailed reading about Istanbul's population: İnalcık: 'Istanbul', pp.243–4; Zafer Toprak, 'Nüfus: Fetihten 1950'ye', *Dünden Bugüne İstanbul Ansiklopedisi,* vol.6, pp.108–11.
13. Since the late-seventeenth century various imperial decrees and orders had been issued to discourage and stop immigration to Istanbul. For detailed reading: Münir Aktepe, 'İstanbul'un nüfus mes'elesine dair bazı vesikalar', *Tarih Dergisi* 9/13 (1958), pp.1-31.
14. Osman Nuri Ergin, *Mecelle-i Umûr-ı Belediyye* (Istanbul, 1995), vol.3, p.1,266. Ergin's *Mecelle-i Umûr-ı Belediyye* was first published in 1922 in five volumes in Ottoman Turkish. It was republished in Modern Turkish alphabet in eight volumes in 1995. The new edition is referred to in this book.
15. Zeynep Çelik, *The Remaking of Istanbul: Portrait of an Ottoman City in the Nineteenth Century* (Berkeley, 1993), p.23.
16. Osman Nuri Ergin, *Türkiyede Şehirciliğin Tarihi İnkişafı* (Istanbul, 1936), p.82.
17. İnalcık: 'Istanbul', p.234.
18. The tulip was the preferred symbol and cultivar of the era. The interest in tulip display was extraordinary. Hundreds of different types of bulbs were planted, tulip gardens were created, competitions were organised and even an imperial decree issued to prevent price speculation in the markets in 1722. When the

craze for tulips was at its peak, some of the rarest bulbs could be sold for up to one thousand gold pieces. As a result, this period (1718–30) became commonly known as the 'Tulip Era', a name given by Ahmed Refik (Altınay), a twentieth-century Turkish historian. For detailed reading about the Tulip Era: Ahmed Refik, *Lâle Devri* (Istanbul, 1932); For architecture in the Tulip Era: Cezar: *Osmanlı Başkenti*, pp.215–51; Shirine Hamadeh, 'Ottoman expressions of early modernity and the "inevitable" question of Westernisation', *Journal of the Society of Architectural Historians* 63/1 (March, 2004), pp.32–51; Shirine Hamadeh, *The City's Pleasures: Istanbul in the Eighteenth Century* (Seattle, 2008).

19. Madeline C. Zilfi, 'Women and society in the Tulip Era 1718–1730' in Amira Sonbol (ed), *Women, the Family and Divorce Laws in Islamic History* (Syracuse, 1996), pp.290–307.
20. Ahmed Refik: *Lâle Devri*, pp.35–71.
21. For detailed information about the first Turkish press: William J. Watson, 'Ibrâhim Müteferrika and Turkish Incunabula', *Journal of the American Oriental Society* 88/3 (1968), pp.435–41.
22. Cezar: *Osmanlı Başkenti*, p.213.
23. For a detailed reading about *Sa'dabad* and the architectural expressions presented see: Hamadeh: 'Ottoman expressions', pp.38–43.
24. Robert W. Olson, *The Siege of Mosul and Ottoman-Persian Relations, 1718-1743: a Study of Rebellion in the Capital and War in the Provinces of the Ottoman Empire* (Bloomington, 1975), pp.65–83.
25. H. Sahillioğlu, 'Sıvış year crises in the Ottoman Empire', in M. A. Cook (ed), *Studies in the Economic History of the Middle East: from the Rise of Islam to the Present Day* (London, 1970), p.245. The Ottoman administration made similar decreases in currency in the subsequent decades to pay for the increasing military expenses: Münir Aktepe, *Patrona İsyanı (1730)* (Istanbul: 1958), pp19–21.
26. Olson: *The Siege of Mosul*, p.66; Aktepe: *Patrona İsyanı*, pp.3–18.
27. Aktepe: 'İstanbul'un nüfus', pp.6–8.
28. Olson: *The Siege of Mosul*, pp.66–71.
29. For a detailed review of the fires in the late-Ottoman period: Cezar: *Osmanlı Başkenti*, pp.352–445.
30. For the Patrona Halil Rebellion: Olson, *The Siege of Mosul*, pp.65–83; A. H. de Groot, 'Patrona Khalil', *Encyclopaedia of Islam*, vol.8, p.287; Aktepe: *Patrona İsyanı*.
31. In this period Said Efendi, the son of Yirmisekiz Çelebi Mehmed Efendi, was sent to France with a new bunch of capitulations, commercial concessions given to European states since the sixteenth century. He came back with two warships and a group of French military personnel, resulting in the beginning of the long-lasting modernisation of the Ottoman army. The opening of the *Hendesehane* (Geometry School) and the establishment of a special division of the *Humbarahane* (Training School for Bombardiers) in 1734 by Claude Alexandre Comte de Bonneval, a French officer who later professed to Islam and took the name of Ahmed, were the two important events that opened the doors of the army to European military advisors. For detailed information on the *Hendesehane*

and *Humbarahane*: Niyazi Berkes, *The Development of Secularism in Turkey* (New York, 1998), pp.45–50.

32. The *Sebil* of Hacı Bekir Ağa, constructed in 1738–39 within the Grand Bazaar, was the first known building ornamented with baroque motifs in Istanbul. The *Sebil* of Mehmed Emin Ağa in Dolmabahçe, built in 1739–40, was the first known building constructed completely in baroque style: Cezar: *Osmanlı Başkenti*, p.271.

33. For detailed information on Nuruosmaniye Mosque: Doğan Kuban, 'Nuruosmaniye Külliyesi', *Dünden Bugüne İstanbul Ansiklopedisi*, vol.VI, pp.100–3; Cezar: *Osmanlı Başkenti*, pp.272–4; and Ayda Arel, *Onsekizinci Yüzyıl İstanbul Mimarisinde Batılılaşma Süreci* (Istanbul, 1975), pp.59–63.

34. Stanford J. Shaw, *Between Old and New; the Ottoman Empire Under Sultan Selim III, 1789-1807* (Cambridge, 1971), p180.

35. Selim III established a consultative council, *Meclis-i Meşveret*, which included about 200 notables, military officers and *ulema*, to provide advice on the problems of the Empire. He then further asked for the preparation of detailed reform proposals from his 23 advisors, two of whom were European: Shaw: *Between Old and New*, pp.71–111.

36. Berkes: *The Development*, pp.75–78.

37. For Abdullah Efendi's memorandum: Reşat Kaynar, *Mustafa Reşit Paşa ve Tanzimat* (Ankara, 1991), pp.4–13.

38. For the emergence of new Ottoman bureaucracy in the early nineteenth century: Kemal H. Karpat, *Ottoman Population 1830–1914; Demographic and Social Characteristics* (Madison 1985), pp.91–5.

39. Ergin: *Mecelle-i*, vol.3, pp.1,265–8.

40. Ergin, *Türkiyede Şehirciliğin*, p.121; Musa Çadırcı, 'Türkiye'de muhtarlık teşkilatının kurulması üzerine', *Belleten* 36/135 (1970), pp.409–20.

41. For detailed information on the *Tanzimat* see: Halil İnalcık, 'Sened-i İttifak ve Gülhane Hatt-i Hümâyûnu', *Belleten* 28/109–112 (1964), pp.603–22; Erik J. Zürcher, *Turkey; A Modern History* (London, 2004), pp.50–70; Berkes: *The Development*, pp.137–200.

42. For detailed reading about the influence of bureaucracy in the *Tanzimat* period: İlber Ortaylı, *İmparatorluğun En Uzun Yüzyılı* (Istanbul, 2000), pp. 89–122; Berand Lewis, *The Emergence of Modern Turkey* (New York, 2002), pp.103–28.

43. M. Cavid Baysun, 'Mustafa Reşid Paşa'nın siyasî yazıları', *Tarih Dergisi* 11/15 (September, 1960), pp.124–7.

44. The 1826 census records show that Istanbul's population, including Dersaadet, Eyüp, Galata and Üsküdar, was 359,089. For detailed information about Istanbul's population throughout the nineteenth century: Karpat: *Ottoman Population*, pp.86–106.

45. For detailed summary of the fires in Istanbul during the nineteenth century: Cezar: *Osmanlı Başkenti*, pp.415–45.

46. Charles White, *Three Years in Constantinople; Or Domestic Manners of the Turks in 1844* (London, 1846), vol.3, p.324.

47. This part of Chapter 1 concerning the 1839 development policy was published

in: Murat Gül and Richard Lamb, 'Mapping, regularizing and modernizing Ottoman Istanbul; aspects of the genesis of the 1839 Development Policy', *Urban History* 31/3 (2004), pp.420–36.
48. This summary of the official document is based on the simplified modern Turkish translation of the original. Ergin's new edition, *Mecelle-i Umûr-ı Belediyye*, provides the original Ottoman Turkish document in the Latin alphabet: vol.3, pp.1,240–43.
49. *Divan-ı Hümayun Buyruldu ve İlmuhaber Defteri, 25 Rebiülevvel 1255* (8 June 1839), p.11, cited in Ergin: *Mecelle-i*, vol.3, pp.1,240–43.
50. Çelik: *The Remaking of Istanbul*, p.50. Ergin also considers Moltke as the author of the 1839 development policy: Ergin: *Mecelle-i*, vol.3, pp.1,243–44; and *İstanbulda İmar ve İskân Hareketleri* (Istanbul, 1938), pp.28–33; .
51. In 1835 Moltke obtained permission from the Prussian government to go to Istanbul on six month's leave. However, the Ottoman administration made an official request in 1836 to the Prussian government through the Prussian Embassy in Istanbul to extend Moltke's stay in Turkey. Consequently, Moltke remained in Turkey and became a military adviser to the Ottoman army until 1839. For detailed information: F. E. Whitton, *Moltke* (London, 1921), pp.30–42; William O'Connor Morris, *Moltke: A Biographical and Critical Study* (London, 1893), pp.13–18.
52. Moltke graduated from the Military Staff College in Berlin in 1826. In the spring of 1828 he was sent to the Topographical Office in Berlin, and was subsequently appointed to prepare topographical surveys under the supervision of the chief of staff of the Prussian army, General von Müffling. For detailed information on Moltke's life and his military career: Whitton: *Moltke*. In addition to the surveys of Istanbul and the Bosphorus, Moltke, during his service in Turkey, drew maps of several other towns and cities, both in Anatolia and in the Empire's European provinces including: Nizip, Urfa, Samsun, Maraş, Musul, Varna, Slistria and various places down the Danube.
53. Mary Herms, *Moltke's Life; Moltke His Life and Character Sketched in Journals, Letters, Memoirs, A Novel, and Autobiographical Notes* (London, 1892), p.16.
54. A letter of W. V. Krauseneck dated 19 August 1837 clearly shows the Prussian government's appreciation for Moltke's surveys and sketches. In his letter Krauseneck, the chief of Prussian General Staff between 1829 and 1848, writes, 'The reports sent by Count Königsmark, your surveys and sketches, as well as an abstract of your report of June 7th concerning your journey in the suite of His Highness the Sultan have been laid before His Majesty the King who expressed his satisfaction. I have also myself examined all these reports and papers with great interest, and I repeat that I have every reason to be satisfied with your contributions and reports, which always bear witness to your special knowledge, and to the clearness and soundness of your views': Herms: *Moltke's Life*, p.127.
55. The first edition of Moltke's map was published by Verlag von Simon Schropp & Comp in Berlin in 1842 at 1:25,000 scale. The map was edited and republished at 1:100,000 scale by H. Kiepert in 1853.

56. Helmuth von Moltke, *Briefe über Zustände und Begebenheiten in der Türkei aus den Jahren 1835 bis 1839* (Berlin, 1893), p.117.
57. Hayrullah Örs (trans), *Moltke'nin Türkiye Mektupları* (Istanbul, 1999), p.107.
58. Moltke's book titled *Briefe über Zustände und Begebenheiten in der Türkei aus den Jahren 1835 bis 1839* (Letters on the Conditions and Events in Turkey 1835-1839) was published in 1893 as the last volume of an eight-volume series of his letters written in various countries where he had worked. The eighth volume includes Moltke's letter dated 22 February 1837, and is the only part of the series translated into Turkish. While many of the letters in this volume have been referenced by several Turkish scholars, a wider reading of the other volumes illustrates that the *Briefe über Zustände und Begebenheiten in der Türkei aus den Jahren 1835 bis 1839* does not comprise all of Moltke's letters from Turkey. Other letters written by him from Turkey were published in volume 4 in 1891.
59. Helmuth von Moltke, *Briefe des General Feldmarschalls Grafen Helmuth von Moltke an Seine Mutter und an Seine Brüder Adolf und Ludwig* (Berlin, 1891), pp.102–4. It was also published in: Clara Bell and Henry W. Fischer (trans), *Letters of Field-Marshal Count Helmuth von Moltke to His Mother and His Brothers* (London: 1891), pp.154–7.
60. Moltke: *Briefe über Zustände*, p.89. Moltke made this statement in one of his other letters to his mother on 20 October 1836: *Briefe des General Feldmarschalls*, pp.98–9.
61. Moltke: *Briefe über Zustände*, p.481.
62. The original text was published in *Daheim*, a German magazine, in 1866. The autobiography was translated into English in Herms: *Moltke's Life*, p.21.
63. Ergin: *Mecelle-i*, vol.3, p.1,244.
64. Lewis: *The Emergence*, pp.94–5; Zürcher: *Turkey*, p.43.
65. Zürcher: *Turkey*, p.43.
66. Emre Aracı, 'Giuseppe Donizetti at the Ottoman Court: a Levantine life', *The Musical Times*, 143/1880 (Autumn 2002), pp.50–3.
67. Zürcher: *Turkey*, pp.44–5.
68. For detailed reading on the military buildings constructed during the nineteenth century: Cezar: *Osmanlı Başkenti*, pp.466–513.
69. Aracı: 'Giuseppe Donizetti', pp.53–4.
70. Steven T. Rosenthal, *The Politics of Dependency: Urban Reform in Istanbul* (Connecticut 1980), p.10; Philip Mansel, *Constantinople: City of the World's Desire 1453–1924* (London, 1995), p.284.
71. White: *Three Years*, vol.1, p.117.
72. MacFarlane: *Turkey*, vol.1 p.58.
73. Moltke: *Briefe über Zustände*, pp.82–3.
74. White: *Three Years*, vol.3, pp.319–23.

Chapter 2

1. Théophile Gautier, 'Constantinople' in *The Louvre–Constantinople*, trans & ed. by F. C. DeSumichrast (Boston, 1901), pp.40-1.
2. Erik J. Zürcher, *Turkey; A Modern History* (London, 2004), p.54.
3. Feroz Ahmad, *Turkey: The Quest for Identity* (Oxford, 2003), p.35.
4. For detailed information about the increased naval traffic in Istanbul ports during

the Crimean War: Wolfgang Müller-Wiener, *Bizans'tan Osmanlı'ya İstanbul Limanı* (Istanbul 1998), pp.112–13.
5. Steven T. Rosenthal, *The Politics of Dependency: Urban Reform in Istanbul* (Connecticut, 1980), p.13.
6. Steven Rosenthal, 'Foreigners and municipal reform in Istanbul: 1855–1865', *International Journal of Middle East Studies* 11/2 (April 1980), p.229.
7. Rosenthal: *The Politics of Dependency*, pp.11–6.
8. *Ibid*, pp.12–3.
9. Osman Nuri Ergin, *Mecelle-i Umûr-ı Belediyye* (Istanbul, 1995), vol.3, pp.1,268–9.
10. *Ibid*, vol.3, pp.1,265–74.
11. *Ibid*, vol.3, pp.1,274–5.
12. *Ibid*, vol.3, p.1,275; Rosenthal: *The Politics of Dependency*, p.39.
13. Ergin: *Mecelle-i*, vol.3, p.1,275.
14. *Ibid*, vol.3, pp.1,278–82.
15. *Ibid*, vol.3, p.1,278; Rosenthal: *The Politics of Dependency*, p.40–1.
16. Ergin: *Mecelle-i*, vol.3, pp.1,297–8.
17. *Ibid*, vol.3, p.1,307.
18. Rosenthal: 'Foreigners and municipal reform', p.233.
19. According to Ergin, even the title of the new experimental municipality was inspired by the *Sixième Arrondissement* of Paris: Ergin: *Mecelle-i*, vol.3, pp.1,307–8.
20. Ergin: *Mecelle-i*, vol.4, pp.1,601–4; Rosenthal: *The Politics of Dependency*, p.52–4.
21. Ergin: *Mecelle-i*, vol.4, pp.1,604–15. For the emergence of modern local governments and municipal organisation in Turkey also see: İlber Ortaylı, *Tanzimat Devrinde Osmanlı Mahalli İdareleri* (Ankara 2000), *Tanzimattan Cumhuriyete Yerel Yönetim Geleneği* (Istanbul 1985).
22. For detailed information about the technical bureau established in the Sixth District: Ergin: *Mecelle-i*, vol.3, pp.1,323–26.
23. Derin Öncel and Figen Orçun Kafesçioğlu, '1858–1860 Galata, Pera ve Pangaltı Planı', *Mimarist* 1 (2005), pp.18–9.
24. Rosenthal: 'Foreigners and municipal reform', p.237.
25. For Server Efendi's period: Rosenthal: *The Politics of Dependency*, pp.141–57.
26. Nur Akın, *19. Yüzyılın İkinci Yarısında Galata ve Pera* (Istanbul, 2002), pp.178–87.
27. For further information about the demolition of the Galata ramparts: Rosenthal: 'Foreigners and municipal reform', p.241.
28. Zeynep Çelik, *The Remaking of Istanbul; Portrait of an Ottoman City in the Nineteenth Century* (Berkeley, 1986), pp.69–70.
29. The exact date of the construction of the Municipal Palace is not known. Referring to newspaper articles of the time, Ergin suggests that the construction started in either 1870 or 1871: Ergin, *Mecelle-i*, vol.3, p.1,335.
30. *The Times*, 11 December 1875.
31. Rosenthal: *The Politics of Dependency*, pp.185–9.
32. Osman Nuri Ergin, *İstanbulda İmar ve İskan Hareketleri* (Istanbul, 1938), p.45.
33. Ergin: *Mecelle-i*, vol.3., pp.1,345–6; Rosenthal: *The Politics of Dependency*, pp.165–6.
34. Ergin: *Mecelle-i*, vol.3., pp.1,346–50 & vol.4, pp.1,615–24; Rosenthal: *The Politics of*

Dependency, p.171.
35. Ergin: *Mecelle-i*, vol.2, pp.963–4.
36. Rosenthal: *The Politics of Dependency*, p.164.
37. Ergin: *Mecelle-i*, vol.3, p.1,224; 'The great fire at Constantinople', *The Times*, 20 September 1865.
38. Ergin: *Mecelle-i*, vol.3, p.1,222.
39. Ergin: *İstanbulda*, p.39.
40. *Ibid*, pp.41–2; For detailed information about the Commission: Ergin: *Mecelle-i*, vol.2, pp.937–62.
41. Ergin: *İstanbulda*, p.43.
42. *Ibid*, p.21.
43. Ergin: *Mecelle-i*, vol.2, p.955.
44. *La Turquie*, 13 June 1873.
45. Baron Haussmann, *Mémoires* (Paris, 2000), pp.868–9.
46. *La Turquie*, 14 February 1873, 19 February 1873 and 12 April 1873.
47. Fâzıl Halil Edhem Bey, director of the Imperial Museum, states that Haussmann worked on the preparation of maps after the fires occurred in the Aksaray region. Again, architect Mazhar Bey claims that Haussmann worked on the opening of a new boulevard from Hagia Sophia and that his project required five million liras but Sultan Abdülaziz did not approve the project. Mimar Mazhar, 'İstanbul'un İmarı ve Eski Eserlerin Muhafazası', *Dergâh Mecmuası*, no.4, cited in Ergin: *Mecele-i*, vol.3, p.1,245.
48. Haussmann's letter to the Ministry of Foreign Affairs dated 23 April 1874: Prime Ministry Archives of the Turkish Republic (Ottoman Archives, Istanbul), Y.EE. 30.6.
49. For a detailed description of building and development controls in the nineteenth-century Ottoman Empire: Ergin: *Mecelle-i*, vol.2, pp.1,031–72; vol.4, pp.1,673–85 and 1,698–1,700; Mustafa Cezar, *Osmanlı Başkenti İstanbul* (Istanbul 2002), pp.311–35.
50. Ergin: *Mecelle-i*, vol.5, pp.2,288–95.
51. A detailed survey for the establishment of the tram lines and their management in Ottoman Istanbul is given in: Ergin: *Mecelle-i*, vol.5, pp.2,398–476.
52. *The Times*, 19 March 1894.
53. For detailed information about the underground project: P. Oberling, 'The Istanbul Tünel', *Archivum Ottomanicum* 4 (1972), pp.217–63.
54. For detailed reading about the Young Ottomans: Zürcher: *Turkey*, pp.66–70.
55. While this dramatic increase within three years may well be a result of an improved and more disciplined census system, it was also the result of approximately 600,000 immigrants who fled to Anatolia and Istanbul from former Ottoman provinces in Europe, the Caucasus and eastern Anatolia. The high percentage of Muslim inhabitants who were born outside Istanbul, approximately 62 per cent, supports this assumption. Stanford J. Shaw, 'The population of Istanbul in the nineteenth century', *International Journal of Middle East Studies* 10/2 (May, 1979), pp. 265–77.
56. Bernard Lewis, *The Emergence of Modern Turkey* (Oxford, 2002), pp.184–7.
57. Zürcher: *Turkey*, pp.62–3; Lewis: *The Emergence*, pp.181–3.
58. Zürcher: *Turkey* pp.81–2.

59. Sibel Bozdoğan, *Modernism and Nation Building; Turkish Architectural Culture in the Early Republic* (Seattle, 2001), pp.23–7.
60. For detailed reading about Islamic Revivalism in Ottoman architecture: *ibid*. pp.22–34.
61. Ergin: *Mecelle-i*, vol.4, pp.1,624–39.
62. Osman Nuri Ergin, *Türkiyede Şehirciliğin Tarihî İnkişafi* (Istanbul, 1936), p.129.
63. A detailed description of the project appeared in an article: 'Bridging the Bosphorus', *The New York Times*, 25 August 1877.
64. 'To Bridge the Bosphorus', *The New York Times*, 21 January 1890 and 'Bridging the Bosphorus', *The Times*, 12 April 1890.
65. Modern readers were first introduced to this project by Turkish historian Hayri Mutluçağ in 1968: 'Boğaziçi köprüsünün yapılması yolunda ilk çabalar', *Belgelerle Türk Tarihi Dergisi* 4 (January 1968), pp.32–8. In his article, Mutluçağ briefly described the project and included extracts of translations of official documents from the Ottoman Archives. Mutluçağ also published a letter written by the editor of *East and West*, a weekly newspaper published in London in 1891, which asked for detailed information about the construction of a bridge over the Bosphorus. In his letter to the imperial translator in the Ottoman Palace, Nasip Abdullah Şebli, the editor of *East and West* asked for detailed information about the project.
66. Transporter bridges consist of a high-level gantry along which a wheeled trolley moves. Beneath the trolley is a cargo-carrying platform, suspended by steel cables, which travels at ground level. Traffic enters the platform at one side of the bridge, and the mobile trolley carries it to the other side. The mobile trolley is moved across the river by steam or electric power, and the level of the car platform being the same as that of the approaches allows the road traffic to pass directly from the shore into the car, and vehicles and pedestrians are then carried bodily across the river. The first transporter bridge was designed in 1872 to cross the River Tees at Middlesbrough, but owing to financial reasons it was never built. For some years thereafter the transporter type of bridge remained more or less a novelty until Palacis, an architect of Bilbao, and Arnodin took out a patent for this system of bridge design. In 1893 they designed and erected a transporter bridge at Portugalte, near Bilbao. The main span of the bridge was 148 feet above high water level and it was built in the form of a suspension bridge with 'stiffening' girders.
67. Zeynep Çelik claims that 'The railroad that ended in Haydarpaşa was to be extended to Üsküdar and from there connected to the Istanbul-Edirne line by means of this bridge': Çelik: *The Remaking*, p.107; Çelik also provides similar claims in: Zeynep Çelik, 'Two projects for fin-de-siècle Istanbul', *Rassegna* 19/72 (1997), p.71.
68. This type of collaboration between architects and engineers can be seen in London's Tower Bridge which was opened in 1894 and is one of Europe's most striking late-Victorian bridges. The design was produced in a highly creative partnership between engineer Sir John Wolfe Barry and architect Horace Jones.
69. Çelik: *The Remaking*, pp.107–9, p.172 (note 3). Wagner's project, which won an

urban design competition for the general regularisation of Vienna in 1893, comprised a detailed rail network in order to establish an effective transport network between the old and new suburbs of Vienna. Wagner was a prominent architect holding various prestigious positions, namely: professor of architecture at the Academy of Fine Arts in Vienna; artistic adviser to the Viennese Transport Commission and adviser to the Commission for the Regulation of the Danube Canal. His circumferential rail routes were first applied in the Ringstrasse connecting the surrounding suburbs to Vienna's historic centre. His proposal also included new infrastructure to improve the supply of drinking water, drainage and gas street lighting in the city. Mata, on the other hand, was the first urban designer to develop the Linear City as an elongated urban form based on a series of functionally specialised parallel sectors. He implemented this design in Madrid.

70. Siegmund Schneider, *Die Deutsche Baghdâd-Bahn und die Projectirte Überbrückung des Bosporus* (Vienna, 1900), p.9.
71. Schneider claimed that German technology, which had already proven its capability in constructing the Pittsburgh and Brooklyn bridges in the United States, could carry out such a great project: *ibid*, p.9.
72. *Ibid*, p.9.
73. Mutluçağ: 'Boğaziçi Köprüsü, p.34.
74. A closer examination of the archival material and the existing literature raises some serious doubts about the above interpretations of the project's context. The existing archival records do not indicate that Arnodin ever visited Istanbul. The title-blocks on the drawings and their very schematic nature and missing topographical data indicate that Arnodin most likely prepared his proposal at Châteauneuf-sur-Loire, Loiret Centre in France.
75. For German interests in the Ottoman Empire and the role of the Baghdad railways see: Murat Özyüksel, *Osmanlı-Alman İlişkilerinin Gelişim Sürecinde Anadolu ve Bağdat Demiryolları* (Istanbul, 1988).
76. Ergin: *İstanbulda İmâr*, pp.46–7.
77. For detailed information about Bouvard's sketches for Istanbul see Zeynep Çelik, 'Bouvard's boulevards; Beaux-Arts planning in Istanbul', *Journal of the Society of Architectural Historians* 43/4 (1984), pp.341–55.
78. Bouvard's watercolour perspectives are kept in Istanbul University Library. They were also published by Çelik in: *The Remaking*, pp.112, 116, 117, 120–1 and 'Bouvard's boulevards'.
79. Ergin: *İstanbulda İmâr*, p.48.
80. Zürcher: *Turkey*, p.80.
81. F. Diodati Thompson, 'Turkey under Abdul Hamid', *The New York Times*, 14 October 1900.
82. Lewis: *The Emergence*, p.228.
83. Prime Ministry Archives of the Turkish Republic (Ottoman Archives, Istanbul), DH.ID.131/3. For detailed information about the loan and the official guarantees: 'City of Constantinople municipal 5 % loan 1909 for £1,000,000 or

£T.1,100,000', *The Times*, 22 March 1910.
84. Ergin: *Mecelle-i*, vol.5, p.3,022.
85. 'Electrical works at Constantinople',*The Times*, 25 August 1909.
86. 'Electric lighting in Constantinople', *The Times*, 5 October 1910.
87. For contracts signed for the establishment of telephone lines in Istanbul: Ergin: *Mecelle-i*, vol.5, pp.2,744–91. The first regular telephone service in Istanbul was established in 1909 at the General Post Office of Istanbul. The capacity of this central service was only 50 lines which were allocated to high ranking bureaucrats and banks. The capacity of the initial central service was further extended in the following years until the concession was given to an international syndicate: Ayşe Hür, 'Telefon', *Dünden Bugüne İstanbul Ansiklopedisi*, vol.7, pp.241–2.
88. 'A telephone system for Constantinople', *The Times*, 23 March 1911.
89. 'The Constantinople Telephone Company', *The Times*, 19 February 1914.
90. Prime Ministry Archives of the Turkish Republic (Ottoman Archives, Istanbul), MV.121/74.
91. Ergin: *Mecelle-i*, vol.5, pp.2,996–9.
92. *Ibid*, vol.5, pp.2,999–3,006.
93. For a detailed analysis of Ottoman Revivalism see Bozdoğan: *Modernism and Nation*, pp.16–55; Bülent Özer, *Rejyonalism Üniversalizm ve Çağdaş Mimarimiz Üzerine Bir Deneme* (Istanbul, 1970), pp.44–6.
94. André Joseph Auric, doctor in mathematical sciences and civil engineer, was born on 1 August 1866 in Orange Vaucluse, France. In September 1909 he resigned his post in the Municipality of Lyon and came to Turkey to work for the Municipality of Istanbul. For his works in Lyon see: Archives Municipales de Lyon, 0524 WP 024 AURIC André, 1906–10.
95. The authorisation of the *Meclis-i Vukela* to allow the Municipality of Istanbul to engage Auric was granted on 3 February 1910. This document and Auric's contract are held in: Prime Ministry Archives of the Turkish Republic (Ottoman Archives, Istanbul), MV.137/6. The government wanted to extend Auric's contract for two years. However, upon the commencement of the First World War the engineer returned to France and this extension was never realised. After this unsuccessful attempt in 1914, Kemalettin Bey was appointed as an advisor to the office which had been established by Auric: Ergin: *Mecelle-i*, vol.5, p.3,012.
96. André Auric, 'Rapport general du service de la préfecture de la ville: Service des eaux potables', *Génie Civil Ottoman* 2 (1911), pp.9–10; 'Canalisation de la des aux de Constantinople', pp.10–11; 'Rapport general du service technique de la préfecture: Etat des taxes proposées poul les bâtisses', *Génie Civil Ottoman* 3 (1911), pp.12–3; 'Rapport general du service technique de la prefecture: Projet de réglement', *Génie Civil Ottoman* 3 (1911), pp.13–4; 'Rapport de la préfecture de la ville: Reglement de voirie–série des prix', *Génie Civil Ottoman* 5 (1912), pp.10–2.
97. André Auric, 'Rapport general du service technique de la préfecture', *Génie Civil Ottoman* 1 (1911), pp.1–4. Another article published in the same journal also provides information about Auric's works in Istanbul: 'La reconstruction de Stamboul', *Génie Civil Ottoman* 1 (1912), pp.4–5.

98. Ergin mentions that in addition to these works, Auric proposed a suspension bridge between Galata and Istanbul. Also Cemil Topuzlu, one of the mayors of Istanbul with whom Auric worked, mentions that he was asked to design a theatre building. Neither project was ever implemented: Ergin: *İstanbulda*, p.50; Cemil Topuzlu, *İstibdad-Meşrutiyet-Cumhuriyet Devirlerinde 80 Yıllık Hatıralarım* (Istanbul, 2002), p.131 and *32 Sene Evvelki, Bugünkü, Yarınki İstanbul* (Istanbul, 1944), p.33.
99. Topuzlu: *İstibdad*, pp.132-4.

Chapter 3

1. George Clerk, 'Istanbul: a city of memoirs', *The Times*, 9 August 1938.
2. In the Turkish political context the meaning of 'secularism' differs from the Anglo-Saxon understanding of the term. In Turkey the major goal of the secularist policies was not only a constitutional separation of political and religious affairs but also the establishment of a strict control on religious life. Moreover, in the early Republican period it sometimes comprised a total disregard for all aspects of Islamic tradition. In this respect, the French term *laicisme* was adapted to Turkish language as *'laiklik'*, and being *'laik'* became one of the most important indicators of the Kemalist reforms. For detailed information see: Şerif Mardin, (a) 'Religion and secularism in Turkey' in Albert Hourani, Phillip Khoury and Mary C. Wilson (eds), *The Modern Middle East* (London, 2004), pp.347–74; Niyazi Berkes, *The Development of Secularism in Turkey* (New York, 1998), pp.479–506; Nuray Mert, *Laiklik Tartışmasına Kavramsal Bir Bakış: Cumhuriyet Kurulurken Laik Düşünce* (Istanbul, 1994).
3. For detailed information about the political events following the Turkish National War of Independence: Bernard Lewis, *The Emergence of Modern Turkey* (New York, 2002); Feroz Ahmad, *The Making of Modern Turkey* (London, 1993); Erik J. Zürcher, *Turkey; A Modern History* (London, 2004).
4. Cited and translated into English in Lewis: *The Emergence*, p.268.
5. Ahmad: *The Making*, pp.80–1.
6. The first opposition party in the Turkish Republic was the *Terakkiperver Cumhuriyet Fırkası* (Progressive Republican Party) founded in November 1924. This new party promoted Western liberal tendencies and opposed the authoritarian character of the new regime. This first democratic experiment, however, was short-lived, and after a Kurdish rebellion broke out in Eastern Anatolia in February 1925, the party was banned in June the same year. For detailed readings about the opposition parties in the early Republican period: Zürcher: *Turkey*, pp.166–75 and 176–79; Ahmad: *The Making*, pp.57–60; Cem Emrence, 'Dünya krizi ve Türkiye'de toplumsal muhalefet: Serbest Cumhuriyet Fırkası' in Murat Yılmaz (ed), *Modern Türkiye'de Siyasi Düşünce: 7 Liberalizm* (Istanbul, 2005), pp.213–6.
7. The term 'Kemalism' or *'Atatürkçülük'*, describing the set of ideas that constitutes the principles of the Republican regime, first emerged in the early 1930s and continued to evolve. As Zürcher argues, Kemalism never became a 'coherent all-embracing ideology' described in detail. Hence Kemalism remained a 'flexible concept' that could be used by many social groups, but mostly by the military

and bureaucratic elite and general academia who called themselves 'Kemalists': Zürcher: *Turkey*, pp.181–2.
8. Ahmad: *The Making*, p.64; Zürcher: *Turkey*, p.177.
9. For detailed information about People's Houses: Neşe G. Yeşilkaya, 'Halkevleri', in Ahmet İnsel (ed) *Modern Türkiye'de Siyasi Düşünce 2: Kemalizm* (Istanbul, 2002), pp.113–18; Neşe G. Yeşilkaya, *Halkevleri, İdeoloji ve Mimarlık* (Istanbul, 1999); İlhan Başgöz and Howard E. Wilson, *Educational Problems in Turkey 1920–1940* (Bloomington, 1968), pp.149–58.
10. Başgöz and Wilson: *Educational Problems*, p154.
11. Yeşilkaya: *Halkevleri*, pp.150–2; 'Halkevleri', p.117.
12. *Mebani-i Resmiyye ve Milliye Üzerindeki Tuğra ve Methiyelerin Kaldırılması Hakkında Kanun* (The Act of Removal of the Coat of Arms and Insignia on Official and National Buildings) gazetted on 16 June 1927. For detailed information on this Act and other practices mentioned above: Beşir Ayvazoğlu, 'Türk muhafazakarlığının kültürel kuruluşu' in Ahmet Çiğdem (ed), *Modern Türkiye'de Siyasi Düşünce: 5 Muhafazakarlık* (Istanbul, 2003), p.509.
13. For detailed information see: Osman Ergin, *Muallim M. Cevdet'in Hayatı, Eserleri ve Kütüphanesi* (Istanbul, 1937), pp.106–27.
14. One of the most vivid examples of this ideology can be found in one of Falih Rıfkı Atay's articles titled 'Mesela Musiki'. Atay wrote 'The Radio administration may consider the appreciation of its *Alla Turca* customers. Cafes, casinos and private venues may make money by trading in Turkish music. But the State shall only support Western music, the schools shall only teach its [Western music's] technique and enjoyment, and the institutions of the Revolution Party [RPP] shall only serve its culture' cited in Ayvazoğlu: 'Türk muhafazakarlığının', pp.510–11; For the removal of classical Turkish music from primary and secondary school curricula and proposal for the conversion of Sultan Ahmet Mosque into an art gallery: Cemal R. Rey, 'Atatürk ve müzik', *Cumhuriyet*, 11 November 1963.
15. *Fotoğrafla Türkiye*, printed in Munich, Germany, by the General Direction of the Press, Ankara c.1940, no page numbers.
16. Cited in Yeşim Arat, 'The project of modernity and women in Turkey', in Sibel Bozdoğan and Reşat Kasaba (eds), *Rethinking Modernity and National Identity in Turkey* (Seattle, 1997), p.99.
17. Arat: 'The project of modernity', p.95.
18. Sibel Bozdoğan, *Modernism and Nation Building; Turkish Architectural Culture in the Early Republic* (Seattle, 2001), p.82.
19. Mardin (a): 'Religion and secularism', p.366.
20. Celâl E. Arseven, *Türk Sanatı Tarihi: Menşeinden Bugüne Kadar Mimari, Heykel, Resim Süsleme ve Tezyini Sanatlar*, vol.VI (Istanbul, c. 1955), p.435.
21. It should be noted that although Turkish architectural historiography provides several rationales for this paradoxical practice of the Kemalist regime, the issue requires a more detailed investigation. It is generally argued that the confluence between the nationalist struggle against Western powers and the nationalistic character of Ottoman Revivalist architecture was an important reason for its acceptance by the

Kemalist regime. Some scholars, such as Sözen and Aslanoğlu, claim that the limited international exposure of Turkish society in the 1920s was the other ground for this practice: Metin Sözen, *Cumhuriyet Dönemi Türk Mimarlığı* (Ankara, 1984), p.29; İnci Aslanoğlu, *Erken Cumhuriyet Dönemi Mimarlığı 1923–1938* (Ankara, 2001), p.30.
22. Bozdoğan: *Modernism and Nation*, pp.47–8.
23. Behçet and Bedrettin, 'Türk inkilap mimarisi', *Mimar* 3/9–10 (1933), pp.265–6.
24. According to an observation by a foreign visitor in 1937, in ten years the government had built 4,041 official buildings, 3,287 public buildings, 352 parks, 261 sporting fields, 190 public promenades, 477 markets, 152 abattoirs, 120 monuments, two poor houses, 24 hospitals, 28 dispensaries and 44 clinics. In addition, 116 cities and towns had been electrified and 212 towns had been supplied with running water: Dragoslav P. Mihajlovic, *La Nouvelle Turquie Economique* (Belgrade, 1937), p.14.
25. Bozdoğan: *Modernism and Nation*, p.157–61.
26. Mardin (a): 'Religion and secularism', p.367.
27. Şerif Mardin (b), 'Religion and secularism in Turkey' in Ergun Özbudun and Ali Kazancıgil (eds), *Atatürk, Founder of a Modern State* (London, 1997), p.214.
28. Mardin (a): 'Religion and secularism', p.368.
29. *Ibid*, p.369.
30. İlhan Tekeli, *Türkiye'de Kentleşme Yazıları* (Ankara, 1982), pp.55–61.
31. *Bayındırlık Dergisi* (1950), p.154, cited in Malcolm D. Rivkin, *Area Development for National Growth* (New York, 1965), p.59.
32. Cemil Topuzlu, *Yarınki İstanbul* (Istanbul, 1937), p.6.
33. For detailed reading about the Village Institutions: M. Asım Karaömerlioğlu, 'The Village Institutes experience in Turkey', *British Journal of Middle Eastern Studies* 25/1 (1998), pp.47–73.
34. Bozdoğan: *Modernism and Nation*, pp.97–105. German agricultural colonies and model farms were used as successful examples for Turkish architects who prepared the ideal village projects for Turkish peasants. Site plans and photographs of the model German villages and model farms were presented in the journal *Arkitekt* in the 1930s. The authors of these articles mostly emphasised the importance and success of the German practices. Zeki Sayar, for example, argued that 'we, like the Germans, must give a great significance to science, specialisation and organisation' to create ideal Turkish villages: Zeki Sayar, 'İç kolonizasyon - Başka Memleketlerde', *Arkitekt* 8 (1936), pp.231–5.
35. For detailed reading: Asım Karaömerlioğlu, 'Türkiye'de köycülük' in İnsel (ed): *Modern Türkiye'de: Kemalizm*, pp.284–97 and 'The People's Houses and the cult of peasant in Turkey' in Sylvia Kedourie (ed), *Turkey Before and After Atatürk* (London, 1999), pp.67–91.
36. Aykut Kansu, 'Tek parti döneminde bir radikal muhafazakar politika mektebi olarak "Sosyal Siyaset"' in Çiğdem (ed): *Muhafazakarlık*, pp.622-31.
37. Ömer L. Barkan, *Türkiye'de Toprak Meselesi, Toplu Eserler I* (Istanbul, 1980), p.26 cited in Karaömerlioğlu: 'The People's Houses', p.73.
38. Nusret K. Köymen, 'Kemalizmin hususiyetleri', *Ülkü* 7/42 (1936), p.418.
39. Nusret K. Köymen, 'Köycülük esasları', *Ülkü* 4/20 (1934), pp.149–50.

40. Karaömerlioğlu: 'The People's Houses', p.76–7. See also: Nusret Köymen, 'Köy seferberliğine doğru', *Ülkü* 1/5 (1934), pp.355–61; Mehmet Saffet, 'Kültür inkılabımız', *Ülkü* 1/5 (1933), pp.351–4; Hilmi A. Malik, 'Kışla ve köy', *Ülkü* 1/3 (1933), pp.237–40; Mehmet Saffet, 'Köycülük nedir', *Ülkü* 1/6 (1933), pp.422–30.
41. Karaömerlioğlu: 'The People's Houses', p.76.
42. For detailed information about the selection of Ankara as the new capital city for Turkey: Gönül Tankut, *Bir Başkentin İmarı* (Istanbul, 1993), pp.44–9.
43. Lewis: *The Emergence*, p.261.
44. Bozdoğan: *Modernism and Nation*, p.68.
45. One of the visual characteristics of the new capital, as described by contemporaries in the 1930s, was the image of 'the city without minarets'. Ankara had not built a new mosque during the 27 years of Kemalist rule, and the Hacı Bayram Mosque, which is located in the old city, remained the sole mosque of the city until the 1950s. Although the construction of Maltepe Mosque under the Democrat Party regime in the 1950s was an important milestone in Ankara's architecture, the real break came with the construction of Kocatepe Mosque in 1987. Minarets have since become a dominant element of the city's skyline, together with Atatürk's mausoleum: Ahmad: *The Making of Modern Turkey*, pp.91–2.
46. Turkey reacted to the Great Depression by cutting its expenditure significantly between 1929 and 1934. The total expenditure in 1929 of TL 214.5 million was gradually reduced and became TL 173.6 million in 1934: Zvi Yehuda Hershlag, *Turkey the Challenge of Growth* (Leiden, 1968), p.61. By comparison, the combined funds allocated to the Office of Redevelopment and Ankara Municipality increased from TL 1.8 million in 1929 to TL 2.1 million in 1930 and TL 2.6 million in 1931. Although the total allocation was reduced to TL 1.7 million in 1932 and to TL 1.5 million in 1933, this figure again increased to TL 1.9 million in 1934: Tankut, *Bir Başkentin*, pp.232–7.
47. Professor J. Brix from the *Charlottenburg Technische Hoschule* in Germany, Leon Jausseley, the French government architect who graduated from the *École de Beaux Arts* in Paris and Herman Jansen, a Berlin based architect and professor who was a student of famous late-nineteenth century architectural theoretician Camillo Sitte, were invited to the urban design competition for Ankara. For detailed information: Tankut: *Bir Başkentin*, pp.66–81.
48. Zeynep Uludağ, 'Cumhuriyet Döneminde Rekreasyon ve Gençlik Parkı Örneği' in Yıldız Sey (ed), *75 Yılda Değişen Kent ve Mimarlık* (Istanbul, 1998), pp.73–4.
49. As in other nationalist regimes of the 1930s (for example Italy and Germany) being youthful and healthy were symbols of Republican culture. In contrast to the old, corrupted and unsound nature of the Ottoman Empire, the young and healthy face of the Republic was idealised by creating such public spaces. For detailed information about this symbolic spatial representation: Bozdoğan: *Modernism and Nation*, pp.75–9.
50. For the works of Western architects in Turkey during the early Republican period see: Bozdoğan: *Modernism and Nation*, pp.70–2; Sözen: *Cumhuriyet Dönemi*, pp.167–

74; Bülent Özer, *Rejyonalism Üniversalizm ve Çağdaş Mimarimiz Üzerine Bir Deneme* (Istanbul, 1970), pp.51–4.
51. The number of provinces in Turkey had changed constantly since the 1920s. Initially, there were 71 provinces. This figure became 74 in 1924, 63 in 1926, 57 in 1933, 62 in 1936, 63 in 1939, 66 in 1954 and 67 in 1957. Since then the number of provinces has increased gradually, and today a total of 81 administrative provinces are located in Turkey: Gökşen Kılınç and Nuran Z. Gülersoy, 'Türkiye'deki ilçelerin kentleşme derecelerine göre il olma potansiyellerinin değerlendirilmesi', *İTÜ Dergisi* 6/1 (March, 2007), p.72.
52. Çağlar Keyder, *Istanbul Between the Global and the Local* (Maryland, 1999), p.11.
53. Philip Mansel, *Constantinople, City of the World's Desire 1453-1924* (London, 1995), pp.416.
54. Zürcher: *Turkey,* p.167.
55. Istanbul was included within the first Five-Year Development Plan which was drawn up by the government on 9 January 1934 and began to operate in May 1934. For detailed information on the first and second Five-Year Development Plans see: Hershlag: *Turkey,* pp.80–2.
56. Cemil Topuzlu, *İstibdad-Meşrutiyet-Cumhuriyet Devirlerinde 80 Yıllık Hatıralarım* (Istanbul, 2002), p.221.
57. 'Ankara–Istanbul', *La Turquie Kemaliste* 47 (1943), pp.38–9, cited in Bozdoğan: *Modernism and Nation,* p.67.
58. Rivkin: *Area Development,* p.77.
59. Ahmad: *The Making,* p.91.

Chapter 4

1. Cemil Topuzlu, *Yarınki İstanbul* (Istanbul, 1937), p.40.
2. The government allocated TL 25,000 in its 1933 budget for the payment of the competitors. The related official correspondence being a letter from the minister for Internal Affairs dated 25 April 1933, a letter from the minister for Finance dated 27 April 1933, a letter of approval from the prime minister's office dated 30 April 1933 and the decree of the Cabinet chaired by Atatürk dated 30 April 1933. These are deposited in: the Prime Ministry Archives of the Turkish Republic (Republican Archives, Ankara), No. 14,300, File No. 243–130, Code: 30..18.1.2, Place No. 36.32..3.
3. Pierre Pinon argues that another French planner, Lamaresquier, was also invited to Istanbul but did not participate in the competition: 'Urban transformation between the 18th and 19th centuries', *Rassegna* 19/72 (1997), p.58.
4. For Agache's report in Turkish see: Alfred Agache, *Büyük İstanbul Tanzim ve İmar Programı* (Istanbul, 1934).
5. J. H. Lambert, *İ'mar Raporu* (Istanbul, 1934), p.104.
6. Herman Ehlgötz, *General Bebauung Plan Istanbul,* held in the Atatürk Library, Catalogue No. B.403; for his report in Turkish see: Herman Ehlgötz, *İstanbul Şehrinin Umumi Planı* (Istanbul, 1934).
7. For the subcommittee's report to the competition jury see: 'İstanbul şehir planı',

Arkitekt 2 (1935), pp.61–8.
8. His application was accompanied by a book and several preliminary design sketches. The originals of his submission, such as the covering letter in which he claimed that he had written to Atatürk, and other attached documents have not been found. However, the official correspondence in the Ministry of Foreign Affairs, Ministry of Interior Affairs and the Presidency of the Republic of Turkey disclose important hints about the contents of Le Corbusier's application. For the official correspondence between the Ministry of Foreign Affairs, Ministry of Interior Affairs and the Presidency see: Enis Kortan, *Le Corbusier Gözüyle Türk Mimarlık ve Şehirciliği* (Ankara, 1983), pp.93–6.
9. Şemsa Demiren, 'Le Corbusier ile mülâkat', *Arkitekt* 19/11–12 (1949), pp.230–1. Le Corbusier's view on this issue is also confirmed by Turgut Cansever in the author's interview with him in December 2001. Cansever claimed that in 1950 Le Corbusier, in his office in Paris, made a similar assessment about his application for a master plan of Istanbul.
10. Wagner's appointment as a consultant to the Municipality of Istanbul and his monthly salary of TL 800 was endorsed by the Cabinet on 28 February 1935. Prime Ministry Archives of Turkish Republic (Republican Archives, Ankara), No.: 20,732, File No.: 243–186, Code: 30..18.1.2, Place No.: 52.14..10.
11. 'Büyük şehirler nasıl tadil edilir?', 'Şehir inşaatında sermayenin rolü', 'Şehircilikte sermayenin yanlış idaresi', 'İnşa etmiyen millet yaşamıyor demektir', 'İstanbul nüfusunun yayılışı ve münakale', 'Cadde inşaası', 'İstanbul'un yol meselesi', 'Zelzele mıntıkası için düşünülmüş mukavim ev projeleri', 'İstanbul şehrinin düzeltilmesi meseleleri', 'İstanbulun seyrisefer meselesi', 'İstanbul'un nüfus meselesi' and 'İstanbul havalisinin plânı' were the titles of Wagner's articles published in *Arkitekt* between 1936 and 1937.
12. For the details of Wagner's proposal for Istanbul and its hinterland: Wagner, 'İstanbul havalisinin plânı', *Arkitekt* 10–11 (1936), pp.301–6 and 12 (1936) 333–7.
13. Burhan Arif, 'İstanbulun plânı', *Mimar* 3/5 (1933), pp.155, 160. Also see: Mimar Abidin, 'Memlekette Türk mimarının yarınki vaz'iyeti', *Mimar* 5 (1933), pp.129–30; Zeki Sayar, 'Yerli ve yabancı mimar', *Arkitekt* 8/2 (1938), p.65.
14. The offer was made to him while he was working on a small urban design scheme for Yalova, a small city located on the south-eastern shores of the Sea of Marmara. While it is widely believed that the work was offered to Prost on the personal invitation of Atatürk, no documents have been found to support this claim.
15. For detailed reading about Prost and his works see: *L'Œuvre de Henri Prost; Architecture et Urbanisme* (Paris, 1960).
16. For Prost's initial contract and its renewals see: Municipality of Istanbul, General Assembly Resolution, 16 May 1939, 18 April 1941 and 16 April 1945.
17. 1,500 ha for the Istanbul Peninsula, 1,400 ha for Galata and Beyoğlu districts and 2800 ha for the Asian side of the city including Üsküdar, Kadıköy and Suadiye districts: 'Revizyon Komisyonu Raporu', 28 February 1953 (unpublished typescript document provided by Aru from his personal archive); *7 Yıl İçinde*

Vilayet ve Belediyece Yapılan İşler 1949–1955 (Istanbul, 1956), p.36.
18. *Cumhuriyet Devrinde İstanbul* (Istanbul, 1949), p.13.
19. Prost stated that the municipality had well prepared maps on a scale of 1:2000 (including the terrains) and 1:500 and aerial photographs that could be used for the preparation of the master plan: Henri Prost, 'Note No. 6' in *İstanbul Hakkında Notlar* (Istanbul, 1938), p.16.
20. Henri Prost, *İstanbul Hakkında Notlar* (Istanbul, 1938).
21. For example, in a letter dated 29 June 1936 he explains his initial assessments and works and indicates the importance of cadastral city maps. Prost, 'Note C', 29 June 1936.
22. Municipality of Istanbul, General Assembly Resolution, 29 April 1938.
23. It should be noted that there is a difference between the approval dates of the master plan report and its maps. The report was approved on 30 June 1939. However, the approval stamp on the maps indicates that they were approved one month earlier than the report on 30 May 1939.
24. Henri Prost, 'İstanbulun nâzım plânını izah eden rapor', 15 October 1937. This report was also published in book form by the Municipality of Istanbul in 1938: *İstanbul Nâzım Plânını İzah Eden Rapor* (Istanbul, 1938). There are some minor discrepancies between the two versions. The report with the approval stamp is referred to in this book.
25. Prost: *İstanbulun Nâzım*, p.5.
26. *Ibid*, p.6–7.
27. *Ibid*, p.9.
28. The roads described in the master plan report were in multiples of three-metre-wide traffic lanes and the plan stipulated a minimum road width of nine metres, extending to 12 and 15 metres with a refuge dividing the lanes for roads wider than 15 metres. The total minimum width of major roads was 20 metres and the maximum 26 metres. Trees on the footpath were to be set back 1.5 metres from the kerb and five metres from the building line. The total width of the major road easements, including the footways and refuges, can be estimated as 39 metres: Prost: *İstanbulun Nâzım*, p.10.
29. Despite his negative attitude to railways, Prost proposed an international central railway terminus in Yenikapı because the existing station in Sirkeci could not be extended and, therefore, was only to be used for electrified suburban trains and other minor trains to service the Sarayburnu Port: Prost: *İstanbulun Nâzım*, p.3; Henri Prost, 'Note No. 4', 25 October 1936. Prost provided more detailed information about these railway stations in one of his later works: 'Note No. 241', 2 December 1941, pp.19–21.
30. Prost: *İstanbulun Nâzım*, p.9.
31. Although it was planned in 1930, due to limited economic resources the construction of Atatürk Bridge started in 1935 and finished in 1940.
32. While the works to open this large street recommended by Auric started in the late-Ottoman period, dare economic conditions during the First World War and the following years, the construction of the first section of this boulevard

could only be completed in 1925 at a cost of TL 160,000: *Yenileşen İstanbul: 1939 Başından 1947 Sonuna Kadar İstanbulda Neler Yapıldı?* (Istanbul 1947), p.14.
33. 'Cumhuriyet devrinde İstanbul Belediyesi ve Hususi İdaresi on senede ne yaptı?', *İstanbul Belediye Mecmuası* 109–10 (1933), p.15.
34. Osman Nuri Ergin, *İstanbul Şehri Rehberi* (Istanbul, 1934).
35. Prost: *İstanbulun Nâzım*, pp.13–6.
36. Henri Prost, 'Note No. 395', 27 July 1945, pp.1-2. Also see: Henri Prost, 'İstanbul' *Arkitekt* 5–6 (1948), p.111.
37. Prost: *İstanbulun Nâzım*, p.12.
38. Prost, 'Note No. 241', 2 December 1942.
39. Prost: *İstanbulun Nâzım*, p.16. For more detailed information about Prost's proposals in Eminönü and Süleymaniye districts: Prost, 'Note No. 219', 3 February 1942.
40. The construction of this road would require the demolition of the old British Embassy building in Tepebaşı. Prost also advised that if this demolition was not considered appropriate, a tunnel could be constructed to connect the upper and lower sections of the road: Prost: *İstanbulun Nâzım*, p.16.
41. *Ibid*, p.17.
42. *Ibid*, p.3. For Prost's assessments about the Golden Horn: Prost, 'Note No.7', (undated).
43. Prost, 'Note No. 11', 22 November 1936; 'Note No. 20', 10 August 1937.
44. Prost, 'Note No 16', 10 December 1936.
45. Prost, 'Note No. 241', 2 December 1942. See also: Prost: 'İstanbul', p.112.
46. This term was translated into the Turkish language as '*serbest sahalar*'.
47. Prost: *İstanbulun Nâzım,* pp.15, 18.
48. *Ibid*, p.4.
49. The road would follow the walls of Topkapı Palace and have a total of six traffic lanes (three in each direction) with a two-metre-wide separation refuge and all the buildings set back five metres from the kerb along a columned arcade. The southern end of the road terminated at a major roundabout servicing the Sirkeci Train Terminus and a proposed bus terminal. Access ways were provided through the palace walls to the ferryboat wharf in the east. For detailed information see: Prost, 'Note No. 168', *'Transformation de l'At Meidan en Application du Plan Directeur'*, 15 October 1940.
50. Prost's contract was renewed on 23 March 1938 to employ him during the implementation works of the master plan: Başvekalet Kararlar Dairesi Müdürlüğü, Karar No. 2/8449, 7 April 1938 is kept in: Prime Ministry Archives of the Turkish Republic (Republican Archives, Ankara), No.: 2/8449, File No.: 243-305, Code: 30..18.1.2, Place No.: 82.25..10. His contract was also renewed again for a period of three years by the government on 11 June 1940: Municipality of Istanbul, General Assembly Resolution, 18 April 1941.
51. For Prost's master plan for the Asian side of Istanbul: Henri Prost, *Anadolu Sahili Nazım Planını İzah Eden Rapor* (Istanbul, 1940); for the master plan for Büyükada: Henri Prost, *Büyükadayı Tanzim ve Güzelleştirme Plânını İzah Eden*

Rapordur (Istanbul, 1941); for the plan prepared for Eyüp district: *Nâzım Plân* (Istanbul, 1941).

52. Prost's first draft act for general planning controls and land use in Istanbul was dated 17 April 1937. He subsequently made amendments to the draft act in 1941 and 1943. However, neither this act nor the other legislative measures proposed by Prost were approved and remained only as draft documents. For Prost's legislative proposals see: Henri Prost, *İstanbul'un Tehavvülâtı II Mevzuat* (Istanbul, 1955).
53. The government had difficulty even making payments for Prost's works. The review of the related official correspondence shows that despite these difficulties, the government paid Prost a total of TL 24,000 for his works both in 1936 and 1937. The decrees issued by the Cabinet chaired by Atatürk on this decision dated 27 January and 11 November 1937 are kept in: Prime Ministry Archives of the Turkish Republic (Republican Archives, Ankara), No. 2/5913, Code: 30..18.1.2, Place No.: 71.6..20 and No. 2/7642, File No.: 127-19, Code: 30..18.1.2, Place No.: 80.92..10.
54. *Harp Yıllarında İstanbul'daki Faaliyetler, İstanbul Valisi ve Belediye Reisi Dr. Lûtfi Kırdar'ın Eylül 1945 Basın Toplantısındaki İzahatı* (İstanbul, 1945), p.3.
55. Municipality of Istanbul, General Assembly Decree, 14 May 1942.
56. Prost: *İstanbulun Nâzım*, p.8.
57. Prost's note dated 28 September 1948 cited in: Akif Bazoğlu, 'İstanbul imarında karşılaşılan güçlükler ve şikâyetler', *Arkitekt* 20/7–10 (1950), p.201.
58. *Ibid*, p.201.
59. The minutes of the Municipality of Istanbul's General Assembly meeting on 16 June 1947 clearly show that the implementation of Prost's plan for Eminönü, Divanyolu and Ankara Caddesi was not considered possible because of financial restrictions.
60. *Yenileşen İstanbul*, p.14.
61. The open-air theatre was planned for a 4,000 seating capacity at a cost of approximately TL 700,000. *Yenileşen İstanbul*, pp.41–2.
62. Henri Prost, 'İstanbul', *Arkitekt* 3-4 (1948), p.84.
63. As noted in Chapter 3, the *mahalle* was the core of social life in traditional Ottoman culture, and one of the aims of the Republican regime was to break traditional social relationships and destroying the power of the *imam* at the local level of the *mahalle*.
64. Martin Wagner, 'İstanbulun münakale tahlili,', *Arkitekt* 7/5-6 (1937), p.145.
65. Prost: *İstanbulun Nâzım*, p.7.
66. As noted in Chapter 3, peasantism had a wide currency among intellectuals and government officials in the late-1920s and 1930s. An indication of the influence of peasantist ideology in urban planning was the appointment of Dr Reşit Galip as a member of the jury that was established for the urban design competition for Ankara in 1928. Galip was among the founders of the Society of the Villagers and the minister for education in the early 1930s. While there is no direct evidence that Prost agreed with peasantist ideology, his failure to estimate

population growth in his plans clearly indicates that his approach was consistent with the overall policies of the government which took all measures to retain the existing social pattern of Turkey.
67. Turkey increased its army from 120,000 to 1.5 million during the Second World War. The share of the Ministry of Defence within the national budget was raised to 50–60 per cent and the official Cost of Living (C.o.L) Index went from 101.4 in 1939 to 416.2 in 1945. Non-governmental inquiries into C.o.L calculated an even sharper rise and it peaked at 600 in April 1943: Z.Y. Hershlag, *Turkey the Challenge of Growth* (Leiden, 1968), p.143.
68. Erik J. Zürcher, *Turkey; A Modern History* (London, 2004), pp.206–7; Feroz Ahmad, *The Turkish Experiment in Democracy 1950–1975* (London, 1977), p.8.
69. The Republican government carried out noteworthy achievements in the mechanisation of agriculture in the late 1920s and the number of tractors in Turkey reached 2,000 in 1931. Yet in the same year this proactive policy was abandoned because of a growing risk of unemployment in the villages. The policy remained unchanged until 1948, resulting in manually driven agriculture in Turkey: Hershlag: *Turkey*, pp.108–14.
70. *Ibid*, pp.133, 143.
71. Turkey's total energy capacity was 107,000 kilowatts in 1945. Of this, 83,000 kilowatts were used in three big cities only: Istanbul, Ankara and İzmir: M. W. Thornburg, G. Spry and G. Soule, *Turkey: An Economic Appraisal* (New York, 1949), p.133. For the number of villages that were electrified: 'Elektrik', *Türkiye 1923–1973 Ansiklopedisi*, vol.2, p.583.
72. After his novels were published in 1950, Makal was jailed on suspicion of Communism. His gaol term was discussed extensively in the press and, following a successful campaign in intellectual circles, he was released and returned to his teaching position in his village. His popularity earned him a public meeting with the newly elected Democrat Party prime minister and new president.
73. Zürcher: *Turkey*, p.206.
74. *Güzelleşen İstanbul* (Istanbul, 1943), no page number.
75. Zürcher: *Turkey*, p.207.
76. Hershlag: *Turkey*, pp.132–3; Kemal Karpat, *Turkey's Politics; The Transition to a Multi-party System* (Princeton, 1959), pp.91, 103.
77. For detailed information about the Capital Levy: *Varlık Vergisi Kanunu ve Bu Kanun Hükümlerinin Şerhi* (Istanbul, 1942). For its implementation and impact on society: Bernard Lewis, *The Emergence of Modern Turkey* (New York, 2002), pp.297–302; Karpat: *Turkey's Politics*, pp.114–17; Faik Ökte, *The Tragedy of the Turkish Capital Tax* (London, 1987).
78. Çağlar Keyder, *State and Class in Turkey: A Study in Capitalist Development* (London, 1987), p.113; Stanford J. Shaw and Ezel Kural Shaw, *History of the Ottoman Empire and Modern Turkey*, vol.2, *The Rise of Modern Turkey, 1808–1975* (Cambridge, 1977), pp.398–9.
79. Karpat: *Turkey's Politics*, pp.139–41. For detailed reading on Turkish foreign policy during WWII: Selim Deringil, *Turkish Foreign Policy During the Second World War:*

An 'Active' Neutrality (Cambridge, 2004), pp.178–9.
80. Ahmad: *The Turkish*, pp.9–10; Zürcher: *Turkey*, pp.208–9. For more detailed information: Deringil: *Turkish Foreign Policy*, pp.178–83.
81. For the original text of İnönü's speech: Kâzım Öztürk, *Cumhurbaşkanları'nın Türkiye Büyük Millet Meclisini Açış Nutukları* (Istanbul, 1969), p.379.
82. Adnan Menderes was born into a landowning family in Aydın in Western Anatolia in 1899. He attended the American College in İzmir, and continued his education at the School of Law in Ankara after he was elected to the National Assembly as the deputy of Aydın in 1931. He did not hold any important political position, with the exception of the RPP's chairmanship in his province, until he became prime minister after the 1950 elections.
83. The Independence Tribunals (*İstiklâl Mahkemeleri*) were special courts established in 1920 to conduct the trials of rebels during the national struggle. These special courts were re-activated between 1923 and 1925 to severely punish the enemies of the regime, and remained in the Turkish legal system until 1949.
84. For detailed reading on the emergence of the Democrat Party: Karpat: *Turkey's Politics*, pp.408–31; Ahmad: *The Turkish*, pp.35–76; Zürcher: *Turkey*, pp.206–18.
85. The elections were brought forward by the government with the aim of pushing the DP to enter the elections without being fully established in the country. More importantly, despite President İnönü's guarantees, the election was far from being fair due to electorate manipulation by the RPP. In many villages and provincial towns the constituents were overwhelmingly illiterate, which meant that deposit ballots had to be marked by state officials and RPP members. Also the voting system was organised to satisfy the ruling RPP's requirements, and the ballot was not secret. The elections were totally controlled by government officials instead of the judiciary and the ballots were counted by the police, gendarmes and RPP officials without any supervision by the opposition party. More importantly, as soon as the results were declared the ballots were destroyed making any check impossible: Zürcher: *Turkey*, p.212; Karpat: *Turkey's Politics*, pp.163–4.
86. *Ibid*, pp.163–4.
87. Hershlag: *Turkey*, p.144; Karpat: *Turkey's Politics*, pp.172–3.
88. Economic and military matters were not the only areas in which Turkey entered into special agreements with the United States. The Turkish government strengthened its relationship with the United States in all areas. For example, a Fulbright agreement for the exchange of scholars was signed between the government and the United States on 27 December 1949: *The Middle East Journal* 4 (1950), p.218.
89. Nihat Erim, the RPP's deputy prime minister, declared, 'If we are not involved in an external disaster, I am very hopeful for the future of the country. In the near future Turkey will become a Little America'. *Cumhuriyet*, 20 September 1949.
90. On 5 June 1947 the secretary of state of the United States, George C. Marshall, spoke at Harvard University and outlined what would become known as the Marshall Plan. This speech marked the official beginning of the Economic Recovery Program. Under the plan the United States provided aid to Europe

to prevent starvation in the major war areas, repair the devastation of those areas as quickly as possible, and begin economic reconstruction. The plan had two major objectives: to prevent the spread of communism in Western Europe and to stabilise the international order in a way favourable to the development of political democracy and free-market economies. For detailed reading and a bibliography about the Economic Recovery Program: *The European Reconstruction, 1948-1961: Bibliography on the Marshall Plan and the Organisation for European Economic Co-operation (OEEC)* (Paris, 1996).

91. The US funds diverted to Turkey between 1946 and 1950 reached around 3 per cent of GNP, allowing imports to increase by 270 per cent over the wartime average: Keyder: *State and Class*, p.119; 'Economic development and crisis: 1950–1980', in Irvin C. Schick and Ertuğrul A. Tonak (eds), *Turkey in Transition: New Perspectives* (New York, 1987), p.294; Hershlag: *Turkey*, pp.150–1.

92. The report drafted by the deputy commissioner, H. E. Hilts, stated that national roads be increased by 5,000 km and provincial routes by 30,000 km. It also suggested the establishment of a semi-autonomous Turkish highway department to carry out the programme. The report was very much appreciated by both the US and Turkish governments and the first works started in 1948 under the Turkish Department of Public Works: H. E. Hilts, 'The highway situation in Turkey: A report of the United States Public Roads Mission to Turkey to the Minister of Public Works of Turkey', Ankara, February 1948. For the Turkish road programme: Robert W. Kerwin, 'The Turkish roads program', *The Middle East Journal* 4 (1950), pp.196–208.

93. The full text of the Turkish–American Roads Agreement is given as Appendix D in the *Fourth Report to Congress on Assistance to Greece and Turkey*, Department of State (Washington, 1948).

94. The Republican government's transportation policy was oriented towards railways. The total railway network in 1923 was 4,086 kilometres and became 6,808 kilometres in 1938 and 7,295 kilometres in 1946: Hershlag: Turkey, pp.233–4. Between 1923 and 1939 the total public investment in road transportation was less than one third of the total investment in the construction of railways: Malcolm D. Rivkin, *Area Development for National Growth: Turkish Precedent* (New York, 1965), pp.63–4.

95. 'Turkey to ratify highway pact; U.S. experts to help in program', *The New York Times*, 17 January 1948. According to the agreement between the Turkish Ministry of Public Works and the Public Roads Group of the American Aid Mission, Turkey would have a total of 20,000 kilometres of all-weather roads, 25,000 kilometres of provincial roads and 100,000–150,000 kilometres of country roads. Five million dollars of the initial US$100 million of military aid granted in 1947 was allocated to the roads programme for the purchase of the essential modern road-making equipment. Subsequently, the United States Economic Cooperation Administration granted an additional US$5 million for the road programme for the financial year 1949-50.

96. The US military saw Turkey's single-track rail system as insufficient because it

could not provide the necessary military manoeuvrability against a Soviet attack. Moreover, it was also considered poor in terms of establishing an effective farm-to-market transportation network for Turkey's agricultural potential, which was vital for Western Europe after the Second World War: Rivkin: *Area Development*, p.105.
97. Doğan Kuban, *Kent ve Mimarlık Üzerine İstanbul Yazıları* (Istanbul, 1998), p.232; Aydın Boysan, 'Adnan Menderes belediyeciliği imar hareketi uygulama ve sonuçları', *Mimarist* 3 (2004), p.28; Burak Boysan, 'Politik hummanın silinmeyen izleri: Halkla ilişkiler stratejisi olarak İstanbul'un imarı', *İstanbul* 4 (1993), p.85.
98. Hershlag: *Turkey*, p.256. In parallel to the increase in machinery, the amount of land cultivated by tractors also increased rapidly. In 1948 the total area farmed by tractors was only 132,000 ha. This figure reached 1,244,000 ha in 1950: Ruşen Keleş, *Türkiye'de Şehirleşme Hareketleri 1927–1960* (Ankara, 1961), p.35.
99. The city's population within the municipal border was 860,558 in 1945. This figure reached 983,041 and 1,268,771 in 1950 and 1955 respectively. It should be noted that in the previous decade Istanbul's population increased by only 20 per cent, the original figure being 741,148 in 1935, reaching 860,558 in 1945: *İstanbul Şehri İstatistik Yıllığı, vol.12, 1953–57*, (Istanbul: 1958).
100. Rivkin: *Area Development*, p.55.
101. Zürcher: *Turkey*, p.214; Andrew Mango, *Atatürk* (London, 2001), p.530; Asım Karaömerlioğlu, 'Köy Enstitüleri' in Ahmet İnsel (ed), *Modern Türkiye'de Siyasi Düşünce: 2 Kemalizm* (Istanbul, 2002), pp.292-3; 'The Village Institutes experience in Turkey', *British Journal of Middle Eastern Studies* 25/1 (1998), pp.65–9.
102. Cemil Topuzlu was a councillor in the Municipal Assembly in 1948: Municipality of Istanbul, General Assembly Resolution, 4 June 1948.
103. Karpat: *Turkey's Politics*, pp.279–81; Binnaz Toprak, *Islam and Political Development in Turkey* (Leiden, 1981), pp.76–8.
104. Karpat: *Turkey's Politics*, pp.158–9.
105. *Ibid*, p.241.

Chapter 5

1. Arnold Leder, 'Party competition in rural Turkey: Agent of change or defender of traditional rule', *Middle Eastern Studies* 15/1 (January 1979), pp.84–6. The DP was also the first major party in modern Turkey whose leaders did not come from the military. One of the interesting characteristics of the DP was the very limited number of deputies in the assembly with a military background. After the 1950 elections the overall number of deputies with military backgrounds in the National Assembly became less than 3 per cent. Also five out of six defence ministers in the Democrat governments of the 1950s were non-military politicians. In contrast, all of the 11 defence ministers who served during the 27-year RPP period were ex-military officers: Nurşen Mazıcı, '27 Mayıs, Kemalizmin restorasyonu mu?' in Ahmet İnsel (ed), *Modern Türkiyede Siyasi Düşünce 2: Kemalizm* (Istanbul, 2002), p.556.
2. Kemal H. Karpat, *Turkey's Politics; The Transition to a Multi Party System* (New Jersey,

1959), p.166. The DP even received support from the illegal Communist Party during the 1950 elections: Çağlar Keyder, *State and Class in Turkey; A Study in Capitalist Development* (London, 1987), p.122.
3. Feroz Ahmad, *The Turkish Experiment in Democracy 1950–1975* (London, 1977), p.45.
4. Halûk Kılçık, *Adnan Menderes'in Konuşmaları-Demeçleri-Makaleleri: 9* (Ankara, 1992), pp.1–17 cited in Tanıl Bora, 'Adnan Menderes' in Murat Yılmaz (ed), *Modern Türkiyede Siyasi Düşünce 7: Liberalizm* (Istanbul, 2005), p.486.
5. The DP's candidates for the 1946 elections comprised: 52 lawyers, 41 landowners, 40 medical doctors, 39 businessmen, 15 retired generals, 14 engineers, 13 teachers and some other professionals. In contrast to the Democrat candidates' demographic plurality, the RPP candidates were mainly retired military personnel, known political figures and high government officials such as ex-governors, etc.: Karpat: *Turkey's Politics*, p.163; Erik J. Zürcher, *Turkey: A Modern History* (London, 2004), p.221.
6. Metin Toker, *Demokrasimizin İsmet Paşalı Yılları 1944–1973: DP'nin Altın Yılları 1950–1954* (Ankara, 1990), pp.26–7, 40–1.
7. The elites considered Menderes a provincial figure with limited capacity to understand and conduct the urban affairs of Istanbul. Doğan Kuban, for example, portrays this view vividly by linking Menderes' rural affiliations to his urban redevelopment projects and criticising him as follows: 'History's role in the urban vision of Anatolian provincials was limited and symbolic. It could be used for ideological purposes, but its cultural sense was limited': Doğan Kuban, *Kent ve Mimarlık Üzerine İstanbul Yazıları* (Istanbul, 1988), p.230.
8. Zürcher: *Turkey*, p.234.
9. Between 1948 and 1959 Turkey was granted a total of US$1,210 million in financial assistance as grants or long-term loans. The allocations decreased gradually from 1950 onwards but started to rise again after 1956, with the significant amount of US$359 million granted in 1958. In addition, Turkey was granted a total of US$60.2 million by the International Bank of Reconstruction and Development between 1956 and 1960. Z. Y. Hershlag, *Turkey the Challenge of Growth* (Leiden, 1968), p.150.
10. One of the most important indicators of this integration was Turkey's wish to join the North Atlantic Treaty Organisation (NATO). In order to qualify for full membership, Turkey sent its troops to Korea in 1950 and became a member of NATO in 1952. For detailed reading about Turkey's membership to NATO: Behçet K. Yeşilbursa, 'Turkey's participation in the Middle East Command and its admission to NATO, 1950–52', *Middle Eastern Studies*, 35/4 (October, 1999), pp.70–102.
11. Bayar used this phrase in the 1957 election campaign: 'In our country we work following the stages of American progress. We are so hopeful that after 30 years this auspicious country will become a little America with a population of 50 million'. *Zafer*, 21 October 1957, cited and translated in Ahmad: *The Turkish Experiment*, note 60, p.71.

12. Sabri Sayarı, 'Adnan Menderes; between democratic and authoritarian populism' in Metin Heper and Sabri Sayarı (eds) *Political Leaders and Democracy in Turkey* (2002), p.70; Zürcher: *Turkey*, p.224.
13. Zürcher: p.224.
14. The proportion of the total land cultivated by tractors within the total cultivated area also increased dramatically during the Democrat period. In 1950, for example, only 1,244,000 ha were farmed by machinery. This figure reached 3,310,000 ha in 1957: Ruşen Keleş, *Türkiyede Şehirleşme Hareketleri 1927-1960* (Ankara, 1961) p.35.
15. Hershlag: *Turkey*, p.356.
16. Malcolm D. Rivkin, *Area Development for National Growth; The Turkish Precedent* (New York, 1965), p.97; Feroz Ahmad, *The Making of Modern Turkey* (New York, 2000), p.116; In 1949 Turkey imported 120,000 tons of cereals. In 1953 it had a capacity to export around 2,000,000 tons of cereals: 'U.S. economic aid helps Turks arm', *The New York Times*, 5 January 1953.
17. Hershlag: *Turkey*, p.366.
18. Rivkin: *Area Development*, pp.110, 113.
19. Kemal H. Karpat, 'Political developments in Turkey, 1950–70', *Middle Eastern Studies* 8/3 (October, 1972), p.354.
20. Edwin J. Cohn, T*urkish Economic Social and Political Change; the Development of a More Prosperous and Open Society* (New York, 1970), p.173; Hershlag: *Turkey*, p.363.
21. Hershlag: *Turkey*, p.173.
22. Prime Ministry State Institute of Statistics Turkey, Census of Population, 20 October 1985, p.XXII.
23. Hershlag: *Turkey*, p.375. Karpat gives the total number of newspapers 131 in 1950 and 560 in 1960: Karpat: 'Political developments', p.355
24. Karpat: 'Political developments', p.355.
25. The strict secular policies of the 1930s and 1940s were mostly accepted in intellectual circles. Their impact on small towns and villages, however, was almost non-existent as the vast majority of the population could retain the Islamic identity despite the government's increased antagonism to Islamic tradition: Karpat: *Turkey's Politics*, p.271.
26. Karpat: 'Political developments', p.353.
27. It should be noted that despite the bill to lift the ban on Arabic *ezan* (call for prayer) being proposed by DP representatives at the Grand National Assembly, the RPP did not oppose this proposal and voted for the amendment of the *Ezan* Act. For wider reading about the DP and the issue of secularism see: Binnaz Toprak, *Islam and Political Development in Turkey* (Leiden, 1981), pp.79–90; Ahmad: *The Turkish Experiment*, pp.365–373.
28. Karpat: *Turkey's Politics*, p.419.
29. The DP received 58 per cent of the total votes—a result that no other political party has achieved in the history of Turkish politics.
30. *Havadis*, 27 February 1957.
31. Tekeli provides the general feeling among the elites and bureaucrats about the relocation of the capital from Istanbul to Ankara: İlhan Tekeli, *Türkiye'de Kentleşme*

Yazıları (Ankara, 1982), p.54.
32. The eminent Turkish poet, Yahya Kemal, vividly expressed the common view of Ankara in the following succinct statement when he was asked 'What do you like best about Ankara?' Kemal responded, 'Returning to Istanbul'.
33. Mükerrem Sarol, a medical doctor and one of Menderes' closest friends since his very early days in politics, writes in his memoirs that all Menderes' friends encouraged him to participate in the elections from Istanbul as it was the most important city of Turkey. Sarol recounts, 'We cannot compare Istanbul with the other 67 provinces of the country. As well as its natural beauties, it is Turkey's most important gate to the West; press, universities, large labour populations, industry, culture, history and, in brief, all other things are located in this city. In my opinion you should be elected from Istanbul, and should enter the National Assembly from this major gate'. Mükerrem Sarol, *Bilinmeyen Menderes I* (Istanbul, 1983), p.109.
34. A Turkish traditional saying for elderly people who want to celebrate a younger person.
35. Memoirs of Aydın Menderes, youngest son of Adnan Menderes, cited in: Mehmet Ali Birand, Can Dündar and Bülent Çaplı, *Demirkırat: Bir Demokrasinin Doğuşu* (Istanbul, 2007), p.46.
36. Cited in Burak Boysan, 'Politik hummanın silinmeyen izleri: Halkla ilişkiler stratejisi olarak İstanbul'un imarı', *İstanbul* 4 (1993), p.84.
37. *Cumhuriyet*, 28 August 1950.
38. Despite Ağaoğlu's promise, Istanbul continued to have an appointed governor and mayor for a long period until March 1957 when the two offices were separated and mayors began to be elected by city dwellers.
39. For the DP's municipal programme for Istanbul see: 'Seçimler ve İstanbulun vaziyeti', *Cumhuriyet*, 28 August 1950.
40. Before Prost was discussed in the Municipal Assembly, there were many articles published in daily newspapers about this issue. Cemil Topuzlu, Muhiddin Üstündağ and Lütfi Kırdar, former mayors of Istanbul, blamed the previous governments and municipal administrations because of the lack of legislative support and inadequate financial assistance. They did not support the removal of Prost: *Cumhuriyet* 5 and 27 December 1950.
41. Municipality of Istanbul, General Assembly Records, 5 December 1950, pp.4–5.
42. Municipality of Istanbul, General Assembly Records, 26 December 1950, pp.7, 12–3.
43. *Ibid*, p.16.
44. *Ibid*, p.7. The debates about the land in Taşlık were extensively published in the Turkish press: *Cumhuriyet* 21, 22 & 24, November 1950 and 27 December 1950.
45. Municipality of Istanbul, General Assembly Records, 26 December 1950, pp.7, 12–13, 15.
46. Municipality of Istanbul, General Assembly Records, p.12.
47. The assembly members also considered that State officials and politicians, rather than Prost, should have been asked these questions. Saim Nuri Uyar, a councillor

of the Municipality of Istanbul, claimed in the meeting that under the monoparty mentality there was no chance to do anything else. He argued that Prost completed his tasks in accordance with the terms of his contract, and requested that the assembly renew Prost's contract for one more year. Similarly, Recep Bilginer, another councillor, argued that as 60 per cent of the application plans were made by people other than Prost, the assembly should have questioned the people who had ignored Prost's reports and recommendations: Municipality of Istanbul, General Assembly Records, 26 December 1950, pp.11–12.

48. Municipality of Istanbul, General Assembly Records, 26 December 1950, pp.8–9.
49. *İl ve Şehirde Geçen Yılda Neler Yapıldı ve Bu Yıl Neler Yapılıyor 1950–1951* (Istanbul, 1951), pp.45–7.
50. *Cumhuriyet*, 19 December 1950.
51. Municipality of Istanbul, General Assembly Records, 26 December 1950, pp.9–10. Also see: 'Prost'un mukavelesinin uzatılmaması kararlaştı', *Cumhuriyet*, 27 December 1950.
52. Municipality of Istanbul, General Assembly Records, 26 December 1950, p.16.
53. Although information about the congress, including its organising committee, strategy and working programme, was found, confirmation of whether the congress was organised as scheduled in 1952 is not possible. For detailed information about the preparation for the congress see: *1952 İstanbul Bölge Kalkınma Kongresi* (Istanbul, 1951).
54. The establishment of the Revision Commission was discussed by the Municipal Assembly of Istanbul at its meeting on 27 February and 15 March 1951: Municipality of Istanbul, General Assembly Records, 27 February and Municipality of Istanbul, General Assembly Resolution, 15 March 1951.
55. 'Revizyon Komisyonu Raporu—H. Prost'un İstanbul şehri için tanzim ettiği imar planlarını tetkik etmek üzere kurulmuş bulunan heyet tarafından hazırlanmıştır' Istanbul, 1954, p.3.
56. *Ibid*, pp.4–22.
57. *Ibid*, pp.22–24.
58. Unpublished typescript reports written to the governor and mayor of Istanbul: 'Altı Aylık İmar Planı Çalışmaları Hakkında Rapor', 28 February 1953; and 'İmar Planı Çalışmaları Hakkında', June 1953. These reports were taken from Kemal Ahmet Aru's personal archives.
59. Patrick Abercrombie, 'İstanbul: Halen hazırlanmakta olan nazım planlardaki teklifler ve metodlar hakkında muvakkat rapor', 26 April 1954, unpublished typscript manuscript from Kemal Ahmet Aru's personal archive.
60. The plan for Beyoğlu District was prepared at 1:5,000 scale, comprising an area of 3,400 ha. The plan covered the whole European section of the city to the north of the Golden Horn. The total population within the boundaries of this area was 347,488 in 1952. In addition to the general plan, detailed implementation plans were also prepared at 1:500 scale. The plan was first endorsed by the Municipal Assembly and then approved by the Department of Public Works on 17 February

1954: *İstanbul İmar Plânı İzah Raporları: I. Beyoğlu Ciheti* (Istanbul, 1954).
61. The plan covered the total area of 6,625 ha (the Istanbul Peninsula and Bakırköy and Eyüp districts). The total population was 582,276 in 1955. The plan estimated its future population as 1,081,080, and was accompanied by a detailed industrial plan for the areas of the Golden Horn and the coastal belt between Yedikule and Bakırköy: *İstanbul İmar Plânı İzah Raporları: 2. İstanbul Ciheti* (Istanbul, 1956).
62. The appendices of the master plan report show that the Municipality of Istanbul forwarded the draft master plan to various public and private agencies for their comments. These agencies included State Maritime Lines, State Railways, the Maritime Bank, İ.E.T.T (Istanbul Electric, Tramway and Tunnel Corporation), the Chamber of Commerce and the Chamber of Industry: *İstanbul İmar Plânı İzah Raporları: 2. İstanbul Ciheti*, pp.19–38.
63. The industrial sites in the Golden Horn region became a controversial issue during the preparation of the master plan. Despite the municipality's wishes to exclude the Golden Horn from industrial activities, this idea was not favoured by the Department of Public Works, Chamber of Commerce and Chamber of Industry and the plan was therefore amended to keep the existing industrial sites in situ alongside the Golden Horn: Municipality of Istanbul, General Assembly Resolutions, 31 March and 13 July 1955; for the responses of the Department of Public Works: Bayındırlık Vekaleti, Yapı ve İmar İşleri Reisliği Yazıları, 28 May and 12 November 1955, cited in *İstanbul İmar Plânı İzah Raporları: 2. İstanbul Ciheti*, pp.19–38.
64. A comprehensive transportation plan for Istanbul was prepared by a French consultancy team in 1952. This project was prepared by Marc Langevin, the director of the Paris Railway Company, and Louis Meizonnet, the chief engineer of Parisian Autonomous Transportation. It included plans, buses, trams and underground railways: M. Langevin and L. Meizonnet, 'Etude des transports d'Istanbul', unpublished typescript report, September 1952.
65. For a detailed review of the urban works that were carried out between 1950 and 1953: *1950–1953 İl ve Şehir Hizmetlerinden: İstanbulun İmarı*, (Istanbul, c.1953).

Chapter 6

1. *Havadis*, 27 February 1957.
2. Samet Ağaoğlu, *Arkadaşım Menderes* (Istanbul, 1967), p42.
3. In August 1958 the government made a large devaluation, and as a result the purchasing power of the Turkish lira decreased from 2.80 to 9.025 against the US dollar. For detailed reading about the economic problems: Z. Y. Hershlag, *Turkey: the Challenge of Growth* (Leiden, 1968), pp.144–9 and pp.178–84. For a summary of the general economic situation in the period: Feroz Ahmad, *The Turkish Experiment in Democracy 1950–1975* (London, 1977), pp.138–9.
4. Kemal H. Karpat, 'Political developments in Turkey, 1950–70', *Middle Eastern Studies* 8/3 (October, 1972), p.356.
5. *Ibid*, pp.354–5.

6. Şerif Mardin (a), 'Religion and secularism in Turkey' in Albert Hourani, Phillip Khoury and Mary C. Wilson (eds), *The Modern Middle East* (London, 2004), p.372; Erik J. Zürcher, *Turkey; A Modern History* (London, 2004), pp.232–4.
7. The cases opened against the Democrat government in historical order are: The Dog Case, 6–7 September Incidents Case, The Baby Case, Vinileks Co. Case, Fraud Case, Vacant Lots Case, Ali Ipar Case, The Mills Case, The Barbara Case, The Secret Payments Case, The Radio Case, The Topkapı Incident Case, The Çanakkale Incident Case, The Kayseri Incident Case, The Democrat İzmir Case, The University Incidents Case, The Expropriation Case, The National Front Case and The Subversion of Constitution Case.
8. Following the military coup, Menderes, Zorlu and Polatkan became the 'martyrs of democracy'. Their remains were exhumed and transferred to new mausoleums in Istanbul with an official state ceremony in 1990. Since then, many streets, parks and public spaces, including the former Vatan Street, the international airport in Izmir and a university in Aydın, home city of the former prime minister, have been named after Menderes.
9. The governors and mayors who were accused of misconducting their duties were: Kemal Hadımlı (12 July – 5 October 1957), Mümtaz Tarhan (25 November 1957 – 17 May 1958), Ethem Yetkiner (17 May – 11 July 1958) and Kemal Aygün (11 June 1958 – 27 May 1960). The other defendants were Dilâver Argun, Emin Kalafat, Medenî Berk, Hayrettin Erkmen and Halûk Şaman: The Verdicts of the Case of Corrupt Expropriation, Section No. 17, Case No 961/8, p.11.
10. The Verdicts of the Case of Corrupt Expropriation, pp.1, 45–6.
11. Records of the Case of Corrupt Expropriation, p.362; The Verdicts of the Case of Corrupt Expropriation, p.31.
12. The chief prosecutor opened this case on the basis of Section 1 of Article 146 of the Turkish Penal Code—an offence to attempt to alter the Constitution by force or forcibly silencing the National Assembly. Although Menderes and the other two defendants were found guilty, the court did not apply a special penalty as it amalgamated the results of this case with the other cases in which the prime minister and others were charged with similar offences: The Verdicts of the Case of Corrupt Expropriation, pp.43–5.
13. Author's interviews with Burhan Apaydın and Talat Asal, Menderes' legal defenders in the Yassıada trials, Istanbul, October 2003.
14. Nedim (1681–1730) was one of the greatest lyric poets of Ottoman Turkish literature. He lived and wrote his famous poems during the Tulip Era. His poems reflect the social and cultural atmosphere of the Tulip Era.
15. Records of the Case of Corrupt Expropriation, 5 May 1961 at 9:10 am, pp.349–62.
16. The trials were held under extraordinary conditions. In many cases the accused were not allowed to speak with their legal representatives or to see the files before the trials. The press was used to create a negative atmosphere against the Democrat administration. Immediately following the coup, newspapers published fabricated front pages with sensational headlines such as, 'The

university students [under the Democratic administration] were killed and their bodies minced in the depots of the State Meat and Fish Corporation' or 'They [the DP] were going to sell Kars and Ardahan [two border provinces in Eastern Turkey] to Russia'. One of the most vivid demonstrations of the unfairness of the trials can be found in the answer of the chief judge of the court, Salim Başol, to one of Menderes' objections to an accusation against him during the trial: 'The power invested in me wants it this way': author's interviews with Apaydın and Asal, Istanbul, October 2003.

17. *İstanbul Şehri İstatistik Yıllığı, vol.12, 1953–57*, (Istanbul: 1958), p.10.
18. In 1952 there were 3,703 private motorcars, 322 buses, 3,213 trucks and pick-ups, 724 motorcycles and 4,251 taxis in Istanbul: M. Langevin and L. Meizonnet, Etude des Transports d'Istanbul, unpublished typescript report, September 1952, p.8. The total number of the motor vehicles (expect for the military vehicles) reached 20,868 in 1955: *İstanbul Vali ve Belediye Reisi Ord. Prof. Dr. F. K. Gökay'ın 1956–1957 Konuşmaları* (Istanbul, 1958), p.17. Çağlar Keyder also estimates the total number of motor vehicles in Istanbul to be 17,000 in 1955 and 35,000 in 1960: 'A tale of two neighbourhoods' in Çağlar Keyder (ed), *Istanbul Between the Global and the Local* (Lanham, 1999), p.175.
19. Ertuğrul Menteşe, 'İstanbul'un seyrüseferi ve metronun faydaları', *Arkitekt* 23/3–6 (1954), p.94.
20. İlhan Tekeli, 'Dolmuş', *Dünden Bugüne İstanbul Ansiklopedisi*, vol.3, pp.97–8.
21. *Akşam*, 24 September 1956; *Hürriyet* and *Cumhuriyet*, 24 September 1956; and *İstanbul Ekpres*, 23 September 1956.
22. The early postwar period saw the mass production of motorcars. Many studies were undertaken in cities around the world to plan and build roads for this form of transport. An example is: Fox, W. Smith and Associates, *London Transportation Study; Phase III*, vol.4 (London, 1968).
23. *Akşam*, 24 September 1956; *Hürriyet* and *Cumhuriyet*, 24 September 1956; and *İstanbul Ekpres*, 23 September 1956.
24. *Istanbul Expres*, 5 and 23 September 1956; *Cumhuriyet*, 29 September 1956; *Akşam*, 23 September 1956
25. Şevket Rado, 'İstanbul'a hala güzel diyebilmek için', *Akşam*, 25 September 1956.
26. Şevket Rado, 'Bütün güzelliğiyle Süleymaniye', *Akşam*, 26 September 1956.
27. Metin Toker, *Demokrasimizin İsmet Paşalı Yılları 1944–1973: DP'nin Altın Yılları 1950–1954* (Ankara, 1990), p230.
28. Zeki Sayar, 'İstanbul'un imârı münasebetiyle', *Arkitekt* 25/284 (1956), p.49.
29. Following the coupe d'état, the National Union Committee established a commission to oversee the preparation of a new constitution by university professors. Onar was appointed as the head of this committee, and he played an important role in the political developments that occurred after the coup.
30. This term has a special meaning in Turkish historiography and refers to the destruction of the Janissaries by Sultan Mahmud II in a bloody massacre on 15–17 June 1826. Later this term became a general colloquialism to describe events or phenomena that are benevolent to the general public.

31. Sıddık S., Onar, 'Mahalli ademi merkeziyet prensibi ve imar işleri', *Cumhuriyet*, 2 July 1957.
32. The total money spent under Republican governments between 1923 and 1949 was TL 19,987,333. This figure increased sharply and reached TL 86,807,787 during the first seven years of the DP administration: *İstanbul'un Kitabı* (Istanbul, c. 1957), p.28.
33. The total money spent on the expropriations during the Republican period (1923–50) was TL 25,845,246. The money spent on expropriations was dramatically increased between 1950 and 1957 and reached TL 335,464,245: *İstanbul'un Kitabı* (Istanbul, c. 1957), p.127. The draft budget for 1958 shows the figure for expropriations and redevelopment works as TL 150 million: Municipality of Istanbul, General Assembly Records, 4 February 1958, pp.4–6.
34. Records of the Case of Corrupt Expropriation, 17 April 1961; The Verdicts of the Case of Corrupt Expropriation, pp.16–31.
35. Records of the Case of Corrupt Expropriation, pp.14–18.
36. İlhan Tekeli, 'İcabında plan' *İstanbul* 4 (1993), p.33; Doğan Kuban, *İstanbul; An Urban History; Byzantion, Constantinopolis, Istanbul* (Istanbul, 1996), pp.430–1.
37. 'Başbakanın aylık basın toplantısı', *İETT Dergisi* 6 (March 1957), p.8.
38. Records of the Case of Corrupt Expropriation, pp.13–14.
39. *İstanbul'un Kitabı*, p.128.
40. Records of the Case of Corrupt Expropriation, p.24.
41. Only 101 of the 317 properties which were subject to the prosecutor's claim of inappropriate expropriations in the Yassıada trial were buildings, with the remainder being either vacant or redundant sites. The official records of the Municipality's Assembly also show that a total of 4,131 properties was expropriated in 1956 and 1957. And according to these records, 2,900 out of the 4,131 properties were buildings while the rest were vacant lands: Municipality of Istanbul, General Assembly Records, 4 February 1958, p.9.
42. *İstanbul'un Kitabı*, pp.59–60.
43. Mükerrem Sarol wrote in his memoirs about Menderes' extensive residences in Istanbul in order to personally conduct the urban redevelopment programme and reports how these residences became a conspicuous matter, even within his party: Mükerrem Sarol, *Bilinmeyen Menderes II* (Istanbul, 1983), pp.726, 739.
44. While his continuous interest in the redevelopment of Istanbul during his trips abroad was extensively voiced during the Yassıada trials, Menderes in his testimony stated that this matter was exaggerated, as his involvement in planning works while abroad occurred only once when he wanted to find out up-to-date information about the Beyazıt–Laleli Road due to the forthcoming winter: Records of the Case of Corrupt Expropriation, p.229. Menderes' directives from abroad were also mentioned at various times during the trials: *Ibid*: pp.44, 47.
45. Mükerrem Sarol, *Bilinmeyen Menderes I* (Istanbul, 1983), pp.304–5.
46. Author's interviews with Aru and Cansever, Istanbul, December 2001.
47. Ağaoğlu: *Arkadaşım*, pp.41–2.
48. Author's interviews with Cansever, Istanbul, December 2001.

49. These stories have always been told in academic lectures, professional meetings and symposiums regarding the redevelopment of Istanbul under the DP administration.
50. Records of the Case of Corrupt Expropriation, p.176.
51. 'Benevolent bomber', *Time*, 12 August 1957, pp.22–3.
52. Doğan Kuban, *Kent ve Mimarlık Üzerine İstanbul Yazıları* (Istanbul, 1998), p.231.
53. Burak Boysan, 'Politik hummanın silinmeyen izleri: Halkla ilişkiler stratejisi olarak İstanbul'un imarı', *İstanbul* 4 (1993), p.86. Author's interviews with Aru and Cansever, Istanbul, December 2001.
54. Boysan: 'Politik hummanın', pp.84–6; Tekeli: 'İcabında plan', p.33; Kuban: *Istanbul*, p.425; author's interviews with Aru and Cansever, Istanbul, December 2001. It should also be noted that such criticisms are not limited to pro-Atatürk scholars and writers but are shared by some Islamist writers as well, for example: Abdurrahman Dilipak, *Menderes Dönemi* (Istanbul, 1990), p.217.
55. Boysan: 'Politik hummanın', pp.84–5; Tekeli: 'İcabında plan', p.33; Kuban: *Istanbul*, p.426; author's interviews with Aru and Cansever in December 2001. The participation of Emin Onat, a professor in architecture at Istanbul Technical University, in Menderes' urban redevelopment programme has always been whispered about in academic circles. It is claimed that he was the 'man behind the curtain' and encouraged Menderes to carry out the demolitions and construction of new roads. It is also avowed that Onat supported the prime minister by saying, 'You are the greatest architect and urban planner of the world'.
56. Records of the Case of Corrupt Expropriation, pp.350–1.
57. *Ibid*, p.351.
58. *Ibid*, p.351.
59. *Ibid*, p.387–8.
60. *Ibid*, p.394.
61. *Ibid*, p.394.
62. Tekeli: 'İcabında plan', p.33; Boysan: 'Politik hummanın', p.88; Kuban: *Istanbul*, p.425.
63. Akpınar: 'The rebuilding', pp.178, 193, 243–4.
64. Boysan: 'Politik hummanın', p.88.
65. Zeki Sayar, 'İstanbul'un imârında şehirci mimarın rolü', *Arkitekt* 25/285 (1956), pp.97–8.
66. Zeki Sayar, 'İstanbulun imarı hakkında düşünceler!', *Arkitekt* 26/286 (1957), p.3, 11. Sayar also published several other articles criticising the urban redevelopment of Istanbul: 'İstanbul'un imârında şehirci mimarın rolü', *Arkitekt* 25/285 (1956) pp.97–8; 'İmar ve eski eserler', *Arkitekt* 26/287 (1957), pp.49–50; 'Beyazıt Meydanından alacağımız ders!', *Arkitekt* 27/291 (1958), pp.53–4.
67. 'Başbakanın Aylık Basın Toplantısı', p.8.
68. Records of the Case of Corrupt Expropriation, p.350.
69. *Ibid*, pp.359–360.
70. Governor and mayor, Gökay, proposed to give an honorary mayorship and coat of arms of Istanbul to Menderes at the Municipality of Istanbul's Assembly

meeting on 1 June 1957. He thanked the Assembly for its support for the redevelopment of Istanbul and, in particular, for the Assembly's encouragement of the construction of a social centre in Florya, the construction of Municipal Palace and the demolitions in Balıkpazarı and Eminönü. He also thanked the Assembly for its endorsement of the increase in the municipal budget from TL 186 million to TL 206 million. The Assembly unanimously accepted his offer and Gökay sent a telegram to the prime minister who was in Tehran at that time: Municipality of Istanbul, General Assembly Records, 1 June 1957, pp.4–5. The honorary mayorship, however, was conferred to Menderes by the new governor, Tarhan, after Gökay's dismissal on 20 March 1958: *Havadis*, 21 March 1958.

71. The Verdicts of the Case of Corrupt Expropriation, p.25.
72. Statements made by other defendants: Mümtaz Tarhan, Hayrettin Erkmen (minister for Working Affairs), Emin Kalafat (deputy prime minister), Halûk Şaman (minister for Working Affairs), Medeni Berk (deputy prime minister), Records of the Case of Corrupt Expropriation, p. 360. Statements made by witnesses: Sedat Erkoğlu (deputy mayor), Mümtaz Naymen (head auditor, Istanbul Governorship), Fahri Cintel (deputy mayor), Akif Göksel (assistant director, Public Works Division, Municipality of Istanbul), İsmail Tamçelik (director, Finance Division, Municipality of Istanbul), Kemal Erpat (assistant director, Urban Redevelopment and Expropriation Division, Municipality of Istanbul) and Fahri Paksoy (director, Urban Redevelopment and Expropriation Division, Municipality of Istanbul), The Verdicts of the Case of Corrupt Expropriation, pp.17–24.
73. Mithat Niyazi Resnelioğlu, an engineer who worked for the Municipality Istanbul for a limited period in 1959, criticised the technical aspects of the urban redevelopment works and claimed that as there were no adequately prepared and updated implementation plans, it was difficult to carry out calculations and determine the proposed routes: Records of the Case of Corrupt Expropriation, pp.338–46.
74. Records of the Case of Corrupt Expropriation, pp.385–8.
75. *Ibid*, pp.388–9, 393.
76. Governor and mayor, Gökay, mentioned the municipality's works in almost all his speeches and press conferences between 1951 and 1955. He particularly emphasised the work of the Board of Advisors to promote the municipality's preparation of the urban renewal programme: *İstanbul Vali ve Belediye Reisi Ord. Prof. Dr. F. K. Gökay'ın 1951–1955 Konuşmaları* (Istanbul: 1957), pp.43, 83, 106, 122, 154, 175, 197–8 and 234–35.
77. Ertuğrul Menteşe, 'İstanbulun imarı', *Arkitekt* 24/279 (1955), pp.27–38.
78. Nuran Zeren, Türkiye'de tarihsel değerlerin korunmasında uygulanmakta olan yöntem çerçevesinde uygulayıcı kuruluşların görüşlerine dayanan bir araştırma, unpublished PhD thesis, İstanbul Teknik Üniversitesi, 1981, pp.35–6.
79. *İstanbul Ekspres*, 23 September 1956. Municipality's initial contact with Högg also mentioned in *İstanbul Vali ve Belediye Reisi Ord. Prof. Dr. F. K. Gökay'ın 1956–1957 Konuşmaları*, pp.102, 106.

80. Municipality of Istanbul, General Assembly Resolution, 956/186, 16 October 1956.
81. The Municipality of Istanbul's Assembly discussed and decided on the appointment of a foreign expert at its meeting on 22 November 1956. An office at Levels 2 and 3, Divanyolu Caddesi, Işık Sokak No. 12–14 was rented for his team: Municipality of Istanbul, General Assembly Records, 1 March 1957, p.6. The Assembly's records show that a total of 60 architects and engineers were working for the Planning and Redevelopment Bureau of the Municipality of Istanbul: Municipality of Istanbul, General Assembly Records, 28 February 1957, p.9.
82. *Cumhuriyet*, 15 January 1957.
83. Hans Högg, 'Istanbul, Ausschnitte aus der Stadterneuerung', *Baumeister* 58/1 (1961), pp.33–52.
84. It is noteworthy that like Prost, Piccinato had planning experience in North African Muslim cities under Italian mandate. For Piccinato's experience in Muslim cities see: Ruben A. Bianchi, 'The work of Luigi Piccinato in Islamic countries 1925–1981', *Environmental Design* (1990), pp.184–91. Piccinato was initially invited to prepare the plans for residential development in the Baruthane district, and he came to Istanbul in early January 1957. His arrival was celebrated in the Turkish press and many articles were published about his proposals. See: *Havadis*,7 January, 9 January and 5 March 1957.
85. Prime Ministry Archives of Turkish Republic (Republican Archives, Ankara), File No.: A4, Code: 30..1.0.0, Place No.: 6.32..10., 18 &19 January 1957.
86. *Havadis*, 9 January 1957.
87. For details of the Bosphorus Bridge project: Prime Ministry Archives of the Turkish Republic (Republican Archives, Ankara), File No.: E8, Code: 30..1.0.0, Place No.: 74.471..7; File No.: E8, Code: 30..1.0.0, Place No.: 74.471..11; File No.: E8, Code: 30..1.0.0, Place No.: 74.473..1; File No.: E8, Code: 30..1.0.0, Place No.: 74.473..10; File No.: A4, Code: 30..1.0.0, Place No.: 7.36..30.
88. Municipality of Istanbul, General Assembly Records, 4 June 1957, pp.4–8.
89. Republic of Turkey, High Council of Immovable Heritage Items and Monuments Resolution No. 29, 8 July 1952.
90. Republic of Turkey, High Council of Immovable Heritage Items and Monuments Resolution No. 413, 22 July 1955.
91. The letters of objections made by the Chamber of Architects, the Turkish Historical Society and The Society of the Preservation of Monuments have been found in the archives of the Republic of Turkey, High Council of Immovable Heritage Items and Monuments.
92. Republic of Turkey, High Council of Immovable Heritage Items and Monuments Resolution No. 514, 17 July 1956. The decision for demolition was reached by seven votes against six. Tahsin Öz, Orhan Çapçı, Ekrem Akurgal, Kamil Su, Ahmed Hamdi Tanpınar, Osman Turan and Behçet Ünsal voted for the demolitions. Kemali Söylemezoğlu, Ali Saim Ülgen, Ali Müfit Mansel, Zeki Faik İzer, Celâl Esad Arseven and Orhan Alsaç voted against the resolution.

93. High Council of Immovable Heritage Items and Monuments Resolution No. 661, 8 July 1957.
94. The council discussed the construction of the coastal road many times at its meetings between June 1956 and February 1958: . Republic of Turkey, High Council of Immovable Heritage Items and Monuments Resolution Nos. 607, 6 June 1956; 637, 17 November 1957; 646, 21 April 1957; 707, 6 August 1957; 810, 23 September 1957; 811, 23 September 1957; 820, 6 October 1957; and 882, 15 February 1958. Approval was also sought in a similar way for the demolition of many buildings on the routes of Vatan and Millet streets and Eminönü–Unkapanı Road.
95. The number of apartment blocks constructed in Istanbul was only 67 in 1945. This figure increased dramatically and became 1,025 in 1950 and 1,722 in 1955: *7 Yıl İçinde Vilâyet ve Belediyece Yapılan İşler 1949–1955* (Istanbul, 1956), p.112.

FIGURE SOURCES

1. Staatsbibliothek zu Berlin, Preussischer Kulturbesitz-Kartenabteilung
2. Staatsbibliothek zu Berlin, Preussischer Kulturbesitz-Kartenabteilung
3. Abdul-Hamid II Collection, Prints & Photographs Division, Library of Congress, LC-USZ62-80986
4. Prints & Photographs Division, Library of Congress, LC-DIG-ppmsca-03774
5. Abdul-Hamid II Collection, Prints & Photographs Division, Library of Congress, LC-USZC4-11685
6. Prints & Photographs Division, Library of Congress, LC-DIG-ppmsca-03804
7. Abdul-Hamid II Collection, Prints & Photographs Division, Library of Congress, LC-USZ62-81206
8. Staatsbibliothek zu Berlin, Preussischer Kulturbesitz-Kartenabteilung
9. Abdul-Hamid II Collection, Prints & Photographs Division, Library of Congress, LC-USZ62-80951
10. Prints & Photographs Division, Library of Congress, LC-USZC4-11857
11. Prints & Photographs Division, Library of Congress, LC-DIG-ppmsca-03048
12. Abdul-Hamid II Collection, Prints & Photographs Division, Library of Congress, LC-USZC4-11677
13. Abdul-Hamid II Collection, Prints & Photographs Division, Library of Congress, LC-USZC4-11649
14. Prime Ministry Archives of the Turkish Republic (Ottoman Archives, Istanbul)

15. Prime Ministry Archives of the Turkish Republic (Ottoman Archives, Istanbul)

16. Reproduced from Siegmund Schneider, *Die Deutsche Baghdâd-Bahn und die Projectirte Überbrückung des Bosporus* (Vienna, 1900)

17. Prints & Photographs Division, Library of Congress, LC-DIG-ppmsca-03895

18. Prints & Photographs Division, Library of Congress, LC-DIG-ppmsc-06062

19. Reproduced from *Génie Civil Ottoman* 1 (1912)

20. Atatürk Library, Istanbul Metropolitan Municipality

21. Reproduced from *Mimar* 9 (1932)

22. Mimar Sinan Fine Arts University, Restoration Department Archives, Istanbul

23. Yapı Kredi History Archives Selahattin Giz Collection, Istanbul

24. Mimar Sinan Fine Arts University, Restoration Department Archives, Istanbul

25. Mimar Sinan Fine Arts University, Restoration Department Archives, Istanbul

26. Mimar Sinan Fine Arts University, Restoration Department Archives, Istanbul

27. Mimar Sinan Fine Arts University, Restoration Department Archives, Istanbul

28. Mimar Sinan Fine Arts University, Restoration Department Archives, Istanbul

29. Mimar Sinan Fine Arts University, Restoration Department Archives, Istanbul

30. Mimar Sinan Fine Arts University, Restoration Department Archives, Istanbul

31. Atatürk Library, Istanbul Metropolitan Municipality

32. Yapı Kredi History Archives Selahattin Giz Collection, Istanbul

33. Yapı Kredi History Archives Selahattin Giz Collection, Istanbul

34. Yapı Kredi History Archives Selahattin Giz Collection, Istanbul

35. Reproduced from *Cumhuriyet Devrinde İstanbul* (Istanbul, İstanbul Belediyesi Neşriyat ve İstatistik Müdürlüğü, 1949)

36. Reproduced from *Güzelleşen İstanbul* (Istanbul: İstanbul Belediyesi, 1943)

37. Reproduced from *Güzelleşen İstanbul* (Istanbul: İstanbul Belediyesi, 1943)

38. Yapı Kredi History Archives Selahattin Giz Collection, Istanbul

FIGURE SOURCES

39. Reproduced from *Cumhuriyet Devrinde İstanbul* (Istanbul, İstanbul Belediyesi Neşriyat ve İstatistik Müdürlüğü, 1949)

40. Reproduced from *Güzelleşen İstanbul* (Istanbul: İstanbul Belediyesi, 1943)

41. Reproduced from *İstanbul'un Kitabı* (Istanbul: İstanbul Vilâyeti Neşriyat ve Turizm Müdürlüğü, c.1957)

42. Reproduced from Hilmi Şahenk, *Bir Zamanlar İstanbul* (İstanbul Büyükşehir Belediyesi Kültür İşleri Daire Başkanlığı, 1996). Courtesy of Istanbul Metropolitan Municipality

43. Reproduced from Hilmi Şahenk, *Bir Zamanlar İstanbul* (İstanbul Büyükşehir Belediyesi Kültür İşleri Daire Başkanlığı, 1996). Courtesy of Istanbul Metropolitan Municipality

44. Reproduced from Hilmi Şahenk, *Bir Zamanlar İstanbul* (İstanbul Büyükşehir Belediyesi Kültür İşleri Daire Başkanlığı, 1996). Courtesy of Istanbul Metropolitan Municipality

45. Author's collection

46. Yapı Kredi History Archives Selahattin Giz Collection, Istanbul

47. Reproduced from Hilmi Şahenk, *Bir Zamanlar İstanbul* (İstanbul Büyükşehir Belediyesi Kültür İşleri Daire Başkanlığı, 1996). Courtesy of Istanbul Metropolitan Municipality

48. Yapı Kredi History Archives Selahattin Giz Collection, Istanbul

49. Reproduced from *Güzelleşen İstanbul* (Istanbul: İstanbul Vilâyeti Neşriyat ve Turizm Müdürlüğü, c. 1957)

50. Prepared by author from various maps obtained from Istanbul Municipality

BIBLIOGRAPHY

7 Yıl İçinde Vilayet ve Belediyece Yapılan İşler 1949–1955 (Istanbul: İstanbul Belediye Matbaası, 1956).

1950-1953 İl ve Şehir Hizmetlerinden: İstanbulun İmarı (Istanbul: Halk Basımevi, c. 1953).

1952 İstanbul Bölge Kalkınma Kongresi (Istanbul: Tan Matbaası, 1951).

'Başbakanın aylık basın toplantısı', *İETT Dergisi* 6 (March 1957), pp.6–8.

Cumhuriyet Devrinde İstanbul (Istanbul: İstanbul Belediyesi Neşriyat ve İstatistik Müdürlüğü, 1949).

'Cumhuriyet devrinde İstanbul Belediyesi ve Hususi İdaresi on senede ne yaptı?', *İstanbul Belediye Mecmuası* 109–10 (1933).

Güzelleşen İstanbul (Istanbul: İstanbul Belediyesi, 1943).

Harp Yıllarında İstanbul'daki Faaliyetler: İstanbul Valisi ve Belediye Reisi Dr. Lûtfi Kırdar'ın Eylül 1945 Basın Toplantısındaki İzahatı (Istanbul: İstanbul Belediye Matbaası, 1945).

İl ve Şehirde Geçen Yıl Neler Yapıldı ve Bu Yıl Neler Yapılıyor 1950–1951 (Istanbul: Belediye Matbaası, 1951).

İstanbul İmar Plânı İzah Raporları: I. Beyoğlu Ciheti (Istanbul: Belediye Matbaası, 1954).

İstanbul İmar Plânı İzah Raporları: II. İstanbul Ciheti (Istanbul: Belediye Matbaası, 1956).

'İstanbul şehir planı', *Arkitekt* 2 (1935), pp.61–8.

İstanbul Şehri İstatistik Yıllığı, vol. 12, *1953–1957* (Istanbul: Belediye Matbaası, 1958).

İstanbul Vali ve Belediye Reisi Ord. Prof. Dr. F. K. Gökay'ın 1949–1951 Konuşmaları (Istanbul: Belediye Matbaası, 1958).

İstanbul Vali ve Belediye Reisi Ord. Prof. Dr. F. K. Gökay'ın 1951–1955 Konuşmaları (Istanbul: İstanbul Belediyesi, 1957).

İstanbul Vali ve Belediye Reisi Ord. Prof. Dr. F. K. Gökay'ın 1956–1957 Konuşmaları (Istanbul: İstanbul Belediye Matbaası, 1958).

İstanbul'un Kitabı (Istanbul: İstanbul Vilâyeti Neşriyat ve Turizm Müdürlüğü, c. 1957).

İstimlâk Yolsuzluğu Davası Tutanakları-Esas No. 961/8 (Records of the Case of Corrupt Expropriation) (unpublished manuscript, Ankara, Grand National Assembly Library).

'La Reconstruction de Stamboul', *Génie Civil Ottoman* 1 (1912), pp.4–5.

L'Œuvre de Henri Prost; Architecture et Urbanisme (Paris: Académie d'Architecture, 1960).

'Revizyon Komisyonu Raporu—H. Prost'un İstanbul şehri için tanzim ettiği imar planlarını tetkik etmek üzere kurulmuş bulunan heyet tarıfından hazırlanmıştır' (Istanbul: Belediye Matbaası, 1954).

The European reconstruction, 1948-1961: Bibliography on the Marshall Plan and the Organisation for European Economic Co-operation (OEEC) (Paris: Organisation for Economic Co-operation and Development, 1996).

Yenileşen İstanbul: 1939 Başından 1947 Sonuna Kadar İstanbulda Neler Yapıldı? (Istanbul: İstanbul Belediye Matbaası, 1947).

Yüksek Adalet Divanı Kararları-İstimlâk Yolsuzlukları Davası Kararı Gerekçesi (High Court of Justice-The Verdicts of the Case of Corrupt Expropriation), Bülüm Sıra No. 17, Esas No 961/8 (unpublished manuscript, Ankara, Grand National Assembly Library).

Abercrombie, Patrick, *Greater London Plan 1944* (London: H.M.S.O., 1945).

—'İstanbul: Halen hazırlanmakta olan nazım plandaki teklifler ve metodlar hakkında muvakkat rapor', 26 April 1954.

Agache, Alfred, *Büyük İstanbul Tanzim ve İmar Programı* (Istanbul: İstanbul Belediye Matbaası, 1934).

Ağaoğlu, Samet, *Arkadaşım Menderes* (Istanbul: Rek-Tur Kitap Servisi, 1967).

Ahmad, Feroz, *The Making of Modern Turkey* (London: Routledge, 1993).

—*Turkey: The Quest for Identity* (Oxford: One Word Publications, 2003).

—*Turkish Experiment in Democracy 1950–1975* (London: C. Hurst for the Royal Institute of International Affairs, 1977).

Ahmed Refik, *Lâle Devri* (Istanbul: Hilmi Kitaphanesi, 1932).

Akın, Nur, *19. Yüzyılın İkinci Yarısında Galata ve Pera* (Istanbul: Literatür Yayınları, 2002).

Akpınar, İpek, The rebuilding of Istanbul after the plan of Henri Prost 1937–1960: From secularisation to Turkish modernisation, unpublished PhD thesis, Bartlett School of Graduate Studies, University of London 2003.

Aktepe, Münir, 'İstanbul'un nüfus mes'elesine dair bazı vesikalar', *Tarih Dergisi* 9/13 (1958), pp.1–31.

—*Patrona İsyanı (1730)* (Istanbul: Edebiyat Fakültesi Yayınları, 1958).

Aracı, Emre, 'Giuseppe Donizetti at the Ottoman Court: a Levantine life', *The Musical Times*, 143/1880 (Autumn 2002), pp.49–56.

Arel, Ayda, *Onsekizinci Yüzyıl İstanbul Mimarisinde Batılılaşma Süreci* (Istanbul: İTÜ Mimarlık Fakültesi, 1975).

Arseven, Celâl Esat, *Türk Sanatı Tarihi: Menşeinden Bugüne Kadar Mimari, Heykel, Resim, Süsleme ve Tezyini Sanatlar*, vol.VI (Istanbul: Maarif Basımevi, c. 1955).

Aslanoğlu, İnci, *Erken Cumhuriyet Dönemi Türk Mimarlığı 1923-1938* (Ankara: ODTÜ Mimarlık Fakültesi Yayınları, 2001).

Auric, André, 'Rapport General du Service Technique de la Préfecture', *Génie Civil Ottoman* 1 (1911), pp.1–4.

Aydemir, Şevket S., *Menderes'in Dramı* (Istanbul: Remzi Kitabevi, 2007).

Başgöz, İlhan and Wilson, Howard E., *Educational Problems in Turkey 1920-1940* (Bloomington: Indiana University Press, 1968).

Baysun, M. Cavid, 'Mustafa Reşid Paşa'nın siyasi yazıları', *Tarih Dergisi* 11/15 (September 1960), pp.121–42.

Bazoğlu, Akif, 'İstanbul imarında karşılaşılan güçlükler ve şikâyetler', *Arkitekt* 20/7–10 (1950), pp.198–202.

Behçet and Bedrettin, 'Türk inkilap mimarisi', *Mimar* 3/9–10 (1933), pp.265–6.

Berkes, Niyazi, *Development of Secularism in Turkey* (New York: Routledge, 1998).

Bianchi, Ruben A., 'The work of Luigi Piccinato in Islamic countries 1925–1981', *Environmental Design* (1990), pp.184–91.

Birand, Mehmet A., Dündar, Can and Çaplı, Bülent, *Demirkırat: Bir Demokrasinin Doğuşu* (Istanbul: Doğan Kitapçılık, 2007).

Boysan, Aydın, 'Adnan Menderes belediyeciliği imar hareketi uygulama ve sonuçları', *Mimarist* 3 (2004), pp.25–31.

Boysan, Burak, 'Politik hummanın silinmeyen izleri: Halkla ilişkiler stratejisi olarak İstanbul'un imarı', *İstanbul* 4 (1993), pp.84–9.

Bozdoğan, Sibel, *Modernism and Nation Building; Turkish Architectural Culture in the Early Republic* (Seattle: University of Washington Press, 2001).

Bozdoğan, Sibel and Kasaba, Reşat, *Rethinking Modernity and National Identity in Turkey* (Seattle: University of Washington Press, 1997).

Burhan Arif, 'İstanbulun plânı', *Mimar* 3/5 (1933), pp.154–61.

Çelik, Zeynep, 'Bouvard's Boulevards: Beaux-Arts planning in Istanbul', *Journal of the Society of Architectural Historians* 43/4 (1984), pp.341–55.

—*The Remaking of Istanbul; Portrait of an Ottoman City in the Nineteenth Century* (Berkeley: University of California Press, 1986).

—'Two projects for fin-de-siècle Istanbul', *Rassegna* 19/72 (1997), pp.71–5.

Cerasi, Maurice, et. al., *The Istanbul Divanyolu; A Case Study in Ottoman Urbanity and Architecture* (Würzburg: ErgonVerlag in Kommission, 2004).

Cezar, Mustafa, *Osmanlı Başkenti İstanbul* (Istanbul: E. K. Aksoy Kültür, Eğitim, Spor ve Sağlık Vakfı, 2002).

—*Tipik Yapılariyle Osmanlı Şehirciliğinde Çarşı ve Klasik Dönem İmar Sistemi* (Istanbul: Mimar Sinan Üniversitesi Yayını, 1985).

Çumralı Sedad and Karay Talat, *Son Değişikliklere Göre Şerhli ve İzahlı Millî Korunma Kanunu* (Ankara: Ulusal Matbaa, 1943).

Demiren, Şemsa, 'Le Corbusier ile mülâkat', *Arkitekt* 19/11-12 (1949), pp.230–1.

Deringil, Selim, *Turkish Foreign Policy During the Second World War; An 'Active' Neutrality* (Cambridge: Cambridge University Press, 2004).

Dilipak, Abdurrahman, *Menderes Dönemi* (Istanbul: Beyan Yayınları, 1990).

Duranay, N., Gürsel, E. and Ural, S., 'Cumhuriyetten bu yana İstanbul planlaması', *Mimarlık* 7 (1972), pp.65–109.

Ehlgötz, Herman, *İstanbul Şehrinin Umumi Planı* (Istanbul: Ahmet Sait Matbaası, 1934).

Ergin, Osman N., *İstanbul Şehri Rehberi* (Istanbul: Matbaacılık ve Neşriyat Türk Anonim Şirketi, 1934).

— *İstanbulda İmar ve İskân Hareketleri* (Istanbul: Bürhaneddin Matbaası, 1938).

—*Mecelle-i Umûr-ı Belediyye* (Istanbul: İstanbul Büyükşehir Belediyesi Kültür İşleri Daire Başkanlığı Yayınları, 1995).

—*Muallim M. Cevdet'in Hayatı Eserleri ve Kütüphanesi*, (Istanbul: Bozkurt Basımevi, 1937).

—*Türkiyede Şehirciliğin Tarihi İnkişafı* (Istanbul: Cumhuriyet Gazete ve Matbaası, 1936).

Gül, Murat and Lamb, Richard, 'Mapping, regularizing and modernizing Ottoman Istanbul; Aspects of the genesis of the 1839 Development Policy', *Urban History* 31/3 (2004), pp.420–36.

—'Urban planning in Istanbul in the early Republican period; Henri Prost's role in tensions among beautification, modernisation and peasantist ideology', *Architectural Theory Review* 9/1 (2004), pp.59–81.

Hamadeh, Shirine, 'Ottoman expressions of early modernity and the "inevitable" question of Westernisation', *Journal of Society of Architectural Historians* 63/1 (March 2004), pp.32–51.

—*The City's Pleasures; Istanbul in the Eighteenth Century* (Seattle: University Washington Press, 2008).

Haussmann, Georges-Eugène, *Mémoires* (Paris: Seuil, 2000).

Herms, Marry, (trans), *Moltke's Life: Moltke His Life and Character Sketched in Journals, Letters, Memoirs, A Novel, and Autobiographical Notes* (London: James R. Osgood, McIlvaine & Co., 1892).

Hershlag, Zvi Yehuda, *Turkey: The Challenge of Growth* (Leiden: E. J. Brill, 1968).

Högg, Hans, 'Istanbul: Ausschnitte aus der Stadterneuerung', *Baumeister* 58/1 (1961), pp.33–52.

İnalcık, Halil, *Volume 1: 1300–1600* of H. İnalcık and D. Quataert (eds), *An Economic and Social History of the Ottoman Empire* (Cambridge: Cambridge University Press, 1994).

—'Sened-i İttifak ve Gülhane Hatt-i Hümâyûnu', *Belleten* 28/109–112 (1964), pp.603–22.

—'The policy of Mehmed II towards the Greek population of Istanbul and the Byzantine buildings of the city', *Dumbarton Oaks Papers* 23 (1969–1970), pp.229–49.

Karaömerlioğlu, M. Asım, 'The People's Houses and the cult of peasant in Turkey' in S. Kedourie (ed), *Turkey Before and After Atatürk* (London: Frank Cass, 1999).

—'The Village Institutes experience in Turkey', *British Journal of Middle Eastern Studies* 25/1 (1998), pp.47–73.

—'Türkiye'de köycülük' in A. İnsel (ed), *Modern Türkiye'de Düşünce Tarihi 2: Kemalizm* (Istanbul: İletişim Yayınları, 2002).

Karpat, Kemal H., *Ottoman Population 1830-1914; Demographic and Social Characteristics* (Madison: University of Wisconsin Press, 1985).

—'Political developments in Turkey, 1950–70', *Middle Eastern Studies* 8/3 (October, 1972), pp.349–75.

—*Turkey's Politics; The Transition to a Multi-party System* (Princeton: Princeton University Press, 1959).

Kaynar, Reşat, *Mustafa Reşit Paşa ve Tanzimat* (Ankara: Türk Tarih Kurumu Basımevi, 1991).

Keleş, Ruşen, *Türkiye'de Şehirleşme Hareketleri 1927–1960* (Ankara: Maliye Enstitüsü, 1961).

Kerwin, Robert W., 'The Turkish roads program', *The Middle East Journal* 4 (1950), pp.196–208.

Keyder, Çağlar, 'A tale of two neighbourhoods' in Ç. Keyder, *Istanbul Between the Global and the Local* (Lanham: Rowman & Littlefield, 1999).

—'Economic development and crisis: 1950–1980' in I. C. Schick and E. A. Tonak (eds), *Turkey in Transition; New Perspectives* (New York: Oxford University Press, 1987).

—*State and Class in Turkey; A Study in Capitalist Development* (London: Verso, 1987).

Kılınç G. and Gülersoy, N. Z., 'Türkiye'deki ilçelerin kentleşme derecelerine göre il olma potansiyellerinin değerlendirilmesi', *İTÜ Dergisi* 6/1 (March, 2007), pp.66–78.

Kortan, Enis, *Le Corbusier Gözüyle Türk Mimarlık ve Şehirciliği* (Ankara: ODTÜ, 1983).

Köymen, Nusret K., 'Kemalizmin hususiyetleri', *Ülkü* 7/42 (1936), pp.416–18.

—'Köy seferberliğine doğru', *Ülkü* 5 (1934), pp.355–61.

—'Köycülük easaları', *Ülkü* 4/20 (1934), pp.145–53.

Kuban, Doğan, *Istanbul An Urban History: Byzantion, Constantinopolis, Istanbul* (Istanbul: The Economic and Social History Foundation of Turkey, 1996).

—*Kent ve Mimarlık Üzerine İstanbul Yazıları* (Istanbul: Yapı Endüstri Merkezi Yayınları, 1998).

Lambert, J. H., *İ'mar Raporu* (Istanbul: Milli Neşriyat Yurdu, 1934).

Langevin, M. and Meizonnet, L., Etude des transport d'Istanbul, September 1952 (unpublished typescript report, Istanbul, Atatürk Library, Istanbul Metropolitan Municipality).

Leder, Arnold, 'Party competition in rural Turkey; Agent of change or defender of traditional rule', *Middle Eastern Studies* 15/1 (January 1979), pp.82–105.

Lewis, Bernard, *The Emergence of Modern Turkey* (New York: Oxford University Press, 2002).

MacFarlane, Charles, *Turkey and its Destiny; The Results of Journeys made in 1847 and 1848 to Examine Into the State of That Country*, vol.1 (London: John Murray, 1850).

Malik, A. Hilmi, 'Kışla ve köy', *Ülkü* 1/3 (1933), pp.237–40.

Mango, Andrew, *Atatürk* (London: John Murray, 2001).

Mansel, Philip, *Constantinople, City of the World's Desire, 1453–1924* (London: John Murray, 1995).

Mardin, Şerif, 'Religion and secularism in Turkey' in E. Özbudun and A. Kazancıgil (eds), *Atatürk, Founder of a Modern State* (London: Hurst & Co., 1997).

—'Religion and secularism in Turkey' in A. Hourani, P. Khoury and M. C. Wilson (eds), *The Modern Middle East* (London: I. B. Tauris, 2004).

Mazıcı, Nurşen, '27 Mayıs, Kemalizmin restorasyonu mu?' in A. İnsel (ed), *Modern Türkiyede Siyasi Düşünce 2: Kemalizm* (Istanbul: İletişim Yayınları, 2002).

Mehmet Saffet, 'Köycülük nedir', *Ülkü* 1/6 (1933), pp.422–30.

—'Kültür inkılabımız', *Ülkü* 1/5 (1933), pp.351–4.

Menteşe, Ertuğtul, 'İstanbulun imarı', *Arkitekt* 24/279 (1955), pp.27–38.

—'İstanbul'un seyrüseferi ve metronun faydaları', *Arkitekt* 23/3–6 (1954), pp.83–96.

Mert, Nuray, *Laiklik Tartışmasına Kavramsal Bir Bakış: Cumhuriyet Kurulurken Laik Düşünce* (Istanbul: Bağlam Yayınları, 1994).

Mihajlovic, Dragoslav P., *La Nouvelle Turquie Economique* (Belgrade: Institut Balkanique, 1937).

Mimar Abidin, 'Memlekette Türk mimarının yarınki vaz'iyeti', *Mimar* 3/5 (1933), pp.129–30.

Moltke, Helmuth von, *Gesammelte Schriften und Denkwürdigkeiten des General-Feldmarschalls / Grafen Helmuth von Moltke, Achter Band – Briefe über Zustände und Begebenheiten in der Türkei aus den Jahren 1835 bis 1839* (Berlin: E.S. Mittler & Sohn, 1893).

—*Gesammelte Schriften und Denkwürdigkeiten des General Feldmarschalls Grafen Helmuth von Moltke Vierter Band – Briefe des General Feldmarschalls Grafen Helmuth von Moltke an Seine Mutter und an Seine Brüder Adolf und Ludwig* (Berlin: E.S. Mittler & Sohn, 1891).

Morris, W. O., *Moltke: A Biographical and Critical Study* (London: Ward & Downey, 1893), pp.13–18.

Müller-Wiener, Wolfgang, *Bizans'tan Osmanlı'ya İstanbul Limanı* (Istanbul: Tarih Vakfı Yurt Yayınları, 1998).

Mutluçağ, Hayri, 'Boğaziçi köprüsünün yapılması yolunda ilk çabalar', *Belgelerle Türk Tarihi Dergisi* 4 (January, 1968), pp.32–8.

Oberling, P., 'The Istanbul Tünel', *Archivum Ottomanicum* 4 (1972), pp.217–63.

Ökte, Faik, *The Tragedy of the Turkish Capital Tax* (London: Croom Helm, 1987).

Olson, Robert W., *The Siege of Mosul and Ottoman-Persian Relations, 1718–1743; A Study of Rebellion in the Capital and War in the Provinces of the Ottoman Empire* (Bloomington: Indiana University, 1975).

Öncel, Derin and Kafesçioğlu, Figen O., '1858–1860 Galata, Pera ve Pangaltı planı', *Mimarist* 1 (2005), pp.18–9.

Örs, Hayrullah (trans), *Moltke'nin Türkiye Mektupları* (Istanbul: Remzi Kitabevi, 1999).

Ortaylı, İlber, *İmparatorluğun En Uzun Yüzyılı* (Istanbul: İletişim Yayınları, 2000).

— *Tanzimat Devrinde Osmanlı Mahallî İdareleri* (Ankara: Türk Tarih Kurumu Basımevi, 2000).

—*Tanzimattan Cumhuriyete Yerel Yönetim Geleneği* (Ankara: Hil Yayın, 1985).

Özer, Bülent, *Rejyonalizm, Ünivresalizm ve Çağdaş Mimarimiz Üzerine Bir Deneme* (İstanbul: İstanbul Teknik Üniversitesi, 1970).

Özfatura, İrfan, 'Depremlerin yapamadığını H. Prost yaptı!, "İthal Neron İstanbul'da"', *Tarih ve Düşünce* 49 (2004), pp.12–18.

Öztürk, Kâzım, *Cumhurbaşkanları'nın Türkiye Büyük Millet Meclisini Açış Nutukları* (İstanbul: Ak Yayınları, 1969).

Özyüksel, Murat, *Osmanlı-Alman İlişkilerinin Gelişim Sürecinde Anadolu ve Bağdat Demiryolları* (İstanbul: Arba, 1988).

Pinon, Pierre, 'Urban transformation between the 18th and 19th centuries', *Rassegna* 19/72 (1997), pp.53–61.

Prost, Henri, *Anadolu Sahili Nazım Planını İzah Eden Rapor* (İstanbul: İstanbul Belediye Matbaası, 1940).

—*Büyükadayı Tanzim ve Güzelleştirme Plânını İzah Eden Rapordur* (İstanbul: İstanbul Belediye Matbaası, 1941).

—'İstanbul', *Arkitekt* 17/3–4 (1948), pp.82–5; *Arkitekt* 17/5–6 (1948), pp.110–12; *Arkitekt* 17/7–8 (1948), pp.169–71.

—*İstanbul Hakkında Notlar* (İstanbul: İstanbul Belediye Matbaası, 1938).

—'İstanbulun nâzım planını izaheden rapor', (report published by İstanbul Belediyesi, 15 October 1937).

—*İstanbul'un Tehavvülâtı II: Mevzuat* (İstanbul: İstanbul Belediye Matbaası, 1955).

Rivkin, Malcolm D., *Area Development for National Growth; The Turkish Precedent* (New York: Praeger, 1965).

Rosenthal, Steven T., 'Foreigners and municipal reform in Istanbul: 1855–1865', *International Journal of Middle East Studies* 11/2 (April 1980), pp.227–45.

—*The Politics of Dependency; Urban Reform in Istanbul* (Connecticut: Greenwood Press, 1980).

Sahillioğlu, H., 'Sıvış year crises in the Ottoman Empire' in M. A. Cook (ed), *Studies in the Economic History of the Middle East; From the Rise of Islam to the Present Day* (London: Oxford University Press, 1970).

Sarol, Mükerrem, *Bilinmeyen Menderes,* vol. I and II (İstanbul: Kervan Yayınları, 1983).

Sayar, Zeki, 'Beyazıt Meydanından alacağımız ders!', *Arkitekt* 27/291 (1958), pp.53–4.

—'İç kolonizasyon - Başka memleketlerde', *Arkitekt* 6/8 (1936), pp.231–5.

—'İmar ve eski eserler', *Arkitekt* 26/287 (1957), pp.49–50.

—'İstanbulun imarı hakkında düşünceler!', *Arkitekt* 26/286 (1957), pp.3, 11.

—'İstanbul'un imârı münasebetiyle', *Arkitekt* 25/284 (1956), pp.49–50.

—'İstanbul'un imârında şehirci mimarın rolü', *Arkitekt* 25/285 (1956), pp.97–8.

—'Yerli ve yabancı mimar', *Arkitekt* 8/2 (1938), p.65.

Schneider, Siegmund, *Die Deutsche Baghdâd-Bahn und die Projectirte Überbrückung des Bosporus* (Vienna: Verlagsbuchhandlung Leopold Weiss, 1900).

Shaw, Stanford J., *Between Old and New; the Ottoman Empire Under Sultan Selim III, 1789-1807* (Cambridge: Harvard University Press, 1971)

— 'The population of Istanbul in the nineteenth century', *International Journal of Middle East Studies*, 10/2 (May, 1979), pp. 265–77.

Shaw, Stanford J. and Shaw, Ezel Kural, *History of the Ottoman Empire and Modern Turkey*, vol.2, *The Rise of Modern Turkey*, 1808–1975 (Cambridge: Cambridge University Pres, 1977)

Sözen, Metin, *Cumhuriyet Devri Türk Mimarlığı* (Ankara: Türkiye İş Bankası Kültür Yayınları, 1984).

Summerson, John, 'Urban forms' in O. Handlin and J. E. Burchard (eds), *The Historian and the City* (Cambridge: MIT Press, 1963).

Tankut, Gönül, *Bir Başkentin İmarı* (Istanbul: Anahtar Kitaplar Yayınevi, 1993).

Tekeli, İlhan, 'İcabında plan', *İstanbul* 4 (1993), pp.26–37.

—*Modernite Aşılırken Kent Planlaması* (Ankara: İmge Kitabevi, 2001).

—*Türkiye'de Kentleşme Yazıları* (Ankara: Turhan Kitabevi Yayınları, 1982).

Thornburg, M. W., Spry, G. and Soule, G., *Turkey: an Economic Appraisal* (New York: Twentieth Century Fund, 1949).

Toker, Metin, *Demokrasimizin İsmet Paşalı Yılları 1944–1973; DP'nin Altın Yılları 1950–1954* (Ankara: Bilgi Yayınevi, 1990).

Toprak, Binnaz, *Islam and Political Development in Turkey* (Leiden: E. J. Brill, 1981)

Topuzlu, Cemil, *32 Sene Evvelki, Bugünkü, Yarınki İstanbul* (Istanbul: Ülkü Basımevi, 1944).

—*İstibdad-Meşrutiyet-Cumhuriyet Devirlerinde 80 Yıllık Hatıralarım* (Istanbul: Topuzlu Yayınları, 2002).

—*Yarınki İstanbul* (Istanbul: Kenan Basımevi ve Klişe Fabrikası, 1937).

Uludağ, Zeynep, 'Cumhuriyet Döneminde Rekreasyon ve Gençlik Parkı Örneği' in Y. Sey (ed), *75 Yılda Değişen Kent ve Mimarlık* (Istanbul: Tarih Vakfı Yayınları, 1998).

Ünsal, Behçet, 'İstanbul'un imarı ve eski eser kaybı', in *Türk Sanatı Tarihi Araştırma ve*

İncelemeleri II (Istanbul: Devlet Güzel Sanatlar Akademisi Türk Sanatı Tarihi Enstitüsü Yayınları, 1969), pp.6–61.

Wagner, Martin, 'İstanbul havalisinin plânı', *Arkitekt* 10–11 (1936), pp.301–6 and 12 (1936) 333–7.

—'İstanbulun münakale tahlili', *Arkitekt* 7/5–6 (1937), pp.143–6.

Watson, William J., 'Ibrâhim Müteferrika and Turkish Incunabula', *Journal of the American Oriental Society* 88/3 (1968), pp.435–41.

Whitton, Frederick E., *Moltke* (London: Constable and Company, 1921).

Yeşilbursa, Behçet K., 'Turkey's participation in the Middle East Command and its admission to NATO 1950–52', *Middle Eastern Studies,* 35/4 (October, 1999), pp.70–102.

Yeşilkaya, Neşe Gürallar, *Halkevleri; İdeoloji ve Mimarlık* (Istanbul: İletişim Yayınları, 1999).

Zeren, Nuran, Türkiye'de tarihsel değerlerin korunmasında uygulanmakta olan yöntem çerçevesinde uygulayıcı kuruluşların görüşlerine dayanan bir araştırma, unpublished PhD thesis, İstanbul Teknik Üniversitesi, 1981.

Zilfi, Madeline C., 'Women and society in the Tulip Era 1718-1730' in A. Sonbol (ed), *Women, the Family and Divorce Laws in Islamic History* (Syracuse: Syracuse University Press, 1996).

Zürcher, Erik J., *Turkey; A Modern History* (London: I. B. Tauris, 2004).

INDEX

Abdülaziz 52, 54, 155, 188*n.47*
Abdülhalim Bey 35
Abdülhamid II 54–7, 59, 63–5
Abdullah Efendi (Tatarcık) 22–3, 28, 172
Abdülmecid 33, 44
Abercrombie, Patrick 138
Acemi Oğlanlar 17
Adnan Menderes Boulevard 154; *see also Vatan Street*
Agache, Alfred 92–94, 96–7
Ağaoğlu, Samet 133, 140, 160, 207*n.38*
Ahmad, Feroz 90
Ahmed III 18–21
Akçer, Faruk 137, 169
Aksaray, 50, 52, 53; in 1839 development policy 28, 30; in Auric's proposals 68–70; in Agache's proposal 93; in Prost's proposal 101, 115; in Board of Advisors' plan 138; in Menderes' press conference 147; during Menderes' redevelopment works 152–154; 188*n.7*
Alleon, Antoine 44–5
Alman Çeşmesi (German Fountain in Sultanahmet Square) 56
aman (mercy) 9
American Public Roads Administration 123
Anadoluhisarı 58
Anatolia, immigration 15, 20, 160, 188*n.55*; railways 54, 56; Baghdad Railways 56, 61; in Republican era 72, 75, 77, 80; occupied after the First World War 71; peasantism 84; moving Ottoman capital 84–5; deputies and ministers 89; living conditions 121; in Moltke's surveys 185*n.52*; Kurdish rebellion 192*n.6*
Anglo–Ottoman Commercial Treaty 25, 41, 42
Ankara 2, 4, 78, 92, 125, 133, 135, 140, 146, 163, 195*n.45*, *46*; railway connection to Istanbul 56; selected as new capital 72, 84–5, 119, 128; ideal city planning model 80; versus Istanbul 84–90, 131, 133 population boom 124; total travel time to Istanbul 129
Ankara Palace Hotel 77
Ankara People's House 83
Ankara Şehremaneti Kanunu 80
Ankara University 77, 125
Antwerp 97
Argun, Dilaver 143, 158, 160, 210*n.9*
Arkan, Seyfi 137
Arkitekt (architectural magazine) 79, 95–6, 149, 164, 167, 194*n.34*
Armenian cemetery in Taksim 106
Armenians of Istanbul 9, 12, 42
Armistice of Mudros 71
Arnodin, Ferdinand Joseph 59–61, 177, 179, 189*n.66*, 190*n.74*
Arseven, Celâl Esat 77, 215*n.92*

Art Deco buildings in Istanbul 79
Artillery Barracks in Taksim 106, 115–6, 179
Aru, Kemal Ahmet 137–8
Âsitane 181*n.6*
Ataköy residential complex 143, 170
Atatürk Boulevard 101–2, 112, 114–5, 149, 152, 155–6, 173
Atatürk Bridge 100–2, 112, 116, 139, 147, 157, 198*n.31*
Atatürk Esplanade 101
Atatürk, Mustafa Kemal 1, 3, 4, 72, 74, 76, 79, 85, 89, 92, 116, 122, 136; delay in visiting Istanbul 88; in Le Corbusier's memoirs 95; in Prost's writings 118, 119; protection act 130; his house in Thessaloniki 141
Atatürk Orman Çiftliği 87
Atik Ali Paşa Complex 50
Auric, André 67–70, 94, 101, 112, 152, 154, 173, 191*n.94, 95*, 192*n.98*
Austria, Holy League 7; member of Concert of Europe 40; horses brought for trams 53; Ottoman alliance in the First World War 71
Ayasofya (Istanbul's district) 112
Aydemir, Şevket Süreyya 1
Aydın (province in Western Anatolia) 122, 132, 202*n.82*, 210*n.8*
Aygün, Kemal 143, 165–6, 210*n.9*
Ayhan, Aydan 142
Ayniyat Vergisi (Payment-in-kind Tax) 120
Azapkapı 38, 53, 139
Aziziye Street 50

Bab-ı Hümayun 28–9
Babıâli 49–50
Bağdat Street 157
Baghdad 161
Baghdad Railway project 56, 60–1
Bahçekapı 28
Bakırköy 36, 94, 170, 209*n.61*
bal kapanı 14

Balat 12
Bank of Provinces (*İller Bankası*) 137, 169
Barbaros Boulevard 157
Barillet-Deschamps, M. 52
Barkan, Ömer Lütfi 82–3
Baruthane 170, 215*n.84*
Başar, Ahmet Hamdi 133
Basra 56
Batum 55
Bayar, Celâl 122, 126, 142–3, 205*n.11*
Bayezid II 13
Bayrakdar Mustafa Paşa 23
Bebek 139, 150
bedesten 13–4, 27
Bedrettin Hamdi 78
Behçet Sabri 78
Berlin 10, 31, 83, 93, 96, 185*n.52, 55*, 195*n.47*
Beşiktaş 18–9, 53, 157, 164; in Auric's proposal 69; in Prost's proposal 102; in Revision Commission's proposal 139; in Yassıada trials 143; in Menderes' press conference 147
Beyazıt 14, 50, 89–91; in 1839 development policy 28; in Auric's proposal 68, 70; in Lambert's proposal 94; in Prost's proposal 102, 112, 120; in Menderes' press conference 147; during Menderes' redevelopment 152–3, 170, 212*n.44*;
Beyazıt Square in 1839 development policy 30; in Bouvard's perspectives 63; in early Republican period 89–91; during Menderes' redevelopment 161, 164
Beykoz 36, 147
Beyoğlu 8, 10, 35; in Agache's proposal 93; in Prost's plans 97–8, 100–104, 106, 112, 197*n.17*; in Board of Advisor's plans 138–9, 208*n.60*; during Menderes' redevelopment 156, 160, 171; during Dalan's works in the 1980s 178

Bilâd-ı Selâse 8, 17
Birinci Milli Mimari (First National Style Architecture) 66
Birmingham 38
Bizerte 60
Black Sea 32, 103, 132, 179
Bosnia-Herzegovina 55
Bosphorus 8, 12, 35–6, 54, 57, 64–5, 71, 173, 179; in Tulip Era 18–9, 21; in 1839 development policy 30; in Moltke's survey 30–33, 185*n.52*; new regulatory measures on naval traffic 41; during the Sixth District's works 48; commencement of steam ferry services 53; bridge proposals in late Ottoman period 58; in Arnodin's proposal 59–62, 189*n.65*; in Auric's proposal 69; Atatürk's tour 88; in Ehlgötz's proposal 95; Prost's bridge proposal 100; in Prost's proposals 102–3, 118–9; suspended bridge proposal in 1950s 139, 149, 169; Högg's doctoral study 168; construction of bridge 178; in Menderes' press conference 147; in Yassıada trials 145; during Menderes' redevelopment 157
Bostancı 118, 157
Botanical Institute building 163
Bouvard, Joseph Antoine, imaginary proposal 62–3, 190*n.78*; visit to Istanbul 66
Brazil 93
Bulgaria 55, 75
Burhan Arif 96
Büyük Çamlıca 49
Büyük Cumhuriyet Meydanı (Great Republic Square) in Sultanahmet 106
Büyükada 107; in Prost's plan 199*n.51*
Büyükdere 32
Byzantion 181*n.6*

Cağaloğlu 112
Cairo 52
Caliphate 73, 85–6, 88, 175
Caméré, M. 52
Camondo, Avram 44–5, 52
Canberra 93
Canonica, Pietro 89, 91
Capital Levy (*Varlık Vergisi*) 121, 128
Çarşamba Pazarı 28
Casablanca 97, 135
Case of Corrupt Expropriation (*İstimlâk Yolsuzluğu Davası*) 143
Celâli İsyanları (revolts) 15
Çemberlitaş 14, 50–1, 182*n.11*; in Prost's proposal 152
Cemil Paşa (Topuzlu) 70, 80, 88–9, 92, 125, 149, 192*n.98*, 204*n.102*, 207*n.40*
Cemiyet-i Umumiye-i Belediye 80
Central Asia 77
Church of the Holy Apostles 12
Cibali 12
Cihangir 79
Çırağan Palace old palace 35; Abdülaziz's death 54; in Menderes' press conference 147
Çırçır 112
Cisr-i Cedid (bridge over the Golden Horn) 28
Clerk, Sir George 72
Coficci, G. 46
Cold War period 129
Committee of Union and Progress (CUP) 64–5, 67
Communist threat in Europe 123
Compagnie Internationale du Chemin de Fer de Bosphore 59
Comte de Bonneval, Claude Alexandre 183*n.31*
Concert of Europe 40, 45
Congress of Vienna 40
çöplük subaşısı 17
Côte d'Azur 97
Crédit Mobilier 52
Creil 93
Crimean War 4–5, 40–1, 44, 53
Çubuk Dam in Ankara 87

Cuno, Helmuth 66
Cyprus 55, 141

D'Aronco, Raimondo 57
Dalan, Bedrettin 178
Danger, René 97
Dardanelles Moltke's survey 30, 33; Högg's doctoral study 168
Darius 61
Darülfünun 35–7
Dautry, Raoul 97
Davies, B. R. xiii
Davud Paşa 32
Dedeağaç 54
Democrat Party ix, 1–6, 123, 172; establishment 122; in 1946 elections 122, 202*n.85*; in 1950 elections 125–6; in 1950 municipal elections 126; representative of large stratum of society 127–8, 204*n.1*, 205*n.5*; economic and social developments 128–131, 206*n.27*; Istanbul under DP in early 1950s 131–9; economic and political difficulties 140–2; closed by the military junta 142–3; redevelopment programme 145, 148–150, 152, 154, 156, 159–60, 162, 167, 171–2, 174–6, 180*n.2*, 212*n.32*,
Dersaadet 8, 17, 181*n2*, *n.6*; 1826 census 184*n.44*
Dersaadet Belediye Kanunu 57
Dersaadet Teşkilat-ı Belediyesi 64
Dersaadet Tramvay Şirketi 53
d'Espèrey, Franchet 71
Deutsches-Syndikat für Städtebauliche Arbeiten in der Türkei 66, 70
Direklerarası 145
Divan (Privy Council of the Ottoman Empire) 9
Divanyolu 14, 50–1, 152, 182*n.11*, 200*n.59*, 215*n.81*; in 1839 development policy 28–9; *see also mese*
Dolmabahçe 102, 106, 156–7, 184*n.32*
Dolmabahçe Mosque 118

Dolmabahçe Palace 41, 43–4, 71
dolmuş (shared taxi) 146
Donizetti, Domenico G. Maria 34
Donizetti, Giuseppe 34, 36
d'Ostaya, G. 46
Dunkerque 93
Duparchy, M. 52
Duyun-u Umumiye 58

Eads, James Buchanan 58–9
Ebniye Kanunu 34, 53
Ebniye Nizamı (1796) 23
Ebniye Nizamnamesi 33–4, 53
Ebniye-i Hassa Müdürlüğü 25, 29, 35
École des Beaux-Arts 57
École Nationale Supérieure des Beaux-Arts de Paris 93, 97, 195*n.47*
Edirne 14, 41, 54
Edirnekapı 14, 89; in 1839 development policy 28, 30; in Auric's proposal 68, in Prost's proposal 106
Egesel, Ömer Altay 144–5
Egli, Ernst 79, 87
Eğrikapı 28, 30
Egypt 25, 52
Ehlgötz, Hermann 92–6
Elçi Han 50
Eldem, Sedad Hakkı 170
Elsaesser, Martin 87
Emekli Sandığı (Pension Fund for Public Servants) 150
Emin Muhlis Efendi 44
Eminönü: commercial district 14–15; in 1839 development policy 30; connected to Karaköy 39, 64, 67; street regularisations 49; in Prost's plans 102, 106, 109, 110–13, 118, 173, 199*n.39*, 200*n.59*; in Menderes' redevelopment 147; 150–1, 155, 161, 166, 214*n.70*, 216*n.94*
Emirgan 118
Emlak Kredi Bankası 139
Erbel, Cevat 137–8, 169
Erbhof regulations 82, 127

Erdoğan, Recep Tayyip 179
Ergin, Osman Nuri 29, 49, 187*n.19*, *29*, 192*n.98*
Erol, Nevzat 170
Erzurum 85
European Recovery Programme 123
Evkaf Nezareti (Ministry of Endowments) 29
Eyüp 8, 181*n.2*; 1826 census 184*n.44*; in 1839 development policy 28, 30; industrial plants in late Ottoman era 36, 38; in Auric's proposals 68; in Prost's proposals 102, 107; in Menderes' press conference 147
Eyyüb el-Ensari (companion of Prophet Muhammed) 8
ezan (ceasing the ban on its recital) 130, 206*n.27*

Fatih 30, 41–2, 89, 93
Fatih Mosque 12, 16
Fâzıl Halil Edhem Bey 52, 188*n.47*
Fener 12
Ferhad Paşa 44
Feriköy 44, 69
Feshane 36, 38
fez 36, 38, 73–4, 78
Fez 97
Figuière, Antoine 49
Fincancılar Street 50
Fındıkoğlu, Ziayeddin Fahri 82
Fine Arts Academy (*Güzel Sanatlar Akademisi and Sanayi-i Nefise Mektebi*) 55, 77; name change 79; student proposal for Istanbul 81; members in Revision Commission 137
First World War 4–5, 64, 70–2, 88, 175, 191*n.95*, 198*n.32*
Florya 79, 102, 147, 155, 170, 214*n.70*
Fontainebleau 20
Forum Constantini 14
Forum Tauri 14, 120, 182*n.8*

Fossati, Gaspare Trajano 36–7
France 19, 82; Ottoman alliance in the Crimean War 40; influence in 1856 imperial edict 41; Arnodin's bridges 60, 190*n.74*; in the Triple Entente 71; Said Efendi's visit 183*n.31*; Auric's life and work 191*n.94*, *n.95*
Franchini, Septime 45
Frankish population of Galata 12
Franko Efendi 44
Free Republican Party (*Serbest Cumhuriyet Fırkası*) 74–5
French Revolution 44, 75
Fuad Paşa 51

Galata 8, 12, 19, 38, 42, 45–6, 48–50, 52–3, 59, 65–6, 139, 181*n.2*, 182*n.12*, 184*n.44*, 197*n.17*; European distinctiveness 25, 36, 41; in Moltke's letters 32; in Prost's plans 100, 102, 139; in Menderes' press conference 147
Galata Bridge 46, 63–5, 67, 101–2, 113, 147, 156
Galatasaray 34, 69, 110
Gallipoli campaigns 72
Gautier, Théophile 40
Gavand, Eugène Henri 53
Gayrimenkul Eski Eserler ve Anıtlar Yüksek Kurulu (High Council of Immovable Heritage Items and Monuments) 167, 169, 170, 175
Gayrimenkul Eski Eserler ve Anıtlar Yüksek Kurulu Talimatnamesi (Regulation for the High Council of Immovable Heritage Items and Monuments) 167
gecekondu (shanty buildings) emergence on public lands 125; growth 139, 146, 159, 178; in Menderes' press conference 147
Genç Osmanlılar (Young Ottomans) 54–6
Gençlik Parkı (Youth Park in Ankara) 86

General Directorate of Highways (*Karayolları Genel Müdürlüğü*) establishment 124; its role in the redevelopment of Istanbul 150, 162, 168

Génie Civil Ottoman (engineering journal of the 1910s) 69

Genoese ramparts of Galata 47

Genoeses of Istanbul 8, 32

Germany 82, 93, 96, 168, 195*n.47*; Ottoman alliance 56, 71; authoritarian regime 75, 121, 127, 195*n.49*; Turkey declares war 122

Gökalp, Ziya 66

Gökay, Fahrettin Kerim 97, 131, 162, 167, 213–4*n.70,76*; removal from his office 158; his testimony in Yassıada trials 165; meeting with Högg in Germany 168

Gökdoğan, Mukbil 137–8

Golden Horn 7–8, 12–14, 25, 36, 49, 63, 89, 93–4, 173; in Tulip Era 19, 21; in 1839 development policy 28, 30; industrialisation 38, 103, 107, 138, 139; bridges over 38–9, 53, 64, 93, 112, 162; increased naval traffic during the Crimean War 41; in Auric's proposal 68–9; in Prost's proposals 98, 100–3, 107, 110, 112, 116; in Board of Advisors' proposal 138–9, 208*n.60*, 209*n.61*, *63*; in Menderes' press conference 147; during Menderes' redevelopment 151, 155, 157, 162; during Dalan's operations in 1980s 178

Göztepe 118

Grand Bazaar (*Kapalı Çarşı*) 14, 22, 184*n.32*; decrease in rental income during the nineteenth century 36; in Prost's proposals 98, 173

Grand National Assembly in Ankara 72, 85, 89; building 87; political opposition to RPP after Second World War 122; after 1946 elections 123; election of Bayar as president of Turkey 126; Menderes' speech after 1950 election 127; changed demographic structure after 1950 elections 128; DP representatives accused in Yassıada Trials 143; lift the ban on Arabic *ezan* 206*n.27*

Grand Tour 22

Grande Rue de Pera 36, 42; installation of gas lighting 44; linked to Karaköy 46; in a British correspondent's report 47; in Auric's proposals 69; name change 88; in Prost's proposal 102

Great Britain xiii, member of the Concert of Europe 40; influence in 1856 imperial edict 41; Cyprus ceded to 55; in the Triple Entente 71; buses for Istanbul Municipality 121

Greece, occupying Anatolia 71–2; in Marshall Plan 123

Greek community of Istanbul 8–9, 12; political and economic privileges 42; represented in *İntizam-ı Şehir Komisyonu* 44; represented in the Sixth District 45; affected by 6–7 September 1955 incidents 141

Gregorian Calendar 5, 74

Gropius, Walter 96

Gülek, Kasım 124

Gülhane Hatt-ı Şerifi 26

Gülhane Park 70

Gümüşsuyu 79

Güneş Dil Teorisi (Sun Language Theory) 77

Güven, Muhittin 137

Hacı Bayram Mosque 195*n.45*

Hacı Hüssam Efendi 44

Hadid, Zaha 178

Hagia Sophia 14, 16, 35–6, 50, 52, 94, 188*n.47*; converted into the Grand Mosque of Istanbul 12; converted into museum 75; Prost's surveys 97; in Prost's reports 119

Halil Edhem Bey 66
*hamal*s of Istanbul 27
Hamam of Beyazıt 170
Hamam of Çemberlitaş 50–1
Hamidiye Bridge 60, 62
Han of Hasan Paşa 153, 170
Handan, Mehmed Ali 137
Hanover 168
*han*s of Istanbul 13–14, 25, 27
Hanson, Charles 45
Harik-i Kebir (the Great Fire of 1865) 49
Hasköy 12
Hassa Mimarbaşılığı 17
Hassa Mimarlar Ocağı 17; replaced with *Ebniye-i Hassa Müdürlüğü* 25
Hat Act (*Şapka Kanunu*) 73
Hatt-ı Hümayun of 1856 41
Haussmann, Georges-Eugéne 3, 58, 100, 168; his visit to Istanbul 52, 188*n.47, 48*
Haydar Bey 89
Haydarpaşa, railway connection to İzmit 54; railway terminus building 66; in Ehlgötz's proposals 95; in Prost's proposals 102–3; in Menderes' redevelopment 157; in Arnodin's proposal 189*n.67*
Hénard, Eugène 97
Hendesehane 183*n.31*
Hendese-i Mülkiye Mektebi 57
Hereke 38
Hilton Hotel 139, 170
Hilts, H. E. 123, 203*n.92*
Hippodrome of Constantinople, in Bouvard's proposals 63; in Lambert's proposal 94; recovery attempts by Prost 106–7, 120
Hirsch, Baron Maurice de 53
Hittites 77
Högg, Hans 168–9, 214*n.79*
Holzmeister, Clemenz 87
Humbarahane 183*n.31*
Hungary, fire fighting experts from 47; horses brought for trams 53; Ottoman alliance in the First World War 71
hürremabad 20
Hüseyin Bey 51

İbrahim Edhem Paşa 56
İbrahim Müteferrika 19
İbrahim Paşa (Grand Vizier of Ahmed III) 18–19; his execution 21
İhtisab Nazırlığı 24
İmar Kanunu (1956) 168
India 119
İnönü, İsmet 86, 116, 128, 142, 149, 202*n.85*; elected as president of Turkey 116; title *Milli Şef* (National Chief) 122; transfer of land in Taşlık 134, 136
İnönü Promenade (*Gezisi*) 116–8
International Monetary Fund 123
İntizam-ı Şehir Komisyonu (Commission of the Order of the City) 44–5
İşçi Sigortaları Kurumu (Workers' Insurance Agency) 143, 150, 154
Islahat-ı Turuk Komisyonu (Commission of Road Upgrading) 49–50, 152
İsmail Paşa (Viceroy of Egypt) 52
Istanbul, population and immigration 8, 9, 12, 14, 15, 20, 27, 42, 55, 64, 88, 94, 96, 97, 110, 120, 124, 130, 139, 146, 165, 168, 176, 178, 182*n.12*, 184*n.44*, 188*n.55*, 204*n.99*, 208*n.60*; names 12, 181*n.6*; fires 14, 20, 27, 47, 49, 52, 69; trams 53, 66, 146; tunnel (underground) 53, 121; electricity supply 65, 130; telephone services 65–6, 191*n.87*; number of motor vehicles 119, 146, 211*n.18*
Istanbul–Edirne motorway 101, 138, 152–3
İstanbul Efendisi (the *kadı* of Dersaadet) 17
İstanbul İmar Talimatnamesi (Istanbul Redevelopment Regulation, 1956) 168

Istanbul Technical University 137–8, 213*n.55*
İstanbul ve Bilâd-ı Selâsede Yapılacak Ebniyenin Suver-i İnşasiyyesine Dair Nizâmnâme (Regulation on Construction Methods in Istanbul) 53
İstiklâl Mahkemeleri (Independence Tribunals) 122, 202*n.83*
İstiklâl Street 88, 102; *see also Grande Rue de Pera*
İstinye 157
Italy 9; occupied Anatolia 71; authoritarian regime 75, 121, 195*n.49*
İzmir, Storari works 49; special administrative structure: governor mayor 87; Prost's works 97, 118; electricity supply 201*n.71*
İzmit 38, 54, 86

Jacobin reforms 75
Janissaries 20; rebellion against the *Nizam-ı Cedid* and murder of Selim III 23, 35; loss of status and abolishment 23–4, 43, 211*n.30*; in Moltke's writings 32
Jansen, Hermann 86–7, 124, 195*n.47*
Japan 122
Jasmund, August 57, 60
Jewish community of Istanbul 9, 12, 19, 42
Justinian (Byzantine Emperor) 12

Kabataş 69
kadı 17, 43; loss of administrative power 24
Kadıköy 57, 66, 197*n.17*; in Moltke's writings 32; People's House building 79; in Prost's proposals 118; in Menderes' redevelopment 157
Kadırga 28, 30
Kağıthane 18–19
Kâmil Bey 45

Kandilli 59, 61
Karaköy 39, 64, 66; linked to the Grande Rue de Pera 46; linked to Galata by underground tunnel 53; Passenger Terminal 79; in Prost's proposals 102, 104, 110; in Revision Commission plans 139; in Menderes' press conference 147; in Sayar's article 149–50; during Menderes' redevelopment works 156–7
Karaköy Square 102, 147, 156–7
Kartal 178
Kasımpaşa 45, 69, 116
Kastamonu 74
Kayseri 85
Kazlıçeşme 125
Kemalettin Bey 66, 77–8, 191*n.95*
Kemalism 74, 78, 83, 192*n.7*
Kemalist, principles 3; modernisation project 6; elite 141; ideology 82, 97, 118, 124; project 119; reforms 76–7, 82, 92, 192*n.2*; regime 77–8, 81, 87, 121, 127, 193*n.21*, 195*n.45*
Kemalists 75, 77, 78, 85, 86, 124, 128, 130, 175, 193*n.7*
Kennedy Street 155, 158, 170
Kırdar, Lütfi 97, 109, 134, 207*n.40*
Kısıklı 118
kocabaşı 24–5
Konstantiniyye 181*n.6*
Konya 56, 85
Köprülü, Fuat 122, 132–3
Köprülü Mehmed Paşa 51
Koraltan, Refik 122
Korean War 141, 205*n.10*
Köymen, Nusret Kemal 83–4
Kraatz, L. 10
Küçükayasofya 36
Küçükçekmece 152, 178
Kumkapı 12, 94
Kurtuluş (Tatavla) 45, 69, 102
Kuruçeşme 103
Kütahya 85

Laleli 152, 212*n.44*; mosque 153
Lambert, A. O. 58–9
Lambert, Jacques Henri 92–4, 96, 106, 176
Launay, Marie de 47
Le Corbusier 95–6, 197*n.8, 9*
Leeds 38
Leningrad 83
Levent 139; Houses 157
Lewis, Bernard 64, 85
London, Ottoman Embassy 22; Reşid Paşa's diplomatic service 26; stock market 64; in Köymen's writings 83; Greater Plan by Abercrombie 138
Lörcher, Carl 89
Lyautey (Marechal) 97
Lyon 67, 191*n.94*

MacFarlane, Charles 7
Maçka 34, 106
Maçka Park 118, 134, 136
Madrid 60, 190*n.69*
mahalle 17, 24–5, 28, 79–80, 119, 200*n.63*
Mahmud I 21
Mahmud II 4, 23–5, 30, 33–6, 38, 43, 73, 211*n.30*
Mahmudiye (Ottoman military march) 34
Makal, Mahmut 121, 201*n.72*
Malatya 86
Malta 73
Manchester 38
Manifaturacılar Çarşısı (Textile Merchants Bazaar) 147, 167
Marcuis de Bonnac 19
Mardin, Şerif 79
Marrakech 97
Marshall Plan 123, 176, 202*n.90*
Maschinenfabrik Augsburg-Nürnberg 65
Mata, Arturo Soria 60, 190*n.69*
Mazhar Bey 52, 188*n.47*
Mecca 125
Meclis-i Vâlâ-i Ahkâm-i Adliyye (Supreme Council of Judicial Ordinance) 24, 43–4

Mehmed II (the Conquer) 8, 12, 17, 71, 131, 160
Mehmed VI (Vahdettin) 73
Mehmed Ali Paşa (Governor of Egypt) 25
Mehmed Salih Efendi 44
Meknes 97
Mekteb-i Şahane-i Tıbbiye (Imperial School of Medicine) 57
Menderes, Adnan 1–6, 124, 128, 202*n.82*; his speech at Grand National Assembly in 1945 122, 127; appointment as prime minister 126; elites' opinion of 128, 205*n.7*; prioritising agriculture 129; views on religious expression 131; reconquering Istanbul 131, 140; view of importance of Istanbul in elections 132–3; political ban and trials in Yassıada 142–5, 161–166, redevelopment programme 146–152, 154, 157–169, 172, 173–4, 176–9
Menemen 74
Menteşe, Ertuğrul 137, 167, 171
mese 14, 29, 50; *see also: Divanyolu*
Mesopotamia 77
Mevlevihanekapısı 28, 30, 68
Miğerdiç, Ohannes 44
Millet Street 101, 153–6, 173, 216*n.94*
Milli Birlik Komitesi (National Unity Committee) 142–3
Milli Korunma Kanunu (National Protection Act) 121
Mimar (architectural magazine) 79
Moda (fashion magazine) 76
Moine, M. L. 36
Moltke, Helmuth von 30–3, 38, 177, 185*n.50–2, n.54-5*, 186n.*58, 60*
Mondrokles (Corinthian architect) 61
Mongeri, Giulio 79, 89, 91
Morocco 97, 119
Moscow 83
Muallem Asakir-i Mansure-i Muhammediye (Trained Victorious Troops of Muhammed) 24

muhtar (headman in *mahalle*s) 24–5
muhtesip 17
Munich 168
Municipal Palace of Istanbul 139, 170, 214*n.70*
Murad V 54
Müşavirler Heyeti (Board of Advisors) 137–8, 155, 167–9, 214*n.76*
Mustafa IV 23
Mustafa Reşid Paşa 26

Nafia Nezareti 25
nahiye 17, 87
naib 17
Napoleon III 52, 168
National Socialists in Germany 96
NATO 129, 132, 142, 205*n.10*
Naum, Theodore 45
New York 83, 90, 93
Nizam-ı Cedid (New Order) 21, 23
North Africa 97, 118, 175
Notre Dame de Paris 75
Nuruosmaniye Mosque 16, 21–2

Olympic Stadium (Park) 101, 106, 154
Onar, Sıddık Sami 150, 211*n.29*
Onat, Emin 138, 213*n.55*
open-air theatre 106, 118, 200*n.61*
Ordu Street 50, 152–3, 156
Ortaköy 66, 69
Ottoman Empire 2, 4, 9, 13, 24, 33, 86–7, 90, 173; beginning of decline 7, 8; during Tulip Era 18, 20; during Mahmud II's reign 25; Moltke's arrival 30; during Crimean War and member of Concert of Europe 40–1, 45; dire financial conditions and Georges-Eugéne Haussmann 52; bankruptcy 54; war with Russia 55; under Abdülhamid II's reign 55–8, 61–3; under Young Turks administration 64; collapse 70–1; contrasted with new Republic 73, 75, 77, 84

Ottoman Parliament 26, 55, 57, 63
Ottoman Revivalist architecture 66, 67, 77–9, 193*n.21*
Ottomanism 55–6

Pangaltı 45, 47
Paris 3, 22, 45, 52, 57, 62, 75, 83, 92–3, 97, 100, 118, 136, 148, 168, 197*n.9*
Park Hotel 157, 163
Paşabahçe 64; Glass and Bottle Factory 88
Patrona Halil 20
peasantism 82, 200*n.66*
peasantist, movement 5; ideology 82–4, 120, 200*n.66*; end of utopia 124; policies 127; rhetoric 176;
Pendik 103, 138, 157
People's Houses (*Halkevleri*) 75
People's Rooms 75
Pera 7–8, 25; in Moltke's writings 32; increased land values 36; 'boom town' 41–2; municipal administration 45, 47; Great Fire of 1870 47; improved transport 53; wealthier citizens 59; in Auric's proposals 69
Persian, influence in Tulip Era 18–20; removal of Persian words from Turkish 77, 119
Pervititch, Jacques 89, 101
Piccinato, Luigi 169, 171, 215*n.84*
Poitiers 93
Poland 7
Polatkan, Hasan 143, 210*n.8*
Portugal 9
Praetorian Guard of Imperial Rome 24
Prix de Rome 97
Prost 2, 4–6, 93, 149, 152, 154, 156, 169, 173–9, 180*n.3*; refusal to join the 1933 design competition 92; Le Corbusier's competitor 95; works prior to Istanbul 97; contract 97, 107, 134, 135, 136, 197*n.14, 16*, 199*n.50*, 200*n.53*, 208*n.47*; aims of master plan 98–107; implementation

of master plan 107–118; complaints about municipality 111; appreciation of Kemalist reforms 118–120; shortcomings of master plan 124–5; decommissioning 134–6; criticisms from the Revision Commission 137; consistency with Revision Commission's plans 138–9; reference to by Menderes during Yassıada Trials 166
Prussia 40

Rabat 97
Radio House of Istanbul 116
Rado, Şevket 148
Ragıp Gümüşpala Street 151, 155
Ragıp Paşa Library 153
Refik Mustafa 44
Republican Monument in Taksim 89, 91, 117; in Sultanahmet proposed by Prost 107
Republican People's Party (RPP), Third Congress and its emblem 74; management of People's Houses 75; after the Second World War 122–3, 125–6, 202$n.85$; demographic character in contrast with DP 127–9, 204$n.1$, 205$n.5$; negative views in Municipal Assembly 136; severe opposition to DP 141; during Arabic *ezan* discussions 206$n.27$
Revelaki, David 44
Revizyon Komisyonu (Revision Commission) 136–7, 167, 174, 177–8, 208$n.54$
Rio de Janeiro 93
Ritter, Otto 66
Röpke, Wilhelm 83
Rosenthal, Steven 41, 45
Rouen 60
Rumelihisarı 58–9, 61
Rusçuk 23
Russia 7, 40, 55, 71, 122, 123

Sa'dabad 19–20
Said Efendi 19, 183$n.31$
Saint Raphael 97
Saint Tropez 97
Salih Münir Paşa 62
Salih Paşa 44
Salıpazarı 138, 147, 157
Samatya 12
San Francisco 122
Sandal Bedesteni 173
Saraçhane 112, 114–5
Sarayburnu 28, 54, 59–60, 68, 95, 102, 106, 110, 120
Sarc, Ömer Celâl 82
Sarol, Mükerrem 159, 207$n.33$, 212$n.43$
Sasemann, Victor 61
Sayar, Zeki 149, 164, 194$n.34$
Schneider, Siegmund 60–1, 190$n.71$
Schreider, M. 66
Schütte, Wilhelm 87
Schütte-Lihotzky, Margarete 87
Sea of Marmara 8, 30, 32, 38, 48–9, 54, 65, 68, 93–5, 98, 101, 103, 106, 119, 138, 142, 147, 155, 158, 170, 173, 179, 197$n.14$
Sebastopol 41
Second World War 2, 6, 109, 120, 124, 133, 138, 176, 201$n.67$, 204$n.96$
Şehremaneti (municipality) 43–5, 48, 64, 80
Şehremini (Istanbul's district) 112
Şehremini (mayor) 43–4, 48, 51, 66, 89
Şehzadebaşı 101, 145, 147
Selim I 13
Selim III 21–4, 35–6, 184$n.35$
Selimiye Barracks 36
Server Efendi 46, 48
şeyhülislam 24
Shaw, Stanford 21
Silahtarağa power plant 65–6, 121
Silivrikapı 28, 30, 68
Simkeşhane 153, 170
Sirkeci 50, 54, 106–8, 110, 112, 155,

170, 198*n.29*
Sirkeci Train Terminus 57, 60, 199*n.49*
Şirket-i Hayriye 53
Şişhane 47, 69, 116
Şişli 47, 79, 106, 116
Sitte, Camillo 86, 195*n.47*
Sivas 85
Sixth District 45–50, 57
Sixth District's Municipal Palace 47–8, 187*n.29*
Société Anonyme Ottomane des Téléphones de Constantinople 65
Société des Chemin de Fer Orientaux 53
Sofia 54
Soviet Russia 122, 123, 132, 204*n.96*
Sozialpolitic 82
Spain 9
Storari, Luigi 49
Sublime Porte 26
Süleyman I (The Magnificent) 13
Süleymaniye (Istanbul's district) 94, 109, 173
Süleymaniye Mosque 13, 102, 147, 149, 161, 163, 199*n.39*
Sultan Ahmet Mosque 75, 94, 106; offered as an art gallery 193*n.14*
Sultanahmet, Square 56, 106–7, 182*n.11*; district 93–4, 108, 110, 139, 152
Sumerians 77
sürgün (forced relocation) 9
Surname Act 76
Sütlüce 89
Syria 56

Taksim, under Sixth District 45, 47; in Auric's proposal 69; in late 1930s 79; Republican Monument 89, 91; in Prost's proposals 100, 102, 104, 106, 110, 115–7; in Board of Advisors' plans 139; in Menderes' press conference 147; in 2012 plans 179
Takvim-i Vakayi 34
Tanzimat, edict 26–7, 33; reforms 26, 54; era 26, 35, 41, 55; bureaucrats 51, 55

Tarabya 32, 48, 52
Tarhan, Mümtaz 152, 210*n.9*, 214*n.70*, 72
Tarlabaşı Street 139; Boulevard 178
Taşlık 134, 136, 207*n.44*
Taut, Bruno 87
Tehran 161, 214*n.70*
Tepebaşı 47, 102, 110, 199*n.40*
Theodosian Walls 8, 14, 29–30, 68, 95, 98, 119, 153, 155
Theodosius 161
Thessaloniki 141
Toker, Metin 128, 149
Tophane 28, 30, 45, 49, 53, 69, 102, 139, 147
Topkapı 53, 68, 106, 112, 152–5
Topkapı Palace 16, 18, 30, 35, 37, 41, 54, 70, 103, 182*n.8*, 199*n.49*
Toulon 97
Translation Office (*Tercüme Odası*) 34, 44, 61
Treaty of Carlowitz 7
Treaty of Küçük Kaynarca 21
Treaty of Lausanne 72, 85
Treaty of Passarowitz 7
Treaty of Sèvres 71
Triple Entente 71
Truman Doctrine 123
Truman, Harry 123
Tulip Era 18–20, 183*n.18*, 210*n.14*
Turgut Özal Boulevard 153
Türk Dil Kurumu (Turkish Language Society) 77
Türk Ocakları (Turkish Hearts) 75
Türk Tarih Kurumu (Turkish Historical Society) 77, 170, 215*n.91*
Türk Tarih Tezi (Turkish Historical Thesis) 77
Türk Yüksek Mimarlar Birliği (Turkish Union of Architects) 137
Türk Yüksek Mühendisleri Birliği (Turkish Union of Engineers) 137
Tuzla 103, 138
Twentieth Century Fund 123

ulema 17, 23–4, 184*n.35*
Ülkü (political magazine of the 1930s and 1940s) 83
un kapanı 14
United Nations 122
United States of America, the DP's closer ties 3; electrical lamps imported from 63; Lambert's works 93; migration by Wagner 96; establishment of alliance after Second World War 122–4, 202*n.88, 90,* 203*n.91, 92, 95, 96*; economic aid 123–4, 205*n.9*; intensified relations in DP era 129
Unkapanı 28, 30, 38, 53, 68, 101–2, 112, 114–5, 155, 216*n.94*
Ünsal, Behçet 137, 215*n.92*
Üsküdar 8, 36, 49, 57, 65, 181*n.2,* 184*n.44,* 197*n.17*; during Tulip Era 18–19; during Crimean War 41; in Arnodin's scheme 59–60, 189*n.67*; in Prost's proposal 118; in Menderes' press conference 147
Üstündağ, Muhittin 97, 107, 207*n.40*
Usul-i Mimari-yi Osmani (Principles of Ottoman Architecture) 56

Vak'a-i Hayriye (The Auspicious or Benevolent Event) 24, 150, 211*n.30*
Valens Aqueducts 16
Vallaury, Alexandre 57
Vatan Street 152, 154, 156, 173, 210*n.8,* 216*n.94*
Vedat Bey 66, 77, 79
Vefa 112
Venice 7
Vienna 7, 22, 40, 44, 47, 56, 60, 83, 190*n.69*
Villa Medici 97
village institutes (*köy enstitüleri*) 82, 124

Wagner, Martin 95–7, 119, 176, 197*n.10*
Wagner, Otto 60, 189–90*n.69*

Washington 90
White, Charles 38

yağ kapanı 14
Yalıköşkü 28, 30
Yassıada trials 142–3, 145–6, 150–2, 161–2, 165, 210*n.13,* 212*n.41, 44;*
Yeang, Ken 178
Yedigün (fashion magazine) 76
Yedikule 28, 36, 53, 68, 106, 138, 155, 209*n.61*
yemiş kapanı 14
Yenen, Mithat 137, 169
Yeni Mimari (New Architecture) 78
Yeni Mosque 15, 49, 63, 102, 111
Yenibahçe 94, 101, 106, 154
Yenikapı 12, 68–9, 93–4, 101–2, 138, 147, 155, 198*n.29*
Yeşilköy 36, 66, 94–5, 155; airport 102, 147
Yıldız, palace 63; groves in Prost's proposal 118; in Menderes' press conference 147
Yirmisekiz Çelebi Mehmed Efendi 19, 183*n.31*
Young Turks 63–4
Yüksek Adalet Divanı (High Court of Justice) 142, 144,
Yüksek Soruşturma Kurulu (Higher Investigation Commission)142
Yusuf Efendi 44

Zeytinburnu 36, 125
Zirai Donatım Kurumu (Agricultural Equipment Agency) 143
Zorlu, Fatin Rüştü 143, 210*n.8*

Printed and bound by CPI Group (UK) Ltd, Croydon, CR0 4YY
20/03/2026
02075557-0018